African Women and
Their Networks
of Support

African Women and Their Networks of Support

Intervening Connections

Edited by
Elene Cloete, Martha Ndakalako-Bannikov,
and Mariah C. Stember

LEXINGTON BOOKS
Lanham • Boulder • New York • London

Published by Lexington Books
An imprint of The Rowman & Littlefield Publishing Group, Inc.
4501 Forbes Boulevard, Suite 200, Lanham, Maryland 20706
www.rowman.com

6 Tinworth Street, London SE11 5AL, United Kingdom

British Library Cataloguing in Publication Information Available

Library of Congress Cataloging-in-Publication Data Available

ISBN 978-1-7936-0739-3 (cloth)
ISBN 978-1-7936-0740-9 (electronic)

Library of Congress Control Number: 2020944233

Contents

Introduction

Intervening Connections: Below the Sightline

Elene Cloete, Martha Ndakalako-Bannikov, and Mariah C. Stember

This book explores African women's interventions toward social and political change. In deciding on a title for this volume, we wanted to consider both the individual and the collective and capture the dialectic relationship between these different ways of being in the world. We also wanted to deeply examine Mohanty and Carter's (2018) claim that significant connections exist between the personal and the political, and as a result, women's personal stories inform and are informed by the networks they find themselves in. In this case, intervention refers both to women's individual interventions to initiate change and to those networks women are situated in that actively intervene in and question the status quo. Chapters in this collection therefore consider how women, in their different cultural, social, and political spaces, find innovative strategies to address their concerns and voice their underrepresented perspectives. More often than not, these perspectives are molded in either formal or informal networks of support that provide women with the necessary peer-based foundation to deal with gender discrimination, violence, and subjugation. On other occasions, women's strategies toward change are driven by specific individuals who set the transformative agenda and trajectory toward social change. Women's efforts and support networks are therefore never uniform. Instead, they vary, using either local or international ties, representing different individual and generational voices, and relying on both virtual and traditional forms of connectedness.

Women's networking efforts have not gone unnoticed. In fact, scholars are persistently documenting women's innovative interventions toward social change in both financial and political terms. Examples of such interventions include women's microfinancing groups (Abwunza 1995; Van Rooyen et al. 2012), coalition-building efforts to address violence against women (Tsikata 2009; Mama 2005), and support networks during and following conflict (Lloyd 1999; Meintjes 2001; Utas 2005; Willoughby-Herald 2014). Women's networks have also culminated in more structured social movements that actively mobilize for gender equality, human rights, and political representation. While some of these movements have been defined and shaped by national boundaries, others extend across regional and international territories (Badri and Tripp 2017; Batliwala 2008; Bauer 2011; Fallon 2008; Hassim 2006; Ranchod 2013). Scholars' contributions over the past two decades confirm women's formal and informal strategies to unite and mobilize around commonly shared interests and issues.

Despite such attention, larger national and international events continue to overshadow both the inequalities African women experience and their efforts to address such inequalities. For example, Islamophobic discourse eclipses the commitment of devoted Muslim women toward gender equality, and ideologically driven narratives accompanying the global refugee crisis conceal the persistent efforts migrant African women make to rebuild their and their families' lives. Generally, legislators worldwide have yet to fully acknowledge, let alone work toward rectifying, the global gender-based violence (GBV) epidemic, despite women's persistent demands for such action. This volume, therefore, builds on existing scholars and activists' work to shed light on African women's informal and formal networking efforts to address inequality. We highlight other similar below-the-sightline connections and coalitions women forge to help each other, which frequently remain hidden from national attention. We are also committed to underscoring the systemic oppression that has led to the emergence of these networks. We argue that such networks are indicative of underlying discriminatory structures. We therefore guard against mere description of women's networks and their strategies in overcoming such discrimination without considering what such underlying structures look like, and how women are addressing and destabilizing these oppressions. This volume is therefore interested in what the presence of women's networks and the emergence of certain interventions can tell us about their immediate social worlds. Moreover, what specific conditions necessitate such networking initiatives in the first place?

We are inspired by the work of Purkayasthra and Subramaniam (2004) and their examination of both informal and formal networking among rural women in West Africa and Southeast Asia. In these networks, we also recognize solidarity aimed at altering the status quo, driven in most cases by frustrations around gender inequality. We argue that in such unity of purpose resides the power of women's networks and their accompanying interventions to bring about social change. We also draw from Gouws and Coetzee's (2019) special issue focused on African women's movements and manifestations of feminist activism. Contributing authors of this special issue articulate not only where but also how women voice their activism toward changing the status quo. This book adds to contributions like these by focusing specifically on African women both on the continent and in the diaspora.

In documenting African women's networks of intervention, we wanted to include interpretations from disciplines outside the social sciences. We were especially intrigued by how contributions from the humanities, communication studies, and journalism can illustrate the blurred lines between theory, representations, imagined realities, and women's lived conditions. Our interests also encompass the expanding role and prominence of information and communications technologies (ICTs) and social media in African women's lives. We, therefore, wanted to include mention of women's online networking efforts, similar to those analyzed by, among others, Buskens and Webb (2008, 2014). In doing so, we seek to underscore women's innovative tactics toward altering their social environments. With these objectives in mind, we asked the following questions: What constitutes women's interventions and accompanying support networks across different social and political contexts? How do African women's networking initiatives advocate for a redirection of political and social energies? Additionally, how do such initiatives challenge the social and epistemic spaces in which African women are circumscribed?

We invited our fellow feminist scholars from diverse academic traditions to consider these questions. Employing their different disciplinary lenses, we asked that they assist us in shedding light on the networking efforts of African women, whether that be women's real-life connections or as they are described and forged through literary works both on and offline. Through such collaboration, we consider how different scholarly backgrounds and by implication different methodological positions identify, describe, and analyze women's networks. We are excited about how this variety in scholarly perspectives contributes to a collective celebration of African women's networking to overcome their immediate challenges, but also how these perspectives confirm such networks' pertinent roles in and beyond representative and historic narratives. This book's chapters, therefore, exemplify our interdisciplinary collaborations and document the variety of interventions and networks developed and driven by African women.

TAKING NOTE OF WOMEN'S NETWORKS

Capturing the essence of women's networks and exploring their interventions to address gender injustices is productive for at least three reasons. First, it provides opportunities for collective sharing and learning among women. Such sharing allows women to consider the similarities and nuanced differences in their efforts across national, social, and ethnic boundaries. Through sharing, women not only gain additional encouragement to continue their work toward securing gender equity and equality, but they can also expand their networks to ensure greater access to resources and expertise necessary to sustain their interventions. Second, exploring women's interventions to better their social worlds sheds light on the courage, innovation, and accompanying strategies of women to deal with everyday struggles for gender equality and equity. Within such strategies, we recognize not only women's agency but also how the mere existence of the need to utilize such agency points to deeper, underlying issues that continue to plague women. Lastly, an analysis of how women network around gender issues can bring attention to women's activism and the frequently accompanying social movements. In considering women's interventions and network efforts as they manifest across various cultural and social landscapes, ideas around gender activism can become more nuanced in description and thus avoid one-size-fits-all discourses around African feminist activism.

Networks for Shared Awareness

Learning about African women's interventions and existing networks acts as motivation for women elsewhere. Without a doubt, the United Nations' series of World Conferences on Women which took place in 1975, 1980, 1985, and 1995 (UN Women 2013) set the tone for international collaboration. The conferences, perhaps better than any other example, show the great potential of allied forces: of women around the world rallying together and supporting one another in an international effort at solidarity. The 1985 Nairobi Conference, in particular, saw African women leaders and groups emerge on the international scene, actively questioning the prominence of Western feminism and articulating how the needs of African women differ from those in other contexts. These and related questions also emerged in the first Women in Africa and the African Diaspora Conference in 1992 held in Nsukka, Nigeria. This interdisciplinary conference drew African women and women scholars from all over the world and aimed at linking both academics and nonacademics working toward women's equality in Africa. Along with questions regarding the presence of white women at the conference, the term "feminist" was heavily contested. Attendees debated the differences in experience and in feminist approach between African feminisms and black U.S. feminism, highlighting the particularity of location in feminist approaches as well as shared concerns that must be approached with these particularities in mind (Nnaemeka 1998). The 1995 Beijing Conference for Women brought further visibility to the power of women's networks with more than 30,000 participants attending a parallel nonprofit organization forum (Riles 2010), instilling international networking and what Dufour et al. (2010) would label "solidarity beyond borders." Such networks afford complex, creative solidarities in a transnational "context of extreme diversity" (3).

No doubt, establishing cross-border linkages translates into cross-cultural learning opportunities. This kind of learning is especially evident in the efforts of organizations such as the Association for Women's Rights in Development which encourage women to learn from others' successes and challenges. Cross-cultural learning is also evident in the work of nonprofit practitioners and the diffusion of gender rights education across borders. For example, the nonprofit organization, Tostan, supports such learning exchanges between Senegal and Mali (Monkman, Miles, and Easton 2007; Cislaghi 2018). Opportunities for such cross-cultural learning and subsequent networking can enable women to not only learn from others' experiences but build on these to sharpen their activist strategies.

Women's Agency

Women's connectedness signals their acts of agency toward futures of gender equity and equality. Such agency manifests itself in different ways, ranging from the strategies women employ in their informal savings groups to make sound financial decisions and improve their households' food security, to the actions women take to publicly critique repressive states and discriminatory societal norms. Bailey's (2012) analysis of African women asylum seekers and refugees in the UK points to another example of such agency. The migrant women in Bailey's study recognize their shared experiences in enduring prejudice and the invisibility that comes with their migration status. The frustrations surrounding these experiences in combination with their often limited access to social resources have brought these women together and motivated them to develop their own networks of support. Their grassroots movement toward supporting each other and other women with refugee status developed into their own full-fledged nonprofit organization, the African Women's Empowerment Forum (AWEF). In reference to Ralston's work (2006) and considering AWEF's networking efforts, Bailey (2012) argues that agency is about being "conscious actors, not passive subjects in the various situations in which [women] find themselves." Agency is therefore visible where women, inspired and driven by their own consciousness to exert influence in their social worlds, act to bring about the changes needed to overcome their immediate struggles.

A consideration of women's agency should not downplay the structural and systemic subjection that requires women to deploy their agency in the first place. Merely considering and subsequently describing women's purposeful actions in addressing and improving their situations—or in other words their agency—is just the first stage of analysis. Rather, the fact that women need to act as agents for change at all requires an analysis regarding why such efforts are necessary in the first place. In this case, the presence of women's interventions and evidence of their supportive networks signal embedded social issues. For example, while South African informal savings groups, or *stokvels*, create additional financial safety nets for women, these networks' ongoing popularity can also point to the gendered nature of more mainstream financial institutions, and thus the historic exclusion of black women from the country's finance sectors. Stokvels function as credit and savings groups, with members making a fixed monthly contribution to a shared fund that is then later redistributed among the same people following an agreed-upon cycle of repayments (Verhoef 2002).[1] Even though stokvels are often labeled as an alternative to mainstream savings options, they are surely no small change. On the contrary, an estimated 800,000 stokvels, representing about 11.5 million people, or an estimate 20 percent of the country's total population, collectively managed $4 billion in 2017 (Chutel 2018). For many women, these savings groups not only help them overcome sudden cash shortages but have also become a venue for women to increase their social capital. The presence of such networks therefore leads us to consider why these networks exist and why they remain necessary. When considering women's agency, in other words, we must be conscious not to overemphasize women's strategies in dealing with structural injustices without recognizing the importance of first identifying and then deconstructing these structures.

It is also important to recognize that women's individual and collective actions toward challenging underlying structures of gender oppression do not always bring about the immediate results they wished for. Instead, they often face tremendous backlash, as was the case in the northern Nigerian state of Sokoto, in 2019, following women's localized versions of the #MeToo movement. Called the #ArewaMeToo, women in this Nigerian state joined women in the rest of the country to actively speak out against gender violence and sexual harassment. Their actions were however questioned with intense political severity, with police arresting activists and leadership banning the #ArewaMeToo Movement followed by further harassment—some might say retaliation—against gender activists (Campbell 2019). However, in her foundational work on patriarchal dominance and its various forms, Kandiyoti (1988) reminds us that "even though individual power tactics do little to alter the structurally unfavorable terms of the overall patriarchal script, women become experts in maximizing their own life chances" (280). Persistence as well as collecting ongoing expertise to deal with challenging situations is therefore key in ensuring the eventual overturn of underlying structures of systematic oppression.

The women featured in this volume share similar stories and personal biographies of women at the forefront of initiating change, but who must be patient in seeing immediate results. Without a doubt these women ignite their agency, or inherent capabilities, to question the status quo and initiate the much-needed change for more gender equal societies. But, as many of the following chapters describe, this is not easy, nor does it happen overnight. Instead, processes leading toward gradual change require patience and persistence.

It can however be equally challenging for women's networks, activists, and organizations to maintain their momentum and to sustain ongoing support. One area where such momentum is crucial is within the political landscape, especially following regime changes. One such example is the 2018–2019 revolution in Sudan, which successfully brought an end to Omar Hassan al-Bashir's thirty-year rule. Women played a significant role during this revolution. Comprising an estimated 60–70 percent of demonstrators during the uprisings, women demanded not only a change in political order but also fair and equitable rights for themselves (Lynch 2019). It is precisely women's involvement that made the 2018–2019 revolution different from the country's 1964 and 1985 regime change. Such involvement contributed to the country's highest number of women in the transitional government (that will take the country into the planned 2022 election), as well as the first ever woman appointed as chief justice (Berridge 2019). But, as many activists argue, the end of one regime does not necessarily guarantee gender equality in the next. On the contrary, as Sudanese women and groups like *No to Women's Oppression* have shared, the real work only starts *after* the revolution (Trew 2019). This work includes vigilance to ensure that their revolutionary demands are prioritized, that women's representation in government increases, and that they remain included in important political and legal conversations.

Networks for Solidarity

Women's varied actions in developing and maintaining networks trouble commonplace perceptions of gender and activism. One such perception is one-size-fits-all feminism not necessarily influenced by social, cultural, or national boundaries. Thanks to the various waves of feminism, the contributions of intersectional feminist scholars, and feminist voices from the Global South, homogenizing perceptions of feminism are now recognized as obviously problematic. Instead, nuanced, multifaceted understandings of feminism confirm that women's struggles vary, and recognize that gender is performed differently in different contexts (Butler 2004). The differences in such performances are especially interesting when considering local manifestations of regional and global women's networks and accompanying movements. The recent #MeToo Movement,[2] for example, illustrates just how a movement of global recognition, speaking to commonly shared issues, has been adopted, or in some cases, even ignored in local contexts (The Conversation 2019). Examples of the movement's manifestation in an African context include South Africa and Nigeria (Peyton 2019), and with the #MeTooEthiopia (Griffin 2019) movement emerging among diaspora populations in the United States. Despite these manifestations, the momentum of African versions of #MeToo was not nearly the same as their Western counterparts. This is not because of a lack of interest or limited cases of sexual abuse. Instead, such slow momentum is embedded in cultural contexts which normalize violence against women. Women are also afraid of being stigmatized when sharing their experiences publicly, and legal and penal systems are frequently not proactive enough in addressing cases of GBV (Times Live Africa 2018), or protecting victims from their perpetrators. Despite different contexts, African women still bring attention to their frustrations with GBV. They do this, however, in ways that align with their social and cultural contexts.

There is a delicate balance between articulating differences and a complete dismissal of any generalizations (Mohanty 2003). We argue that it is in the recognition and maintenance of such a balance underscoring solidarity where activists and scholars can cover greater grounds toward rectifying gender inequality. In this regard and considering the close correlation between feminism and the praxis of conscientization,[3] Amina Mama (2018) reminds us that "building solidarities is primarily a task of conscientization. We have to be constantly in a process of becoming alert to the things that divide and oppress us in historically specific ways if we are to strengthen an alternative political culture, one that is premised on different kinds of relationships. It is about how we connect" (location 1517).

In what follows, we adhere to Mama's call and recognize the solidarity women develop around issues of gender discrimination. Such solidarity, embedded in women's networks and bolstered by the interventions of individual women, should remain one of feminism's primary objectives.

Throughout the chapters we recognize women's dependence on their social networks. This ranges from activists relying on their online networks to disseminate information about upcoming protest actions, as is the case with #TheTotalShutDown, to international networking of Zanzibari gender advocates to strategize with their global partners around commonly shared issues. Here, dependency does not signify an inability or reluctance to be autonomous, but rather connectivity with other women as a source of strength. As Amina Mama (2018) reminds us, "Individuals cannot bring about change on their own" (location 1627). Instead, they need structures and networks of support that help enable envisioned futures. Ideas around solidarity and sisterhood are present, throughout this volume.

Overview of Chapters

The book is organized into nine chapters that capture the spaces in which women's interventions happen. This includes both the communicative and the geographical spaces in which women situate and operate their networks. As our contributors illustrate, these networks can function in real time, span across national boundaries, and as a result work against racial, ethnic, and socioeconomic divisions. Women's networks of support can also be virtual in nature, creating digital spaces in which women unite against commonly shared inequities, fears, and subjugation. This ranges from the engagement opportunities provided by social media platforms, to the possibility ICTs provide in connecting African women with those elsewhere in the world. Similar to networks developed in real time and through face-to-face interaction, virtual communities provide women with the structures of support to which they might otherwise have little to no access. Additionally, women's interventions can take place in imagined spaces. Here we consider the interventions happening within the literary field where authors develop narratives that not only write women-centered histories and presents but also consider futures that are Afrocentric and defined by gender equality. But, just as women intervene in virtual and imagined spaces, such interventions also happen in discursive spaces. Here, women are actively considering ways of challenging and subsequently reconstructing discourses around gender norms and male dominance.

WOMEN'S CONNECTEDNESS: INTERVENTIONS' KEY SPACES AND CENTRAL CHARACTERISTICS

National Connections: Coalition-building around gender rights issues within the parameters of the nation-state is an effective strategy women use to mobilize and gain attention from national politicians and state legislators (Mama 2018). More often than not, such mobilization is rooted in informal networks developed around the various hardships that women face. In Senegal, as Riley (chapter 1) documents, such informal networks have taken shape in women's associations, mostly acting as savings groups to provide members additional financial support in economically lean times. These groups and their women leaders embody what Riley recognizes as *teraanga* (from *teral*), the popular Wolof concept "that implies the generous and civic-minded intentions of individuals embedded in acts of giving, hospitality, and general socialization" (page 21). But because of their popularity and obvious success in helping women overcome the struggles of limited resources, these associations have also become powerful spaces used by politicians to garner support. While such support can allow women to make certain demands in exchange for their political support, it also opens space for patronage networks (Beck 2003). Women's associations in Senegal are also prime spaces for political parties to identify potential women candidates, especially after the implementation of gender quotas, or *parité*, actively increasing women's participation in

government. In this case, the Senegalese state is seeing women's representation in public office as one way to operationalize its commitment toward
including women in national politics (Creevey 2006), and join the ranks of
other African states and their increased inclusion of women in legislative and
state positions (Britton and Bauer 2006; Bauer 2011). Against this national
backdrop of women's networks and the dynamics surrounding national politics, Riley introduces us to two women leaders whose biographies and current
lives are not only testament to women's selfless investment in their communities (in this case women's associations) but also in their personal ambitions to
obtain political recognition.

Transnational Networks: Although comparisons can be made between
different contexts, transnational feminism has often been dominated by so-
called Western feminist movements, and has tended to disproportionately
focus on white, educated, "Western" feminist priorities. This was the critique
of especially African women in 1985 during the third UN World Conference
on Women in Nairobi, and it remains a concern more than thirty years later. It
is for this and other reasons that scholars warn against valorizing the solidarity associated with transnational feminisms (Abu-Lughold 2002) and question the applicability of universal human rights to local *contexts* (Hodgson
2011; Levitt and Merry 2009; Merry 2006; Emecheta 2007).

That said, a cold dismissal of transnational learning is however too drastic.
A complete write-off would deny the commonalities African women share
with others when it comes to religion, politics, and cultural connections. In
response, Badri and Tripp (2017) argue for a sort of decolonized knowledge
in which "African movements themselves have shaped and are shaping
global understandings of women's rights and feminism" (1). Ott (chapter
2) introduces us to such transnational connections as they have developed
between Muslim women from Zanzibar and a transnational network of
Muslim women's rights activists from Singapore, Malaysia, and Indonesia.
In this case, an existing national coalition of women activists in Zanzibar
advocates for women's rights to adjudicate Islamic legal cases as *kadhis*
(Islamic judges). In doing so, the coalition draws from the experiences
of other Muslim women, primarily in Southeast Asia, who have already
engaged in such advocacy efforts. Such international connections are not
only about learning from others' experiences, and using such experiences as
examples to argue for gender reform but also about showing the road ahead
to those who have yet to undergo such activism. Networks like the Malaysia-
based Sisters in Islam, can act as the motivating signpost for women in
Zanzibar, conjuring a vision of how gender equity and equality may eventually materialize in Zanzibar. But as Ott finds, despite such international connectivity, Zanzibari gender activists remain adherent to their local contexts.
In addition to centering their advocacy efforts in Islamic knowledge-based

solidarity, they also sustain notions of national connectedness by working to establish *umoja*, a Kiswahili philosophy that implies solidarity, unity, and relational personhood.

Virtual Spaces, Virtual Networks: The Arab Spring solidified the connection between social media and social movements (Bruns et al. 2014; Jamali 2014). Not only did ICTs become a key mobilizing mechanism for social movements, instantaneously sharing updates, locations, and warnings on planned protest actions, but it has also become a public space where social movements can make their frustration with the status quo visible. This ranges from political exclusion and repressive governance to people's limited access to land. Similarly, African women's movements use social media platforms as vehicles for communication between members and toward the general public, sharing their frustrations with structural gender inequalities (Mutsvairo 2016). In fact, women across the continent have taken to social media to strengthen their mobilizations. Recent activism includes protests in Sudan, with women actively involved in civil society's political uprisings. And as Ali (2019) confirms, social media played an instrumental role during these political actions.

Women across the continent have also looked toward ICTs and social media for support in addressing violence against women. It is this confluence of ICTs, accompanying social media spaces and women's efforts to address violence against women that are the main focus of Cloete's (chapter 3) contribution. Cloete argues that South African women's strategies in dealing with GBV manifest itself in both visible and invisible spaces. The latter pertains to closed online groups and provides group members with immediate support through lifesaving mechanisms such as digital "emergency buttons" and location-sharing to be used in the face of GBV. Other forms of more directly visible activism take shape as groups engage in visible public outcry, taking their frustrations about persistent GBV to the streets. #TheTotalShutDown movement exemplifies both these strategies. Employing both online communication and public protest, the movement demands action from South African politicians and legislators toward rectifying the country's record high levels of GBV.

Since it officially took to the streets on August 1, 2018, #TheTotalShutDown movement has actively engaged the public sphere. A primary goal of such engagement is not only to insist on structural change coming from the legislature and government offices but also to keep the state accountable for implementing such changes. Deploying social media, these actions make women's frustrations around GBV clearly visible, and also signify their commitment to hold state actors accountable.

As a space that encourages public conversations and subsequently enacts political participation, the public sphere, as Habermas (1962) imagined, is a discursive arena critical of the state. But, as Nancy Fraser (1990) and others have argued, theorizing over the public sphere as enabler of democratic rigor does not always acknowledge the subaltern's exclusion from the public sphere. It may similarly overlook the counterpublics that are created as a result of such exclusion. Taking such considerations as a vantage point, Ndakalako-Bannikov (chapter 4) explores how Namibians used Facebook to reflect upon their country's gender dynamics. In this case, such reflections are grounded in a fictional Facebook narrative, *The Dream of a Kwanyama Girl*, which describes the lives of young Namibian women in the country's capital, Windhoek, and their subjection to conservative gender expectations and sexual violence. Because of its online location, the narrative encourages comments and elicits subsequent online discussions with readers actively confronting the subject matter. Through enabling such discussions, as Ndakalako-Bannikov illustrates, Namibians are using Facebook as an alternative space, or a counterpublic, to converse over the prominence of misogyny, GBV, and patronage in Namibia. In this instance, ICTs are providing people with an alternative space, as a means of circumventing possible patriarchal intervention, removed from possible patriarchal intimidation, to share their opinions about gender discrimination. Arguably, these conversations that are happening within online networks are needed to agitate the broader public in supporting gender activists' actions toward eventual equity and equality.

In addition to the counterpublic emerging from *The Dream of a Kwanyama Girl*, and the online conversations resulting from the Facebook publication, it is the narrative itself that exposes gender relations in Namibia. The characters in the narrative, mostly women from different generations, bring to life the various struggles ambitious urban women face when subjected to gender norms and expectations. *The Dream of a Kwanyama Girl*'s melodramatic representation of women's lives unfolds, as Ndakalako-Bannikov argues, in the wider societal context of a social drama (Turner 1990). Social dramas are social processes that emerge out of conflict situations and disrupt the routine cycle of everyday living, revealing the tensions in a society that are otherwise concealed by the day-to-day. Ndakalako-Bannikov's chapter describes a social drama in which representation demands critical engagement with lived reality.

Literacy Spaces, Alternative Futures: Women's efforts to make gender discrimination visible and to challenge gender inequalities extend beyond social justice movements, the public sphere, and online spaces. They involve interventions in literary culture and similar creative spaces with women creatively using their skills to critique and dismantle patriarchal hegemony. As Cockburn (chapter 5) illustrates, the fictional works of many Caribbean women authors stage active interventions both within the Caribbean anglophone literary tradition and Caribbean culture to contest and alter stagnant, colonial understandings of the region and its women, and to envision possibilities for ideological liberation. Driving such interventions are women authors' creative ways of inserting not only themselves into the literary canon but also the stories of Caribbean women and girls. Key to Cockburn's argument is the concept of Afrocentricity, a mode of liberatory thought and action that centers African and black diasporic experiences and perspectives, placing black subjectivity at the center, and defining blackness as an ethical stance "against all forms of oppression, racism, classism, homophobia, patriarchy, child abuse, pedophilia, and white racial domination" (Asante 2003). In centering African folklore and traditions, Cockburn does not construct a monolithic or essential notion of African culture, a critique common to Afrocentricity. Rather, Cockburn demonstrates the social specificity of the Caribbean and its relationship to the continentâ—simultaneously severed and made possible by the trade in enslaved peoples and colonialism. In this chapter, Afrocentricity is tied to Afrofuturism as a means of envisioning a Caribbean future free of "the vestiges of Europeanized minds" (Asante vii). Cockburn provides an overview of how women have and continue to intervene in both the Caribbean literary tradition and world literature more broadly, creating an aesthetic of decoloniality. As Cockburn writes, "This is decolonization of the mind in action: women familiarize themselves with the patriarchal regulations hidden within all institutions (religious, legal, educational) and actively interrogate society using the philosophies of their oppressors as catalysts" (page 123). This statement is very much in line with much of the women's efforts described in this volume.

Spaces of Discursive Intervention: A central theme present in all contributing chapters is women's resistance to gender oppression. We argue that such resistance is not only opposition to oppression but instead the beginning stages of "imagin[ing] and enact[ing] a different kind of future" (Eisenstein 2018). Such resistance also pertains to normative discourse on gender, sexuality, and femininity that perpetuate perceptions of women as passive, indecisive, and subservient. In this case, women are working to alter such discourses, actively defying the gender norms perpetuated by such discourses and insisting on alternative perceptions of women, sexuality, and femininity. In the context of the Kenyan Truth, Justice, and Reconciliation Commission, Awino (chapter 6) insists on a reconstructed discourse that considers women's experiences during war and conflict in more nuanced ways. In the context of the 1984 Wagalla Massacre in northeast Kenya and the public hearings that followed decades later, Awino recognizes narratives of exhortation as a central component of women's testimonies. This involves women calling on others to come together around the injustices surrounding the massacre—to testify about these in the hopes of eventual restorative justice. As one woman stated:

Women we are still alive and have to ask for our rights. Let us stand in unity. Let us be together as that is when our problems will come to an end . . . I am calling upon women as we have to come forward. The Truth, Justice and Reconciliation Commission, is telling us that we have to be aware of our rights. We need to claim our rights, so that we can be given land and education.

Gender advocates have campaigned successfully around the inclusion of women in restorative justice processes. Yet, as Awino reminds us, there is still work to be done with regard to how women's testimonies are interpreted. Too often the public interprets women's stories about their experiences during conflict, war, and violence as told by passive victims who suffered bodily and in some cases emotional harm (Borer 2009; Ephgrave 2015). It is undeniable that women suffered tremendous sexual violence during the Wagalla Massacre. But, as the different sets of narratives emerging from Awino's chapter exemplify, such a narrow single narrative undermines other injustices, including political, economic, and civil rights violations. Furthermore, a narrow focus conceals the preexisting structural injustices that allowed the Massacre to occur in the first place. By not allowing other themes related to these kinds of violations to come to the forefront, processes around restorative justice are incomplete.

The resistance to and subsequent reconstruction of discourse is also at the heart of Aromona's (chapter 7) work. Aromona considers how "sexual scripts" in combination with "token resistance" impact Nigerian women's sexual behavior and sexual consciousness. As the norms that inform sexual interactions (Simon and Gagnon 1986), sexual scripts, Aromona argues, negatively impact women's control over their bodies and in the process silence their voices as far as their sexual needs and rights are concerned. Token resistance—the refusal of sexual advances by women when in fact they wish to engage in sexual activity—in turn, draws from such sexual scripts. Derived from traditional sexual scripts, token resistance implies that men initiated sex while women are passive recipients (Krahé, Scheinberger-Olwig, and Kolpin 2000). It also highlights the continuation of the age-old gendered expectation that women must behave chastely and protect their sexual innocence. Aware of the power of this discourse over their relationship and bodies, the young women in Aromona's chapter are resisting, and more so, reconstructing these scripts around their sexual desires, needs, and essentially their gender rights. These women are therefore developing new practices that move beyond scripted gender stereotypes, enabling clear and honest communication between partners in the process.

Domestic Interactions: The final two chapters of the volume bring the reader home and into the private and domestic space. The private sphere is often associated with domesticity and corresponding gender norms. And historically, particularly in the cases of classical patriarchal societies, such norms have been imposed upon women with accompanying expectations of motherhood. On the other hand, men and in this case fathers as well are assigned outward-looking roles. They are assigned outward roles with community action focused on the public sphere. They represent their families and by implication their immediate communities in the public sphere, and when needed, protect their communities from outside threats and potential dangers. Such dichotomous thinking is also present in public discourse pertaining to conflict and war. While women continue to sustain the domestic spaces of home and fulfill their motherly obligations, it is men who are supposed to enable their supposed inherent militant side and fight for their communities and sometimes country's objectives, sovereignty, and eventual prosperity. Feminist scholars complicate such gendered assumptions commonly associated with war and conflict, arguing that these roles are often more complicated than perceived (Lorentzen and Turpin 1998). Sometimes women even manipulate their assigned gender roles to participate in broader regional and national objectives. Stember (chapter 8) discusses women's roles during the struggle against apartheid in Namibia. As she illustrates, women mobilized these supposed domestic roles in service of the liberation movement's broader objectives of political freedom. Stember frames women's wartime contributions within the quotidian and extraordinary, arguing that contexts of conflict effectively trouble that which was once considered normal. In manipulating the quotidian to strengthen the national liberation movement, women also drew extensively from informal networks located within the perceived normal to bolster the liberation army's resources, share news about the struggle's progress, and to gain both national and international support. In this regard, women effectively contributed to the country's eventual political freedom in 1990.

The Namibian women Stember features reformulated particular understandings of the domestic in an effort to support the struggles against apartheid. In this case, they manipulated actions associated with domestic spaces and changed these into extraordinary spaces of political engagement. At times, however, displacement because of war and conflict completely removes women from these otherwise normal domestic realms. They are then forced to turn the extraordinary reality of living in a turbulent political and cultural environment into a "new normal," which in turn allows them to develop new domestic and familial roots. Bolton's (chapter 9) conversations with African migrant women in the American Midwest exemplify such resilience. In describing the daily lives and acculturation processes of refugee women, Bolton underscores the diverse range of challenges faced by women from the diaspora when reestablishing themselves and their families in new social and cultural contexts. They navigate new social spaces, seek financial stability, and negotiate dominant, and often discriminatory immigrant ideologies. And as refugees from mostly conflict-ridden areas of Africa, they also must deal with the recurring trauma of violence and war. While working to integrate into their new society, the women Bolton features have few choices, but stake their claim on resilience. Such resilience is exemplified in their patience during various processes that will gain them eventual acceptance into their new communities. This ranges from navigating health services to helping their children adapt to new school environments. Central to these women's resilience are their interactions with other refugee women. Through such connections, Bolton argues, women from the African diaspora communities become better equipped to make new lives and new domestic spaces for themselves and their families.

This volume's contributors illustrate the varied ways women's interventions are addressing and eventually altering the status quo. Ranging from the domestic to the literary, and speaking to changes in legislation and gender discourse, our contributors collectively argue for an equal representation of women and their rights. Such arguments happen not only in different social and national contexts but also from different disciplinary angles. It is the combination of both African women's networking efforts, as well as our contributors' (all women) interpretations of such efforts that are at the core of the chapters to follow.

NOTES

1. For a developed typology of stokvels, including the variety of labels assigned to these savings groups, different societal functions, as well as associated historical contexts, please see Verhoef (2002).

2. Originally started in 2006 by black American activist Tarana Burke, the #MeToo Movement surfaced again in 2017, when American actor Alyssa Milano used the same hashtag to make allegations of sexual assault against movie producer Harvey Weinstein.

3. Developed by Marxist scholar Paulo Freire, conscientization refers to the process of developing, strengthening, and changing consciousness (Montero 2014).

REFERENCES

Abu-Lughod, Lila. 2002. "Do Muslim Women Really Need Saving? Anthropological Reflections on Cultural Relativism and Its Others." *American Anthropologist* 104, 3: 783–790.

Abwunza, Judith. 1995. "'Silika—To Make Our Lives Shine': Women's Groups in Maragoli, Kenya." *Anthropologica* 37, 1: 27–48.

Ali, Nada Mustafa. 2019. "Sudanese Women's Groups on Facebook and #Civil_ Disobedience: Nairat or Thairat? (Radiant or Revolutionary?)." *African Studies Review* 62, 2: 103–126.

Asante, Molefi K. 2003. *Afrocentricity: The Theory of Social Change*. Chicago: African American Images.

Badri, Balghis, and Aili Mari Tripp. 2017. *Women's Activism in Africa: Struggles for Rights and Representation*. New York: Zed Books Ltd.

Bailey, Olga Guedes. 2012. "Migrant African Women: Tales of Agency and Belonging." *Ethnic and Racial Studies* 35, 5: 850–867.

Batliwala, Srilatha. 2008. *Changing Their World: Concepts and Practices of Women's Movements*. Toronto: Association for Women's Rights in Development (AWID).

Bauer, Gretchen. 2011. "Update on the Women's Movement in Botswana: Have Women Stopped Talking?" *African Studies Review* 54, 2: 23–46.

Bauer, Gretchen, and Hannah Evelyn Britton. 2006. *Women in African Parliaments*. Boulder: Lynne Rienner Publishers.

Beck, Linda J. 2003. "Democratization and the Hidden Public: The Impact of Patronage Networks on Senegalese Women." *Comparative Politics* 35, 2: 147–169.

Berridge, Willow. 2019. "The Sudan Uprising and Its Possibilities: Regional Revolution, Generational Revolution, and an End to Islamist Politics?" *Conflict Research Programme Blog*. London School of Economics and Political Science. Blog Entry, October 23, 2019.

Borer, Tristan Anne. 2009. "Gendered War and Gendered Peace: Truth Commissions and Postconflict Gender Violence: Lessons from South Africa." *Violence Against Women* 15, 10: 1169–1193.

Bruns, Axel, Tim Highfield, and Jean Burgess. 2014. "The Arab Spring and Its Social Media Audiences: English and Arabic Twitter Users and Their Networks." In *Cyberactivism on the Participatory Web*, 96–128. New York and London: Routledge.

Buskens, Ineke, and Anne Webb. 2009. *African Women & ICTs: Investigating Technology, Gender and Empowerment*. London and New York: ZED Books.

Buskens, Ineke, and Anne Webb. 2014. *Women and ICT in Africa and the Middle East: Changing Selves, Changing Societies*. London and New York: ZED Books.

Butler, Judith. 2004. *Undoing Gender*. New York and London: Routledge.

Campbell, John. 2019. "Nigeria's Sultan of Sokoto Bans #MeToo Movement." *Council on Foreign Relations*. Accessed December 10, 2019. https://www.cfr.org/blog/nigerias-sultan-sokoto-bans-metoo-movement

Chutel, Lynsey. 2018. "It's Time to Digitize the Shared Savings Method African Grandmothers Have Used for Years." *Quartz Africa*, April 26. Accessed February 2, 2020. https://qz.com/africa/1262927/stokvels-are-worth-billions-and-this-app-aims-to-bring-collective-savings-into-the-21st-century/

Cislaghi, Beniamino, and Lori Heise. 2018. "Using Social Norms Theory for Health Promotion in Low-income Countries." *Health Promotion International* 34, 2: 616–623.

Creevey, Lucy E. 2006. "Senegal: Contending with Religious Constraints." In *Women in African Parliaments*, edited by Gretchen Bauer and Hannah Britton. Boulder: Lynne Rienner Publishers.

Dufour, Pascale, Dominique Masson, and Dominique Caouette. 2010. *Solidarities Beyond Borders: Transnationalizing Women's Movements*. Vancouver: University of British Columbia Press.

Eisenstein, Zillah. 2018. "Toward a New Feminist Politics of Possibility and Solidarity." In *Feminist Freedom Warriors*, edited by Chandra T. Mohanty and Linda E. Carty. Chicago: Haymarket Books.

Emecheta, Buchi. 2007. "Feminism with a Small 'f.'" In *African Literature: An Anthology of Criticism and Theory*, edited by Tejumola Olaniyan and Ato Quayson. Boston: Blackwell Publishing.

Ephgrave, Nicole. 2015. "Women's Testimony and Collective Memory: Lessons from South Africa's TRC and Rwanda's Gacaca Courts." *European Journal of Women's Studies* 22, 2: 177–190.

Fallon, Kathleen. 2008. *Democracy and the Rise of Women's Movements in Sub-Saharan Africa*. Baltimore: Johns Hopkins University Press.

Fraser, Nancy. 1990. "Rethinking the Public Sphere: A Contribution to the Critique of Actually Existing Democracy." *Social Text* 25/26: 56–80.

Gouws, Amanda, and Azille Coetzee. 2019. *Women's Movements and Feminist Activism*. Abingdon-on-Thames: Taylor & Francis.

Griffin, Tamerra. 2019. "'Surviving R. Kelly' Kicked Off a #MeToo Movement in East Africa." *Buzzfeed News*. https://www.buzzfeednews.com/article/tamerragriffi n/ethiopia-me-too-surviving-r-kelly

Habermas, Jürgen. 1989. *The Structural Transformation of the Public Sphere: An Inquiry into a Category of Bourgeois Society*. Translated by Thomas Burger. Cambridge, MA: Massachusetts Institute of Technology Press.

Hassim, Shireen. 2006. *Women's Organizations and Democracy in South Africa: Contesting Authority*. Madison: University of Wisconsin Press.

Hodgson, Dorothy L. 2011. "'These Are Not Our Priorities': Maasai Women, Human Rights, and the Problem of Culture." In *Gender and Culture at the Limit of Rights*, 138. Philadelphia, PA: University of Pennsylvania Press.

Jamali, Reza. 2014. *Online Arab Spring: Social Media and Fundamental Change*. Cambridge: Chandos Publishing.

Jolaade, Adeogun Tolulope, and Isola Abidemi Abiola. 2016. "Patriarchy and Customary Law as Major Cogs in the Wheel of Women's Peace Building in South Sudan." *Journal of Gender, Information and Development in Africa* 5: 53–75.

Kandiyoti, Deniz. 1988. "Bargaining with Patriarchy." *Gender & Society* 2, 3: 274–290.

Krahé, Barbara, Renate Scheinberger-Olwig, and Susanne Kolpin. 2000. "Ambiguous Communication of Sexual Intentions as a Risk Marker of Sexual Aggression." *Sex Roles* 42: 313–337.

Levitt, Peggy, and Sally Merry. 2009. "Vernacularization on the Ground: Local Uses of Global Women's Rights in Peru, China, India and the United States." *Global Networks* 9, 4: 441–461.

Lloyd, Catherine. 1999. "Organising Across Borders: Algerian Women's Associations in a Period of Conflict." *Review of African Political Economy* 26, 82: 479–490.

Lorentzen, Lois Ann, and Jennifer E Turpin. 1998. *The Women and War Reader.* New York: New York University Press.

Lynch, Justine. 2019. "Women Fueled Sudan's Revolution, But Then They Were Pushed Aside." *Independent.* Accessed February 10, 2020. https://www.independ ent.co.uk/news/world/africa/sudan-revolution-women-uprising-democratic-tran sition-army-bashir-a9038786.html

Mama, Amina. 2018. "Bridging Through Time." In *Feminist Freedom Warriors*, edited by Chandra T. Mohanty and Linda E. Carty. Chicago: Haymarket Books. Kindle.

Meintjes, Sheila, Anu Pillay, and Meredith Turshen. 2001. *The Aftermath: Women in Post-conflict Transformation.* London and New York: Zed Books.

Merry, Sally Engle. 2006. "Transnational Human Rights and Local Activism: Mapping the Middle." *American Anthropologist* 108, 1: 38–51.

Mohanty, Chandra T. 2003. *Feminism Without Borders: Decolonizing Theory, Practicing Solidarity.* Durham: Duke University Press.

Mohanty, Chandra T. and Linda E. Carty. 2018. Feminist Freedom Warriors. Chicago: Haymarket Books. Kindle.

Monkman, Karen, Rebecca Miles, and Peter Easton. 2007. "The Transformatory Potential of a Village Empowerment Program: The Tostan Replication in Mali." *Women's Studies International Forum* 30, 6: 451–464.

Montero, Maritza. 2014. Conscientization. In: Teo T. (eds) *Encyclopedia of Critical Psychology.* Springer, New York, NY. https://doi-org.www2.lib.ku.edu/10.1007/978-1-4614-5583-7_55.

Mutsvairo, Bruce. 2016. *Digital Activism in the Social Media Era.* New York: Springer.

Nnaemeka, Obioma. 1998. "This Women's Business: Beyond Politics and History (Thoughts on the First WAAD Conference)." In *Sisterhood, Feminisms and Power: From Africa to the Diaspora*, edited by Obioma Nnaemeka, 351–388. Trenton and Asmara: Africa World Press.

Peyton, Nellie. 2019. "Nigeria Has #MeToo Moment after Popular Pastor Is Accused of Rape." https://www.reuters.com/article/us-nigeria-women-rape/nigeria-has-metoo-moment-after-popular-pastor-is-accused-of-rape-idUSKCN1TW3KE

Purkayastha, Bandana, and Mangala Subramaniam. 2004. *The Power of Women's Informal Networks: Lessons in Social Change from South Asia and West Africa.* New York: Lexington Books.

Ralston, Helen. 2006. "Citizenship, Identity, Agency and Resistance Among Canadian and Australian Women of South Asian Origin." In *Women, Migration and Citizenship*, edited by Evangelia Tastsoglou and Alexandra Dobrowolsky, 197–214. Aldershot, UK and Burlington, VT: Ashgate.

Ranchod, Sarita. 2013. "African Feminist Uprisings: Getting Our Knickers in Knots." *Feminist Africa* 18: 112–116.

Riles, Annelise. 2001. *The Network Inside Out.* Ann Arbor: University of Michigan Press.

Rouf, Kazi Abdur. 2015. "Grameen Bank Services to Women in Development (WID), Gender and Development (GAD), Women in Business (WIB), Women and Development (WAD) and Women in Environment (WED) Approach in Bangladesh." *International Journal of Research Studies in Management* 5: 2.

Simon, William, and John H Gagnon. 1986. "Sexual Scripts: Permanence and Change." *Archives of Sexual Behavior* 15, 2: 97–120.

The Conversation. 2019. "#MeToo Isn't Big in Africa. But Women Have Launched Their Own Versions." Accessed September 15, 2019. https://theconversation.com /metoo-isnt-big-in-africa-but-women-have-launched-their-own-versions-112328

Times Live Africa. 2018. "Stigma, Blame Means African Women Wary to Say #MeToo." Accessed September 15, 2019. https://www.timeslive.co.za/news/af rica/2018-10-05-stigma-blame-means-african-women-wary-to-say-metoo/

Trew, Bel. 2019. "Women Do Not Protest to Be Fetishised: Their Bravery Should Be Better Supported." *Independent*, December 2019. Accessed February 10, 2020. https://www.independent.co.uk/voices/woman-protests-sudan-egypt-turkey-supp ort-a9238131.html

Tsikata, Dzodzi. 2009. "Women's Organizing in Ghana Since the 1990s: From Individual Organizations to Three Coalitions." *Development* 52, 2: 185–192.

Turner, Victor. 1987 "The Anthropology of Performance." In *The Anthropology of Performance*, 72–98. New York: PAJ Publications.

UN Women. 2013. "World Conferences on Women." *UN Women: How We Work*. https://www.unwomen.org/en/how-we-work/intergovernmental-support/world -conferences-on-women

Utas, Mats. 2005. "Victimcy, Girlfriending, Soldiering: Tactic Agency in a Young Woman's Social Navigation of the Liberian War Zone." *Anthropological Quarterly* 78, 2: 403–430.

Van Rooyen, Carina, Ruth Stewart, and Thea De Wet. 2012. "The Impact of Microfinance in Sub-Saharan Africa: A Systematic Review of the Evidence." *World Development* 40, 11: 2249–2262.

Verhoef, Grietjie. 2002. "Stokvels and Economic Empowerment: The Case of African Women in South Africa, c. 1930–1998." In *Women and Credit: Researching the Past, Refiguring the Future*, edited by Bevery Lemire, Ruth Pearson, and Gail Grace Campbell. Oxford & New York: Berg Publishing.

Willoughby-Herard, Tiffany. 2014. "'The Only One Who Was Thought to Know the Pulse of the People': Black Women's Politics in the Era of Post-racial Discourse." *Cultural Dynamics* 26, 1: 73–90.

Chapter 1

Sama Jigéen

Women and Women-Led Associations in a New Era of Politics in Dakar, Senegal

Emily Jenan Riley

Yarax, Dakar, July 13th 2017, with Mously Diakhaté at a meeting with her Jappoo Jëf ci Jamm (Solidarity, Aid, and Peace) *associational members.*

17 days until the parliamentary election.

On the rooftop of a newly constructed building that looks towards the Port of Dakar, a group of women sat in a semicircle of chairs listening intently as their peers gave testimony to the support they received from their leader. It was the eve of the 2017 parliamentary elections, and they were meeting with their representative in parliament, Honorable Mously Diakhaté who also happened to be the leader of the association that gathered them. She sat amongst them wearing a striking pink dress with a black shawl for public discretion or for use to cover her head during prayer. *Jappoo Jëf ci Jamm* (Solidarity, Aid, and Peace), or *A3J*, was initiated by Mously to invest in income-generating activities of women in her district of Yarax and Hann Bel Air. The A3J group was like other groups focused on development, but also served as political support groups that were her base in political campaigns. One member stood up in front of the group and gave an emotional testimony of Mously's influence, saying "*Mously, mës na ma teral, mës na ma bëgg*" (Mously, she has always helped me, she has always loved me). Mously was behind her occupying her gaze on her rings, shyly rotating them around her fingers. The rest of the group erupted in chanting, "Dignity alone, those who don't have it, go nowhere," "*Jom rekk, ku ko amul du dem,*" while banging on metal bowls to keep rhythm.

Camberene, Dakar, June 12th 2017 At the Home of Awa Ka.

48 days until the parliamentary election.

Fifteen or so women sat together on a woven mat, each with their various items to sell such as mint, fabric, or handmade soap as they did every Monday. One woman was busily making *àttaaya*, the sweet mint jasmine tea and staple for afternoons among friends. They drank tea and chatted while waiting for their association leader Awa Ka to arrive with a special guest, a current parliamentary representative of President Macky Sall's coalition, *Benno Bokk Yaakaar* [A Shared Vision] from Pikine, Awa Niang. When Awa Ka arrived with Awa Niang and introduced her to the group, everyone stood up and began clapping while one woman sang out to mark their arrival, "Awa has arrived and she came with the honorable representative." *Awa ñëw na, da and ak honorable deputé.* Awa Ka presented the representative to her association. "This is my group, we work hard, we don't have much, but we work for whatever President Macky wants," she says as the women chose poignant moments to cheer, "we have nothing else but that." In a plug for her association, Awa Ka directs a question to Awa Niang, "if you can do anything. Since before Macky was president, we have been behind him and we haven't received anything. And you know the support people in Camberene have given. You and I have been together a long time." She emphasized, "we don't know anything else but people." *Xamunu lenneen lu dul nit.*

Mously and Awa have two general things in common. First, both are vying for a coveted position in parliament. Mously was fighting to hold onto her seat in parliament, and Awa was looking to cash in her social capital for a spot on the presidential party's roster. Second, they see women's associations and social relationships as the gateway to make this happen: politics as a resource for their social and economic development. The woman's praise for Mously demonstrates an affinity for her as a source of wealth and support, and as the women note here, *teraanga* (from *teral*), the popular Wolof concept that implies the generous and civic-minded intentions of individuals embedded in acts of giving, hospitality, and general socialization. I have argued elsewhere that in the context of politics in Senegal, women who are particularly adept at the art of *teraanga*—fortifying their relationships through financial and social prestations—have garnered significant support and success in state as well as local politics (Riley 2019). Senegalese society is run on social debt which is highly monetized. Ismael Moya argues that in Dakar especially, "there is no domain in social life in which money does not play a continuing role. Money is central to the economy as well as matrimonial relations and kinship, politics, or religious practice" (2015, 156). Because of the centrality of money to all social relations, people are also always indebted to one person or another as they nurture the network of friends and family members. The insistence on framing Mously's financial support for the association as a form of care suggests something moral as much as economic, and illustrates the long-term investments made by women like Mously and the numerous associations throughout the city of Dakar.

These investments, in the form of monetary contributions to kickstart projects or providing encouragement for said projects, create what Buggenhagen states "is intended to bestow the rights and obligations due to kin onto non-kin in order to expand one's circuit of exchange" (2012, 34) or what Vincent Foucher calls "performing munificence" (2007, 115)—a political strategy of generosity and patronage between a male politician and his female or male supporters. I argue in this chapter that in the era of women's increasing formal participation in and access to state politics, it is women who form their own female-driven patronage networks in the form of associations. Their performances of munificence, or *teraanga*, cultivate "horizontal" and "vertical" relations of hierarchy and dependence (Creevey 2004) that utilize the arena of politics to advance personal ambitions as well as collective opportunities to intervene in the allocation of state resources and policymaking. Furthermore, their patronage networks allow for women to emerge from the "hidden public" (Beck 2003) of male-dominated networks and, as Bayart (1989, 87) argues, potentially complicate the nature of the African state as a space of engendered inequality.

The types of associations I describe here are some of the most visible ways to rely on social debt in order to pool resources for further forms of exchange such as family ceremonies, marriages and marital/familial relations, or to have funds for other projects. And now, many of these associations have turned their efforts toward women within the state apparatus as their source for economic development. For Mously, on the one hand, the benefit of investing in these associations is having her peers active in ways that spur political support by helping her campaign. For members of these associations, they have access to funds to pay off debts and to create more income. Awa Ka, on the other hand, is the leader of a neighborhood women's association that seeks to benefit from the political capital she has with members of the party. Alternatively, Awa Ka with the help of her members (oftentimes family members) aligns herself with the party in order to launch her own political career. An ancillary benefit is that affiliation with the party helps provide support for the various projects that her members wish to finance. As Kelly points out, Senegalese parties "are often the expression of the ambition of a single politician, whose organization consists of the politician's family, friends, and neighbors who are socially and materially invested in his success . . . and consistently an expedient way to access state resources"

(2019, 8). These relationships are then sustained by the daily demonstrations of *teraanga* from a leader such as Awa in the form of gifting, sociality, and generosity of a woman in Mously's position who has access to these funds.

This chapter is based on ethnographic research I conducted during the summers of 2017 and 2018. In 2017, I accompanied both Mously and Awa[1] during their associational meetings as well as on the campaign trail for the legislative elections. I visited many homes in Camberene and the Yarax-Han Belair-Maristes neighborhoods of Dakar and saw firsthand the personal relationships they had with members of their associations and by extension, the family members and neighbors of their associational members. Beyond in-person meetings, Mously and Awa were constantly in communication with their members via phone calls or WhatsApp voice notes to organize events or simply listen to their grievances and see how they could help. Upon my return to Dakar in 2018, I was able to spend more time with the members as well as take a trip with Mously to the holy city of Touba, in central Senegal. By way of observations, interviews, and primary sources, I demonstrate how associations have become increasingly prominent spaces for women's political participation that is driven by intricate social relationships on many levels.

ASSOCIATIONS: CORNERSTONES OF SOCIAL AND POLITICAL LIFE

Women's associations in Senegal have long been a source of support, financial stability, and a reliable heartbeat to gauge the wellness of communities. Since precolonial times, associations have been how women assert power in their communities as well (Creevey 2004). They range from small groups of friends within a neighborhood that *natt*, share a stretched-out mat designed for socializing and pooling resources, to more robust associations—*mbootaay* in Wolof—with significant membership numbers that are often sponsored by women of greater means. In Dakar, the capital, it seems as though one could map the city neighborhoods based on the reach of associations and its members' residency. *Mbootaay* commonly bear the names of their particular neighborhood or more often the name of its founder. Frequently in the absence of state engagement with communities, it is women's associations that serve as protectorates of families, their health, their economic vitality, and increasingly local political representatives. During the colonial period women experienced a decrease in power, which was reinforced in the postcolonial period. However, as Lucy Creevey argues, Senegalese women's associations did not necessarily change this reality, but rather allowed women to gain resources that allowed them to deal with this reality (Creevey 2004, 68). Women's associations have over the years been the target of private and state-sponsored programs for money-making activities and microfinance loans from private institutions such as banks or nongovernmental organizations (NGOs) (Doligez, Fall, and Oualy 2012). Following Senegal's economic crisis of the 1980s and 1990s, microfinance programs were popularized by international organizations designed to boost small enterprises. Into the 1990s the Senegalese state became more hands-on in terms of regulating bank loans and providing specific funds for qualified projects. By 2003, a Ministry of Development and Microfinance was established, and by 2008 microfinance made up 10.25 percent of funds contributing to the economy (2012). Funded associations, especially those for women, would take part in short trainings on how to preserve fruits, to mill flour, or to dye textiles for eventual sale. Those associations that sought loans but did not have a bank account would find project finance and state-sponsored institutions such as PAMECAS[2] and Crédit Mutuel du Sénégal (state-sponsored institutions) as well as larger banks with microfinance divisions.

Women-led associations continue to be spaces where development projects and agencies such as those mentioned above, focus their efforts. For-profit outfits remain a source of funds for women and their projects of financial need; however, given the high interest rates of these loans and a tough economic climate for microenterprises, women have found creative ways of accessing funding. In this chapter I argue that since the instauration of gender quotas laws in 2010 (which I will refer to as *parité*) has inducted a historic number of women into state politics, women's associations have become both the *source* and beneficiaries of female leadership. To do so, I rely on ethnographic examples and a semibiographical look at Mously and Awa in leadership roles. The relationships between politicians and their associations and networks are established and maintained by formal and everyday displays of *teraanga* such as personal investment in the well-being of associational members via cash and material gifts, and professional support. Women then recognize the opportunity these relationships bear for benefiting from female support that is different from state institutional aide that comes with greater financial risk. In a similar study of members of several Ghanaian women's associations, many argued that "only women can represent women" (Fallon 2004, 82) and that organizations should use women's established informal networks to mobilize women for formal political participation (2004, 84). The women I spoke with also felt that an increase in women holding political offices would directly result in long overdue attention to women's issues that male politicians had historically ignored, and that associations were the natural place to find future female leaders.

PARITÉ AND THE RISE OF FEMALE LEADERS

With every new Senegalese administration, new institutions have capitalized on the power of women's associations. This includes the structural
adjustment programs of the Abdou Diouf era (1981–2000) and its focus on
development projects, mostly spearheaded by NGOs. Additionally, it encom-
passes Abdoulaye Wade's era (2000–2012) of state-sponsored small grants
to women's associations that defined a reciprocal relationship between the
states. In an interview the Senegalese public intellectual and sociologist Dr.
Baba Biaye (2017) noted that the state under Wade began to take over what
NGOs were doing and began promoting women's associations by controlling
where state microcredit funds were destined in hopes for a majority during
elections. For access to funds, their associations were dependent on state-
organized funds funneled through registered programs such as *Groupement
d'Intérêt Économique* (GIE)—Economic Interest Groups or *Groupement de
Promotion Féminin* (Gpf)—Women's Promotional Groups (Creevey 2004,
67). By implication, Wade's democratic party, and the associations receiving
microcredit and finance monies also capitalized on the power of women's
associations, one outcome being the vote to approve gender quotas in 2010.
Since 2012, the Macky Sall administration seems to be increasing the partisan
utilization of women's associations as a source of *militantisme* (fervent support) that was particularly poignant during the 2017 election season.

Kang and Tripp (2018) have documented the importance of domestically
sourced advocacy groups in African countries, especially Senegal, for the
successful advocacy and adoption of gender quota laws. They argue that
past considerations of international organizations driving the fight for gender
equality overlook the contributions of domestic organizations. In the case of
most women's groups in Senegal, the domestic does not simply mean within
the Senegalese territory, but the home as an important space for organizing.
Some of the most involved organizations for gender equality such as the network of women's organizations called *Siggil Jigéen* (Women Rise), or most
famously the *Council for Senegalese Women* (COSEF), began with women
meeting at one another's homes, through *mbootaay* groups. Homes have
been the place or origin for the beginnings of larger coalitions. As Rokhaya
Gassama, a member and trainer for COSEF states, "Long before it was called
parité, it was simply our mothers and grandmothers at home organizing and
calling for women to be able to participate in the life of the nation" (Gassame,
interview on August 5, 2017). Then with help from prominent women who
had broken into the political realm, COSEF and other coalitions helped advocate for the law of *parité* which was passed by the Senegalese Parliament
in 2010. This law mandates equal representation of men and women in all
elected positions through an electoral candidate quota system. The system

was then written into law and requires all political parties to nominate a minimum number of female candidates to their party lists (Rosen 2017). Rumored
to have gained support by President Abdoulaye Wade in order to garner votes
from female electorates, the law ushered in almost 50 percent of women into
parliament in 2012. This new era of women in elected positions formalized
women's participation in national politics.

However, women have always been instrumental to the functioning of
political parties and especially the construction of male politicians' popularity
as I detailed above. What Aminata Diaw (2004) calls the *présence-absence*
of Senegalese women in politics describes the integral role women played
in men's campaigns while remaining absent from the historical imaginary
of Senegalese politics and positions of power. Moreover, what Beck (2003)
similarly calls the "hidden public," women-led associations have historically
been seen as hotbeds for predominantly male-driven patron-client networks,
referring to women that helped with their campaigns as *sama jigéen*, or "my
woman/women" who were associational leaders in strategic neighborhoods
throughout the city and country. They organized rallies, fed attendees, and
provided liveliness (Allerton 2012). Additionally, they served as the visual
representation of the party by wearing matching outfits, *musoor* (head
wraps with party-specific colors), and T-shirts with the candidate's portrait.
However, in the *parité* era, women in political office are brought out of the
shadow of the "hidden publics" and into prominent roles in the state, and the
women-led associations then, become patronage networks driven by women,
for women.

THE 2017 ELECTION

In the early part of summer 2017, parties and newly formed coalitions chose
men and women for their lists. These were in turn submitted to the Ministry
of Elections with a steep fee to achieve formal registration. For parliamentary
elections, there are two types of representatives: those who represent a local
district and those who represent national interests. The national list required
sixty candidates from each party and the departmental lists depended upon the
population size of any given community. Regardless, all lists were mandated
to respect the *parité* law requiring alternating male and female candidates.
If a man was what they called *tête de liste* (the head of the list), the second
in line must be a woman, continuing to alternate down the list. There were a
record number of forty-seven registered parties and coalitions; of these, four
were led by women with a male candidate in second position. Although the
parité law was passed in 2010 and enacted for the 2012 parliamentary elections, parties in 2017 scrambled to find enough women to fill their party list

slots. I was told this was due to a lack of qualified candidates or few women who were interested or known to party veterans. To find women, most male-dominated parties sourced the thousands of associations throughout Dakar in strategic neighborhoods, mostly directed by women. This process was often haphazard. One freelance journalist told me that on the eve of the deadline to register party lists, people were scrambling to meet their quotes minutes before the deadline, asking others if anyone knew the names of women and men they could add to their incomplete lists. Potentially unaware or disconnected from the sophisticated women's associations throughout the city, it remains challenging for the general population of men and women to take women in politics seriously, not just as placeholders but as valuable contributors to state political decision-making.

What follows is a biographical look at Mously Diakhaté and Awa Ka. Both women are members of the party in power, *Benno Bokk Yaakaar,* and although they differ in their political successes, they share common strategies. Their stories allow for an intimate look at female leadership connecting the workings of local associations to national state politics.

MOUSLY DIAKHATÉ

Humble and Virtuous Beginnings

> *Moukhsinatou Diakhaté cannot represent anything but the heritage of a child of religious education. When she was born, it was Serigne Abdou Ahad Mbacké who baptized her, giving her the name of Moukhsinatou Mbacké, his own daughter. It is also Serigne Abdou Lahad Mbacké who gave her away in marriage to his son Serigne Sidy.*[3]
>
> —Serigne Mahmadane Mbacké, *Du Daara à l'Hemicycle*

In her autobiography *Du Daara à l'Hemicycle* (From Quranic School to Parliament), Moukhsinatou (Mously) Diakhaté tells the story of her childhood, her religious upbringing within the Mouride community, and her political career. The second half of the book is reserved for testimonies from her family, friends, and colleagues sharing their connections with Mously and observations of her life. Because she grew up with ties to the religious family *Mbacké*, descendants of Serigne Ahmadou Mbacké,[4] she was educated in the qur'anic school (*daara*). It was not until her adult years that she decided to learn French. Her father was a fervent follower of Serigne Abdou Lahad Mbacké, son of Serigne Touba and third Khalif of the Mourides. During a recent visit with Mously to Touba, the holy city of the Mourides, I came to realize just how important the Serigne was to her as well.

As her relative Serigne Mahmadane Mbacké notes in the opening quote of this section, Mously is the product of a Mouride education. She was once married to Serigne Sidy, who remains her spiritual guide and friend. Her home in Touba was under construction with few amenities except for a full wall-size print of Serigne Abdou Lahad Mbacké, which she touched affectionately upon entering the house. The kitchen was sparsely equipped, but the cabinets were full of mugs with Serigne's portrait on them for entertaining guests. She was preparing for the *magal* (pilgrimage) of Serigne Abdou Lahad where followers gathered to celebrate the birth of the Serigne every year. On the day, she hosts a large gathering at her house where fellow followers of the Serigne meet to share several meals. After arriving and unloading our bags, we immediately went to pay the family members of Serigne Abdou a visit. One house was right next door, as it was the Serigne who had given Mously the land to build her home. "I can't come to Touba and spend the night until I have greeted my religious guides," she said. This included a visit to Serigne Sidy's house each evening, as well as a large lunch with him and other followers at the home of his father, Serigne Abdou.

In addition to being raised within a religious family, Mously had plenty of mentors in the political realm. Her father was a local politician in Tambacounda where she was born. Tambacounda is situated "467 km from Dakar . . . a climate of the Sahel with a heat that is often unbearable, it is a melting-pot of ethnic groups . . . as the town served as a point of commercial transit between Dakar and Niger, Dakar and Kayes in Mali by way of the railroad" (Diakhaté 2011, 30). But it was from the guidance of her grandmother that she sourced her knowledge of local politics. Her grandmother, Fatou Ndiaye, managed a number of neighborhood associations and "was a reference for the women of her neighborhood of Darou Diène (in Tambacounda), where no one made decisions without speaking with her first. She was their *meeru mbootaaye* (mother of the association) and their political leader. She managed money-pooling groups (*lekket*) of women even before I was born" (Diakhaté 2011, 36). Mously stayed with her grandmother until the age of eighteen when she went to live with her mother in the Dakar suburb of Guediawaye.

Mously also worked as a member and leader of several neighborhood associations in the Dakar suburb of Guediawaye. This led her to become one of the most influential women to hold office in the post-*parité* era. Due in part to the increasing size of her associations, she was recognized as having significant influence in her community of Hann-Bel Air. This led her to accept positions as a municipal adviser and then as an assistant to the mayor. She was president of the Women's Alliance for the political party Jëf-Jël, created by an important opposition leader to Abdoulaye Wade's administration, Talla Sylla. Her parliamentary run began in 2007 due to her leadership among the women's group of Sylla's party. Mously has since been reelected twice, now with the current administration's coalition *Benno Bokk Yaakaar* (BBY).

Association Building

The associations she created began as a way for newly married women, who were yet to have children, to get to know one another. Much like sister associations across the city, the women gathered to pool resources together from an initial investment or *lekket*[5] from a woman of resources such as Mously. *Lekket* hold a symbolic role in life cycles, used to catch the baby's shaven hair in preparation for their baptism, collect the contributions for a grieving family, or hold the *soow* (goat's milk) shared by newlyweds in their new home. The structure of the associations vary from a twelve-month calendar cycle where one woman takes the whole pot to use toward whatever expenses she might have, to a system in which the total is evenly divided among the members. Some *lekket* begin with an invested amount from an external or internal donation to which members add or divide among themselves with the expectation of repayment with a small amount of interest depending on the loaning party. Daba Cadou, the coordinator of thirteen *lekket* groups in Yarax established by Mously for And Jappoo Jëf ci Jamm (A3J), was chosen by a male colleague to be introduced to his "*jigéen*" Mously. They have been collaborating ever since. "Bi ma duggee ci Mously ba tey, regrettewuma benn yoon" ("when I started committing myself to work with Mously, I have never regretted it"), she said.

Associations have long been a reality for many women as part of their social networks among family, friends, neighbors, and members from other associations, often religious ones. For example, Daba and her friends in A3J often organized religious conferences and named Mously as the honoree. Mously would attend and reinforce her solidarity by giving gifts of money and encouragement. Although arguably looking for investment from individuals within parties rather than loan institutions to inject money into what had been mostly small member contributions is a newer phenomenon. It is no wonder, then, that they would be a source for politicians to garner supporters by either founding the associations themselves or tapping into an already influential one. While such associations are nothing new, they have become even more relevant as a way for women and their households to cope in a poststructural adjustment reality which has shifted most economic activity to the informal sector (Hannaford and Foley 2015). In addition to providing everyday support, many *mbootaay* ease financial burdens by paying for obligatory family expenses such as funerals, weddings, and baptisms. Such support is necessary, considering that these social events have only increased in fervor and price.

Political Gateways

For the three weeks of allowed campaigning, I shadowed Mously and her campaign team as they visited every small crevice of the tightly packed homes nestled along the seaside neighborhoods of Hann-Bel Air and Yarax. You felt simultaneously squeezed by the walls while also emerging to see the ocean only a few steps away. Mously preferred to campaign within her district alone instead of scouring the Senegalese countryside with other party members. With official aides and family members doubling as assistants in tow, we walked and greeted residents, stopping briefly in the homes of her A3J members to receive prayers and well-wishes. In some cases, the houses were so close together that a short visit would cause a traffic jam as not everyone could fit into the house or courtyard and had to backtrack.

One evening we ended up on a rooftop with an A3J group, the scene depicted at the beginning of this chapter. The purpose was to inform newer members about what the association does and to update older members on any new developments. It was also an occasion for Mously to solicit their support for the election, although she and her associates were careful to make the distinction between the work they were doing with the associates and their political participation. Her A3J technical adviser, Fatima Ndiaye stood in front of the group and gave a report-like speech about the type of funds they had and would continue to receive, and their purpose. She begins with:

> Everything you are involved in, you should know where it started and where it's going. A3J means, Solidarity, Aid, and Peace[6] and is an association created by our Honorable Mously Diakhaté in 2011. She is a woman with courage and dignity who is engaged and even though they told her she couldn't do it, she turned around and created FADES, Economic and Social Development Funds. A3J is involved in politics, but beyond that, it promotes sustainable community development. What does that mean? It means to promote self-sufficiency. When her party took over the government she could have just taken that money and shared it with her family, but she didn't do that. Currently, A3J groups together [form] 250 associations, within Senegal and internationally, right? FADES works on reinforcing personal ability such as teaching those who do not know how to write their own name or training to learn how to plant urban gardens in members' homes.[7]

Fatima continues to frame Mously's investment in A3J members as a sign of generosity and charity because she used her own funds to invest in the association and put her reputation on the line with international donors. "*Du fonds politique. Dama bëgga mu leer, du fonds politique, dafa téye ay biens wam, dem banque di fa leb ngir jàppale jigéen yi. Kooku amul jom?*" ("These are not political finances, I want that to be clear, these are not political finances. She uses her own means, goes to the bank and borrows money to help women. Don't tell me that she doesn't have dignity?"). The women erupted in a chant, *"jom rekk, yombul dooleem amul, jom rekk!"* ("Pure dignity, it's not easy and she doesn't have much strength, just dignity!"). I would hear this same chant at various A3J meetings or rallies during the campaign as it served as Mously's anthem.

Conveying Mously's dedication to the women's associations despite a lack of funds was a way to demonstrate her benevolence and goodwill. Her lack of strength was more of her status as a woman having less "political capital" than actual motivation or money. Alassane Kitane argues that what was once a treasured safety net of a moral identity, *jom*, has become descriptive of the strategies that one employs in order to survive economic difficulty (2010). For many of the women in Mously's sphere, they see her and the political environment as one that can solve their economic problems. "Whatever you do, we do. If you stand up, we stand up. We only wanted someone who would help us. Women do not have those to help them" one member said. When I sat down with Mously for an interview she reflected on her role as the leader of A3J and the opportunities they offer her and her constituents.

> It's not everyone that God gives the opportunity to work with women's associations like I have. I created several women's associations and ensured they were working and then let them continue by themselves while I moved to another project. I have always wanted to work with women. A3J is mixed with men and women but most are dominated by women because I have empathy for them. Because they are tired of associations, money-pooling groups, with movements, with political parties, yet revenues don't come easily. In addition, banks want to kill them because the interest rates for most financial institutions are expensive and the loans do not last long. Senegalese women have a lot of courage to take care of their families. And even if they have a husband, women are the ones taking care of their families about 80 percent of the time.[8]

In this excerpt Mously gives a strong testimony of just how much weight she gives her role as a politician to the successes of the associations. Beyond herself, she sees the state as a more benevolent partner to women's causes, mostly as a third-party financier, saving women from unproductive debt that private financial institutions force upon them. Dr. Biaye argues that one result of the Wade era's emphasis for increased state control of development projects is what he calls the augmentation of "grignoter au dela de la politique" or a strong dependence on the state that has co-opted women's associations as the focal point for state control (Biaye, interview on May 30, 2017). As the state has in many ways usurped major aspects of civil society, development projects that had been overseen by NGOs were now not only offered by the state, but more often initiatives stemming from individual politicians. It then makes sense that Mously's long-term cultivation of relationships with the women was how the funds reach them. She sees this as a kind of personal charity stemming from a shared experience of being a woman. The testimonies of her associational members suggest they feel similarly.

"She has encouraged me to run for mayor of Yarax since the man who is there now doesn't do anything," Daba mentioned (Cadou, interview on June 21, 2019). My interview with Daba took place in the summer of 2019 and we reflected back to the 2017 campaign. She smiled and asked, "Do you remember when our members mentioned how dirty the Yarax market was?" I remembered very clearly indeed that the women recounted having pled with the mayor to have the market cleaned, but to no avail. Upon hearing this, Mously marched down to the market, staged a made-for-TV interview with the women, and used it to publicly shame the mayor. "The next day, the mayor had a cleaning crew down there," Daba said with a smile. "That is the kind of person Mously is, always giving and always finding ways of helping others with dignity."

Ambitious Vulnerabilities

Shame is what I really fear.

—Mously Diakhaté

As part of the campaigning strategy in Mously's district, Yarax, the party asked that she and the other candidate, Ndèye Fatou Diouf campaign together. "I always tell my women that Macky Sall loves Yarax because he chose two of its daughters for the party," said Mously. Ndèye Fatou had been chosen by the president as number two on the party list, whereas Mously was much further down. Mously was uneasy about Ndèye Fatou and worried about her chances for reelection because for each party member elected, 10,000 individual votes for that particular party were required. On our way home from visiting families alongside Ndèye Fatou, Mously whispered to me that the only thing she was afraid of was the shame of people in her district not voting for her, especially after all of her investments. Because one's political livelihood depends on the social capital that someone like Mously can gain, for her to lose in her own district would be a clear rebuke of her as a person.

When the final counts were announced, the coalition *Benno Bokk Yaakaar*, mostly dominated by Alliance pour la Republique Macky Sall's party, won 125 seats of the 165 available. Mously and Ndèye Fatou were elected as representatives for their districts in the department of Dakar. Although Ndèye Fatou was elected as part of the party majority, she did not win in her own district, precisely what Mously feared for herself: the idea that to lose one's own district meant their neighbors and possibly family members do not see them as a viable part of their small world. For Mously, her long-term participation and investment in the women's associations were the source of her political success.

In order to put Mously's story into comparison while reasserting the importance of women's associations and politics, I will turn to Awa Ka. Mously's story has demonstrated an ideal of a woman who has risen through the ranks of associations into a coveted position in the government. Awa's story and a few perspectives from some of her members, however, show the complex efforts from within the associations to be relevant to a political party and use this connection for personal and communal gain.

AWA KA

Beginning Where the People Are

Awa Ka, similar to Mously, was also born into a religious family and community. The Layene are one of the five main Sufi communities in Senegal. Like the Mourides, the Layene community was developed in the late 1800s by founder, Seydina Limamou Laye and Mahdi (who was the second coming of the Prophet Mohammed). The Layene are located among the fishing villages of Yoff, Camberene, and Malika that run along the Presqu'île coastline in present day Dakar. Awa, like many in Camberene is a devout Muslim and Layene.

Upon arriving at her family's home situated in the central neighborhood of Camberene, first built by her father, there is a distinctive mural of the second Khalif of the Layene, Seydina Madione Lahi. The portrait depicts a man in white clothing with a large black turban wrapped around the top of his head and a white cloth wrapped and tucked under his chin. Most families in Camberene, an original Layene village, have similar paintings or photos hanging in the home of a particular *khalif* who has special importance to the family. After the gate was a beautiful tile courtyard big enough for a car, and a long hallway leading into the house. This is where the women sat along the wall of the hallway on the floor or in plastic chairs reserved for guests.

Awa's family and social life revolves around her identity as a Layene, as do her politics. She is a state employee who does not hold political office, but has the attention of the ruling party based on her activities and support for the party via her associations as well as the importance of capturing the Layene vote. She is a self-declared idealist and has a picture of President Macky Sall next to her bed. She speaks about her allegiance to Macky Sall, even when it was not beneficial to her. A childhood friend recounted that her home was always a place to gather after school because her mother would always have leftovers for anyone who was hungry. Awa herself espoused a similar policy, seen by those who know her as the mother-figure of many, with a home that is open to anyone, in the spirit of Seydina Limamou Laye and the principles of the Layene as well as her personal conviction of being at the service of others. "Anyone who comes to her, she never refuses you," says Khady Ka, one of Awa's *mbootaay* members. I was told by other community members that she was the woman who organized Layene women for *Benno Bokk Yaakaar* and held the key to women's activities in Camberene. When I met her in 2017, she was hoping to be honored with a spot on the party's list for all of her help ensuring a victory for Macky Sall in Camberene and neighboring Yoff. Although Awa had not been given the opportunity to serve in the parliament leading up to the 2017 election, her participation has been a pathway for steady investments from the party which serves her associations.

Most members of her associations are women in the neighborhood, close friends, or even distant relatives such as Khady Ka. Khady shared with me that Awa always shared and never kept money to herself. I pressed further, wondering if she had had previous experiences that were not as positive as she made Awa Ka out to be. "Yes, in fact, we had another leader who just kept the money to herself. She didn't share as much as she received from outside donors, and we never really knew how much she was given," Khady said (Ka, interview on June 16, 2019). "Many of us left her and went to Awa." In the case of Khady, although she is a cousin of Awa, it was not their family connections that brought them together; instead, it was Khady's recognition of Awa as an honest, generous, and good person. It was Awa's characteristics and dedication to her members that she showed through *teraanga* and more official associational transactions that attracted these women to her.

Power in Numbers

I first met Awa at one of the association meetings on a Monday evening. I was introduced to her by a mutual friend who said she was the one to see about women and politics. It was difficult to find time to sit down and talk with her as she was always on the go. This is probably not surprising seeing that she's president of several women associations in Camberene. One evening we chatted about her associations. "Each week we contribute 500 cfa ($1) and every once in a while, I add another 25,000 cfa ($50) of my own money." She manages three separate *lekket*. Two are for aggregating money over a year's time to then withdrawing a large sum at the end of the cycle. The third group was named after Awa by her peers so that she would invest in what they called a "social" group, one that is for more immediate needs such as paying for a wedding or funeral. Similar to most associations, members choose a leader, and then name their group after the individual or group, so as to solicit investments from them.

Awa was in charge of all three but named as a sort of godmother for the particular association I was attending. This was the same technique families employed when naming a child, often doing so with the idea in mind that their namesake would be someone of means to help support the child. I asked Khady Ka how she had come to know Awa and what interested her about politics. She replied that she had not known Awa very well, despite being cousins, until Awa brought her into the fold of various political activities. "Politics are what brought us together," she said. When I asked what she meant by politics bringing them together, she said, "If Awa is going some-where [supposedly a political meeting] she asks us to go with her, then we meet at her house and every Monday we gather for our *lekket* that Awa cre-ated to help us. Machallah, she loves people, wants us all to be united. I pray that God makes her representative and gives her, her half."

What I found curious about Khady's statement was there seemed to be a seamless connection between what she called politics and the money-pooling activities for the purposes of development led by Awa. Politics, therefore, was simply another strategy for weathering the economic storms that had become even more viable an option with the increasing number of women in positions of power. For Awa to succeed in obtaining a position within parlia-ment would mean that those who supported her efforts and benefited from her help would also see an increase in funding.

Selfless Ambition

In the weeks leading up to the deadline to submit party lists, people like Awa Ka were running around meetings with party leaders, holding association-sponsored events, and attending large gatherings such as a religious ceremony held by the main group *Femmes de Benno Bokk Yaakaar* (Women of Benno Bokk Yaakaar, or FBBY) with the presence of her members. FBBY was in charge of gathering and supporting the women's groups associated with their party, such as Awa and her members. Despite being reimbursed only slightly for travel to and from the event, Awa and others hoped their presence would add to her chances of gaining a place on the list.

On the evening the lists were announced, it was as if the whole of Dakar was tuned in to the radio as they read off the names for each party and coali-tion. People could be seen huddling around cars or plugged into their ear-phones, one person for each side. I called Awa to see whether she was on the list for Benno Bokk Yaakaar, only to find that she was not. Understandably upset, she said, "I won't campaign for them, and they didn't even place those on the list that have people, they are going to have problems in Dakar." Her words were indignant. For Awa, Macky Sall had made the wrong choice, preferring women who, in her mind, didn't have the people power in the city to gather a majority for the party. Not only this, but she felt the party owed her something for her dedication and crowdsourcing. Her frustration was palpable, and her members were also disappointed, saying the party had let them down. However, when catching up with Awa in the summer of 2019 on the back of the presidential election that saw President Macky Sall reelected, she had changed her tone. In the place of earning a seat in parliament with the president's coalition, she mentioned she had become much more involved in the First Lady Marième Faye's charity organization, *Servir le Sénégal* (Serve Senegal). "Months before the election, I told the First Lady that they needed to start campaigning right away," Awa said. She lobbied with other presidents of communities across Dakar for money that would go to her members as they organized the campaign.

The First Lady suggested that each community receive three million cfa to share among the various associations, of which they calculated ten for each community. I said, no, make it five million. She said okay, dropped 50 million cfa ($85,000) and said the rest would come from the Ministry of Women's Affairs, for a total of 95 million cfa ($160,000) to be given evenly to each community. The thing with Camberene is, we are a community that shares. You can't give to some and not to others. The other thing is, Camberene has a lot of associations (*lekket*), religious groups (*dahira*) and so when I called on all the associations in Camberene for their lists of members, there were 48 groups instead of 10. Granted, there are women who join several associations in order to receive more. I don't care if they do that. You know that road in front of Mbaye Seck's house [asking me about a large open area near our mutual friend's place]? That couldn't even hold all of us. Ha! No one knows how many people were there.

Awa played a video of the meeting that featured the First Lady and several ministers and to my eyes and ears it sounded a lot like a Layene religious gathering with the distinctive *zikr*, or religious chanting, and all of the women dressed in white. Although Awa did not get what she wanted in 2017, she found other ways of remaining in the political arena in order to keep her associations going. She took advantage of the benevolence of the party that seeks to invest in associations such as hers that need funds for money-making projects and have their finger on the pulse of the voting bloc. Their countless stories attest to Awa's generosity through advocacy for members as well as her own investments in their activities. "During Eid, she brought everyone potatoes and onions, which is not easy [inexpensive], and that is not political money, it is her own money. That is *teraanga*," said Khady Ka. Awa's self-less ambition meant that she not only sought funding through her political contacts but also used them to help her members. Something Khady made clear was that this was not the case with their former leader who was ambitious as well as selfish. Awa, on the other hand, saw no difference between her own successes and those of her association.

CONCLUSION

Associations steered predominantly by women have been historically central to the successes of male-led political parties. Men mostly referred to them as *"sama jigéen"* or my women, capitalizing on women's abilities to support their campaigns. Since the 2010 passing of the *parité* law, there has been a noticeable shift. The stories of Mously and Awa demonstrate how the correlation between women's increased active presence in political life and their involvement with various associations provides women with upward mobility and rewards them with people power. These benefits are created and nurtured in many ways by prestations of *teraanga* that seem much like some parts philanthropic ventures and others, political maneuvers. Women's associations are also an important source of supporters, voters, and visibility. People like Awa Ka who manage an extensive network of women also lean on politicians with whom they have connections for intermediary support. At the same time, her members place hope in her ability to ascend to a position of greater power as it may translate to their own access to funds. At the heart of these interactions is the investment in social capital that takes place through instigating and continuing a circulation of money and constant support.

Mously Diakhaté is one of many female politicians that gained their start in politics from within neighborhood associations that have sought support and resources from microcredit institutions. Their membership is contingent on pooling money and creating a community of interdependence between members that goes beyond the association itself. She sees her investments in the associations as a result of her political status to be a viable alternative to the untenable debt women accrue from "the banks and other micro credit institutions that want to kill them [with debt]" (Diakhaté, interview on May 5, 2017). They do not share the same pity for the social realities of financial demand and reimbursement with which Mously has firsthand experience. Instead, their debt to her is a social one, showing up to her events, creating the lively atmosphere so desired at political rallies, and the voting power to bring a party majority.

Several of my interviewees, be they representatives for various parties or those aspiring to break into politics, expressed a hierarchical and circular type of social and financial debt, placing them either at the end or at the center of an interdependence for access to resources and power. Many scholars have tended toward calling this form of patronage politics or clientelism (O'Brien 1975; Fatton 1986). However, what Mously and Awa's stories show is how patronage networks are taking on new forms as women move from leaders of associations to leaders of parties. As women like them gain access to new resources as well as legislative powers, it allows them to pay attention to issues important to women and the households they manage. This is to say that involvement in politics is one of many strategies these women utilize for overcoming oppressions not just in terms of gender inequality, but economic oppression that affects their entire family.

For both Awa Ka and Mously Diakhaté, their participation within women's associations is one of continual renewal that relies on the circulation of social and financial debt. Equally, members of these associations see leaders such as Awa and Mously as both role models of morality and gatekeepers to financial opportunities. As is apparent from their stories, some are successful in attaining their goals of political power, and others fall short. In either case, what attracts their members to them is a shared kinship in the struggle for economic stability and relevance. In other words, they now have someone to "help women." Mously's members reference to her as having *jom*, as Kitane (2010) notes, is a recognition of her using her position of power to affect change, which she (as a product of similar associations) is well placed to do. Similarly with Awa, her members are loyal to her because she has shown a selfless strategy for using politics by way of these associations to improve her and her members' lives. The dignity that Mously and Awa demonstrate is adaptive to changing needs in the community and is expressed through the prestations of *teraanga* in its smallest and most visible forms. These processes ensure that women like them continue to gain support which places women in positions of overturning in equal access to resources based on gender.

NOTES

1. Mously Diakhaté and Awa Ka both gave their written and verbal permission to be interviewed through an accepted IRB process.

2. PAMECAS is an acronym for the Partenariat pour la Mobilisation de l'Epargne et du Crédit au Senegal.

3. *Sokhna Moukhsinatou Diakhaté ne peut incarner que cet heritage de doomu daara. A sa naissance, c'est Serigne Abdou Ahad Mbacké qui l'a baptisée, lui*

donnant le nom Moukhsinatou Mbacké, sa propre fille. C'est aussi Serigne Abdou Lahad Mbacké qui l'a donnée en mariage à son propre fils Serigne Sidy.

4. The religious family Mbacké are descendants of Serigne Ahmadou Mbacké, also known as Serigne Touba. Toube was the founder of the local Muslim Sufi order the Mourides.

5. *Lekket* is the Wolof term for a deep hollow gourd.

6. And Jappoo Jëf ci Jamm.

7. *"Lepp nga yengoo war nga xam fi mu tambali ak fi mu jëm. A3J mooy, And Jappoo Jef ci Jamm, muy association boo xam ne sunu honorable Mously Diakhaté moo ko sës 2011 mooy jigeen bu am jom, am engagement nu ne 'dootoo way' mu wëlbëtiku creer FADES, muy Fonds d'Appui Developpement Economique et Sociales. Reseau A3J day politique mais ginaaw politique day def developpement communauté durable. Loolu mooy lan? Mooy suqali sa am-amu bopp. Ba nu ko falle 2012 menoon na falluwaat na la 'ma am dama koy bokk ak samay mbokk waaye deful loolu.' Tey reseau A3J mu ngi 250 associations du noonu? Ci biir senegal ak a l'internationale. Mu daldi creer FADES mu fonds di def renforcement de capacite manaam ni menul bind seen tuur nu jangal leen na nu bindee. Mu welbatiku def formation microjardinage nan nu defee bey, beyu ker."*

8. *"Du nun ñepp lu la Yalla may nu jaar ci les associations féminines comme man. J'ai crée beaucoup d'associations féminines yoo xamantane bu ci nekk dama ko crée ba mu yegg, ba mu dox quand même ma bàyyi leen ñu doxal man ma dem ci lenneen. Toujours maa ngi bëgga liggéey ci femmes yi. Association bi [A3J] c'est mix homme-femmes, mais quand même dominant des femmes parce que dama leen yërëm. Parce que sonn nañu ci association yi ci tuur yi ci mouvement yi ci parties yi alors que les revenus demewul noonu. Alors que les banques ñu ngi leen di bëgga rey parce que institutions financières yu bare seen taux de pourcentage chère na durée bi gàtt na. Alors que les femmes sénégalaises am nanu courage bu mag a mag pour yorr seen famille yi. Même ñu fi am jëkkër presque ñoo yor seen famille à 80 pourcent."*

REFERENCES

Allerton, C. 2012. "Making Guests, Making 'Liveliness': The Transformative Substances and Sounds of Manggarai Hospitality." *Journal of the Royal Anthropological Institute* 18: s49–s62.

Bayart, Jean-François. 1989. *L'Etat en Afrique: La Politique du Ventre*. Paris: Fayard.

Beck, Linda J. 2003. "Democratization and the Hidden Public: The Impact of Patronage Networks on Senegalese Women." *Comparative Politics* 35(2): 147–169.

Biaye, Baba. 2017. Interview, May 30, 2017.

Buggenhagen, Beth A. 2012. *Muslim Families in Global Senegal: Money Takes Care of Shame*. Bloomington: Indiana University Press.

Cadou, Daba. 2019. Interview, June 21, 2019.

Creevey, Lucy. 2004. "Impacts of Changing Patterns of Women's Association Membership in Senegal." In *The Power of Women's Informal Networks: Lessons in Social Change from South Asia to West Africa*, edited by Bandana Purkayasha and Mangala Subramaniam, 61–74. Lanham, MD: Lexington Books.

Diakhaté, Moukhsinatou (Mously). 2011. *Du Daara a L'Hemicycle*. Dakar: Le Nègre International.

Diakhate, Mously. 2017. Interview, May 5, 2017.

Diaw, Aminata. 2004. "Les Femmes à l'épreuve du Politique: Permanances et Changements." In *Gouverner le Sénégal: Entre Ajustement Structurel et Développement Durable*, edited by Momar-Coumba Diop. Paris: Éditions Karthal.

Doligez, François, François Seck Fall, and Mansa Oualy. 2012. *Expériences de microfinance au Sénégal*. Dakar: Cres – Karthala.

Fallon, Kathleen M. 2004. "Using Informal Networks to Seek Formal Political Participation in Ghana." In *The Power of Women's Informal Networks: Lessons in Social Change from South Asia to West Africa*, edited by Bandana Purkayasha and Mangala Subramaniam, 75–88. Oxford: Lexington Books.

Foucher, Vincent. 2007. "'Blue Marches': Public Performance and Political Turnover in Senegal." In *Staging Politics: Power and Performance in Asia and Africa*, edited by Julia C Strauss, and Donal B Cruise O'Brien, 111–132. London: I.B.Tauris.

Gassama, Rokhaya. 2017. Interview, August 5, 2017.

Hannaford, D, and EE Foley. 2015. "Negotiating Love and Marriage in Contemporary Senegal: A Good Man Is Hard to Find." *African Studies Review* 58(2): 205–225.

Ka, Awa. 2017. Interview, July 4, 2017.

Ka, Khady. 2019. Interview, June 16, 2019.

Kang, Alice J, and Aili Mari Tripp. 2018. "Coalitions Matter: Citizenship, Women, and Quota Adoption in Africa." *Perspectives on Politics* 16 (1): 73–91.

Kelly, Catherine Lena. 2019. *Party Proliferation and Political Contestation in Africa: Senegal in Comparative Perspective*. London: Palgrave Macmillan.

Kitane, Alassane Khodia. 2010. *Le Sénégal Sous Wade: Cahiers d'une Démocratie Sans Démocrates*. Dakar: L'Harmattan.

Moya, Ismaël. 2015. "Unavowed Value: Economy, Comparison, and Hierarchy in Dakar." *HAU: Journal of Ethnographic Theory* 5(1): 151–172.

Ndiaye, Fatimata. 2017. Interview, July 17, 2017.

Riley, Emily Jenan. 2019. "The Politics of Teraanga: Gender, Hospitality, and Power in Senegal." *Political and Legal Anthropology Review* 42(1): 110–124.

Rosen, Jennifer. 2017. "Gender Quotas for Women in National Politics: A Comparative Analysis Across Development Thresholds." *Social Science Research* 66: 82–101.

Chapter 2

"Anything That Departs from Justice to Injustice Is Not Part of the *Shari'a"*

Women's Rights Activism and Islamic Legal Reform in Zanzibar

Jessica Ott

INTRODUCTION

In October 2016, Subira,*[1] a thirty-one-year-old woman from Zanzibar town, entered the offices of the Zanzibar Female Lawyers Association (ZAFELA) seeking legal advice in her quest to receive a divorce from the archipelago's Islamic *kadhi*'s courts. I learned about Subira's case in 2017, when I was engaged in participant observation at ZAFELA's Jang'ombe offices for my dissertation fieldwork and came across her case file. On Subira's client intake form, a ZAFELA social work intern listed her husband's inability to provide for her and their two children and domestic violence as her reasons for wanting a divorce. Rahma,* a ZAFELA paralegal, drafted her legal paperwork, which Subira carried onward to the urban Islamic *kadhi*'s court of Kwerekwe. *Kadhi*'s courts handle all divorce cases in Zanzibar between Muslims, but only recently have ZAFELA paralegals and lawyers begun to complete the legal claim forms of divorce-seeking women, combining their Islamic legal knowledge with local cultural realities.

Seven months later, the *kadhi* (Islamic judge) of Kwerekwe, on Zanzibar's most populous island of Unguja, refused Subira her desired divorce. He handled more divorce cases than the rest of Zanzibar's *kadhis* combined[2] and had a reputation for refusing to grant women a divorce. Rahma sprung to action, appealing the *kadhi*'s ruling to the more authoritative Chief *Kadhi*. In Rahma's appeal, she contested the *Qur'anic* verse upon which the *kadhi* had depended in his ruling: "There's no wrongdoing if spouses are able to come up with a solution between them, and to come up with a solution is more

43

desirable."[3] Rahma explained that the couple had exhausted their problem-solving efforts and that the marriage should be dissolved in order to avoid worse damage. Rahma then cited another *Qur'anic* verse, stating, "God is content to allow the dissolution of a marriage when each person has put forth his or her best effort."[4] Rahma concluded that maintaining a marriage is the responsibility of a husband and wife, and if one of them is defeated in living with the other in a state of love and sympathy, a marriage is irreparable and should be dissolved. Rahma then told Subira to first visit the office of the *mufti*, a state-appointed Islamic juridical scholar who is empowered to make overriding Islamic legal judgments in Zanzibar,[5] before proceeding onward to the Chief *Kadhi*. The *mufti*'s office granted Subira a divorce, rendering her written appeal to the Chief *Kadhi* unnecessary. I was impressed by Rahma's extensive knowledge of Islamic law and asked where she was trained. She matter-of-factly explained that she gained most of her Islamic legal knowledge from her childhood *madrasa* (Islamic school), where she was exposed to all four Sunni schools of Islamic law.[6]

Rahma relies on her knowledge of Islamic jurisprudence as she drafts the legal claim forms of divorce-seeking clients, a task that was until recently relegated to *kadhi*'s court clerks (Stiles 2009). Rahma also relies on her Islamic legal knowledge as she appeals the decisions of district-level *kadhis* to Zanzibar's Chief *Kadhi* and to the *mufti*'s office. A devout Muslim, Rahma uses the client meeting room as a space of prayer and describes her paralegal work as divinely ordained. The role of ZAFELA paralegals and lawyers in writing Islamic legal justifications for divorce and in appealing the decisions of *kadhis* represents the entrée of women as authoritative figures of Islamic legal knowledge in Zanzibar's male-dominated *kadhi*'s courts. This chapter is about the efforts of a broader coalition of Zanzibari women's rights activists who have tried to expand the Islamic legal authority that women like Rahma practice by advocating for women's right to adjudicate Islamic legal cases as *kadhis*.

Zanzibari women's rights activists have been advocating for women's expanded Islamic legal authority for over a decade, which has implications for women's Islamic leadership more broadly. I begin this chapter with a historical overview and a description of women's experiences with Zanzibar's *kadhi*'s courts, which, despite their shortcomings, have long served as a space where women have been able to make claims to their Islamic legal rights. I continue with an overview of the Swahili philosophical concept of *umoja* (unity and solidarity), which has guided Zanzibari women's rights activists in their national and transnational networking. I then explore activists' recent efforts to reform Zanzibar's *kadhi*'s courts, which began with a knowledge exchange between ZAFELA and Malaysia-based Sisters in Islam in 2013 and culminated in a strategic letter to the president of Zanzibar in 2017.

Activists tried and failed to establish support among Zanzibar's Organization of Muslim Clerics (JUMAZA), which ultimately impeded their ability to pass a law that would allow women to serve as *kadhis*. They succeeded in passing other major reforms, including an equitable division of matrimonial property and a higher education requirement for *kadhis*.

Moving forward, Zanzibari women's rights activists are working to cultivate a cadre of young women Islamic scholars, whom they believe will bring about a depatriarchalized Islamic legal system through an ability to empathize with women litigants and a deep knowledge of their faith. It is this vision of a young women-centered and Islamic knowledge-based solidarity that propels Zanzibari women's rights activists like Rahma forward in their work.

HISTORICAL OVERVIEW

Zanzibar is a semiautonomous archipelago off the coast of Tanzania. Historically, Zanzibar was an important base for Indian Ocean traders, coming under Portuguese rule in the early sixteenth century until falling under the control of the Sultan of Oman in the late seventeenth century. The Sultanate of Oman relocated its capital from Muscat to Zanzibar in 1840, benefiting economically from clove plantations, ivory, and the slave trade. Zanzibar became a British protectorate in 1890, which greatly reduced the power of the Sultanate. In December 1963, the British protectorate was abolished, and Zanzibar became a constitutional monarchy under the Sultan, who was overthrown during a violent revolution in January 1964. Soon after the revolution, Zanzibar entered into a contentious union government with then-Tanganyika to form Tanzania and implemented major socialist reforms. Historical divisions in Zanzibar have manifested more recently in political discord between supporters of the ruling CCM party and supporters of the archipelago's main opposition party, Civic United Front (CUF).

Zanzibar's legal history is intertwined with its political history. The archipelago's Islamic *kadhi*'s courts have arbitrated disputes in Zanzibar since at least the start of the nineteenth century (Stiles 2009). Upon Zanzibar becoming a British protectorate in 1890, European laws were superimposed on existing local structures of customary and religious law (Calaguas, Drost, and Fluet 2007), which constricted the jurisdiction of *kadhis* (Islamic judges) to marriage, divorce, and inheritance cases in which relatively small amounts of property were at stake (Stockreiter 2015). After the 1964 revolution, Zanzibar's Islamic legal system was disrupted until its reinstatement in 1985 (Stiles 2009). Today, Zanzibar's legal system is based primarily on British common law, with multilevel magistrate's courts that deal with civil and criminal cases; a high court that maintains unlimited jurisdiction over civil and criminal cases; and Islamic *kadhi*'s courts that deal with cases related to marriage, divorce, and inheritance (Calaguas, Drost, and Fluet 2007). *Kadhi*'s courts have clerks, who play a central role in constructing case arguments and determining the legal viability of cases (Stiles 2009); *ulama* (Islamic scholars), who meet with and advise litigants before *kadhis* hear their cases;[7] and *kadhis*, or Islamic judges. All *kadhis* in Zanzibar follow the *Shafi'i* school of Islamic law (Stiles 2009).

GENDER AND THE *KADHI'S* COURTS IN ZANZIBAR

While Zanzibari women's rights activists more recently have made it their mission to reform the archipelago's Islamic legal system, the *kadhi*'s courts have long served as a space where women have been able to make claims to their Islamic legal rights, most frequently to a divorce. The *kadhi*'s courts have been accessible to and used by women from the precolonial period up until the present day (Stockreiter 2015). In her ethnography of a *kadhi*'s court in Mkokotoni, Zanzibar, Erin Stiles (2009) reported a widespread belief among Zanzibari men that the *kadhi*'s courts were "one-eyed," or more likely to rule in women's favor. In neighboring Kenya, Susan Hirsch (1998) described women's decisions to seek legal recourse in Malindi's *kadhi*'s court as enabling the reworking of patriarchal gender norms, since women who described their marital woes in the semipublic space of the court challenged a gendered Swahili cultural norm of not airing one's dirty laundry in public. At the same time, in order to receive a divorce, women often had to perform the role of the devoted, persevering wife. The *kadhi*'s court in Malindi served as a space for women to challenge some gender norms, while other gender norms were reinforced.

Zanzibari women's rights activists began to discuss their concerns with the archipelago's *kadhi*'s courts in the early 2000s.[8] Then and now, they have been mostly concerned with a high rate of divorce and its economic implications for women. In Zanzibar, men can easily divorce their wives through verbal or written repudiation, while women either have to convince a *kadhi* of their husbands' misdoings to receive a "free" *fasikhi* divorce (court-ordered annulment) or they have to initiate a legal proceeding called *khuluu*, which allows women to divorce their husbands with a payment that is usually in the amount of their original dower (Stiles 2009). While Islamic law mandates that fathers financially support their children, divorced women are often left with inadequate resources to raise their children. And Zanzibari women's rights activists are not alone in their concerns regarding the economic effects of divorce on women and children. In a 2003 newspaper article in the state-affiliated *Zanzibar Leo*, Omar Said Omar, a *kadhi* in urban Kariakoo, held

men primarily responsible for a high rate of divorce, scolding them for fail-
ing to support their families.[9] *Kadhi* Omar also complained about a lack of
perseverance in marriage.

Kadhi Omar's words reflect another worry among women's rights activists
in Zanzibar: the role of *kadhis* as divorce gatekeepers who frequently order
women to remain in unhappy marriages, in order to preserve the sanctity of
marriage. As a coalition, Zanzibari women's rights activists believe in the
sanctity of marriage and worry about the ease with which men are able to
divorce their wives, sometimes unbeknownst to their families. They worry,
too, about the aftermath of divorce, when women are often left to support
children on their own.[10] But they believe in women's right to a divorce,
particularly in instances of mistreatment, and worry that *kadhis* are allowing
a belief in the sanctity of marriage to cloud their better judgment. In a 2018
interview, ZAFELA director Jamila Mahmoud explained:

> Most of the time, the women who go to the *kadhi's* court, they don't even have
> the ability to speak for their rights. So we find that men are the ones who have a
> voice, they pretend they are good and that women are the ones who did wrong.
> And the *kadhis*, because of the notion that women are supposed to obey their
> husbands, even though their husbands have done things that are wrong, the *kad-
> his* say, "Okay, you are a woman, you are supposed to obey your husband. So
> please go back to your husband."[11]

Not only do women's rights activists worry about instances when women are
ordered to stay with their husbands against their wishes, but they also worry
about *kadhis* forcing women to repay their dowers in *khuluu* divorces despite
having adequate legal justification to receive free *fasikhi* divorces.[12] In a 2018
interview, Hawra Shamte, program manager of the Tanzania Media Women's
Association (TAMWA) Zanzibar, explained:

> A woman goes there [to the *kadhi's* court] and asks for a divorce, and they
> directly ask her to pay back the dower without even looking at the circumstances
> of why this woman wants a divorce. Maybe because he causes her to suffer,
> maybe she raises her children all alone, maybe the man doesn't provide food for
> the family, and maybe he is beating her. But when the woman is tired and she is
> trying to get a divorce, these *kadhi's* courts ask her to pay back the husband.[13]

As a coalition, Zanzibari women's rights activists are worried about the financial implications for women of being unfairly forced to repay their dowers
and then support children on their own.

Because *kadhis* arbitrate in divorce cases, they are theoretically charged
with addressing divorce-related settlements like the division of matrimonial

property and child support. However, litigants have the option of channeling property and child support-related cases through Zanzibar's secular government legal system, in part depending on their preferences and in part depending on the amount of money in question.[14] ZAFELA lawyers and paralegals usually advise their clients to formalize child support contracts before proceeding onward to the *kadhi*'s court for a divorce. ZAFELA paralegals and lawyers often mediate in the creation of such contracts, collecting monthly child support payments on behalf of their clients through mobile phone banking systems like M-Pesa. When fathers refuse to formalize child support contracts via ZAFELA mediation, ZAFELA paralegals and lawyers refer their clients to the new government-established children's court, which usually requires fathers to pay a higher monthly child support payment than the Tsh50,000 (~$25) monthly maximum that *kadhis* are able to mandate.

Zanzibar has a dizzying plural legal system, with new legal structures like the children's court and the *mufti*'s office creating a plethora of legal options for litigants. I have seen postdivorce property cases handled by ZAFELA lawyers through legally binding contracts; by *kadhis*; by district, regional, and high court judges in Zanzibar; by the Tanzanian high court; and by the *mufti*'s office, depending on the value of property in question and litigants' preferences.[15]

Just as Zanzibari women were able to choose from different schools of Islamic law as they negotiated their rights during the colonial period (Stockreiter 2015), they to some extent are able to choose from an assortment of civil society, government, and religious legal structures and figures as they negotiate their rights today. A hodgepodge of legal options available to women has even further constricted the already limited jurisdiction of *kadhis*. As Halima,* a ZAFELA lawyer, explained to me in August of 2017, "The *kadhi's* court has no power these days." And while the power of *kadhis* has been reduced, they are still the ultimate decision makers for women seeking divorce. ZAFELA tries to influence *kadhis*' decisions by writing up their clients' legal claim forms, replete with Islamic legal justifications for divorce, but the *kadhi* makes the final call. ZAFELA paralegal Rahma can appeal the decisions of district *kadhis* to the *mufti* or to the Chief *Kadhi*, but the decision-making power in divorce cases ultimately rests within the overarching Islamic legal system.

If *kadhis* wield most of the decision-making power in divorce cases, how can women's rights activists ensure better divorce outcomes for women? This question has guided activists in their recent *kadhi*'s court reform efforts. First, they have advocated for an equitable division of matrimonial property, recognizing that the Islamic and cultural ideal in Zanzibar of separately held spousal property often does not happen in practice. Spouses contribute, in diverse ways, toward maintaining shared homes, which activists want to be recognized in the division of post-divorce property.[16] Second, in conjunction with Zanzibar's Chief Justice, Oscar Makungu, who has long advocated for a higher education requirement among *kadhis*,[17] activists want every *kadhi* on the archipelago to have at least a bachelor's degree in Islamic jurisprudence. Activists believe that if *kadhis* were more versed in Islamic law, they would rule more equitably in divorce cases.[18] Third, and most controversially, activists sought a stipulation that would allow women themselves to adjudicate Islamic legal cases as *kadhis*. They believed that women *kadhis* would be better able to empathize with women and make more gender-equitable rulings. In their efforts to reform Zanzibar's *kadhi*'s courts, activists worked as part of a national coalition of women and children's rights-oriented organizations, just as they were aligned with a transnational network of Muslim women's rights activists from Singapore, Malaysia, and Indonesia. Zanzibari women's rights activists benefited from a spiritual alliance with their transnational peers in all of their advocacy efforts but especially as they controversially advocated for women's divine right to serve as *kadhis*.

CULTIVATING NATIONAL AND TRANSNATIONAL *UMOJA*

In their recent advocacy efforts surrounding *kadhi*'s court reform, Zanzibari women's rights activists worked together as part of a "national"[19] gender coalition, just as they networked with transnational Muslim women's rights activists. In their national and transnational networking, women's rights activists worked to establish *umoja*, a Swahili philosophical tenet that implies solidarity, unity, and relational personhood. As a philosophical concept, *umoja* infers the increased power that a unified whole has over the sum of its parts and was a central tenet of first Tanzanian president Julius Nyerere's political system of *Ujamaa*, or African socialism (Nyerere 1967). Over time, the national and transnational *umoja* cultivated by Zanzibari women's rights activists has become increasingly influenced by a shared Islamic faith.

Women and children's rights organizations in Zanzibar initially formed a national coalition in 2002.[20] Among the leaders of today's gender coalition, TAMWA Zanzibar director Mzuri Issa was a proponent for civil society *umoja* as a journalist with the state-run *Zanzibar Leo* newspaper in the early 2000s. She published an article in 2003 beginning with the Swahili proverb, "*Umoja ni nguvu, utengano ni udhaifu* [unity is strength, division is weakness]," in which she called on civil society organizations to join together to collaboratively address social problems.[21] Like other African countries, Zanzibar experienced a civil society explosion during the millennial era, in part due to its enmeshment in a broader global human rights and democratization movement (Tripp et al. 2009). Mzuri envisioned a gender network in Zanzibar that would be modeled after mainland Tanzania's gender coalition and the Pan-Africanist Organization of African Unity (OAU). It would reflect national and Pan-African *umoja*.

Zanzibari women's rights activists have long drawn on the philosophical tenet of *umoja* in their advocacy efforts, particularly in their ongoing organizing for women's greater political representation. For example, TAMWA-affiliated journalist Shifaa Said Hassan wrote in a 2002 *Zanzibar Leo* article, "*Umoja* . . . is indeed the only weapon that will enable women to be elected."[22] A few years later, in 2005, the women's caucus of Zanzibar's House of Representatives called on women from different political parties to maintain *umoja* in order to ensure women's broader political representation and participation.[23] *Umoja* as a tenet of Zanzibari feminism was front and center among women politicians, voters, and political aspirants in the lead-up to what would be a contentious 2005 election.

I observed the work of Zanzibar's national gender coalition from 2017 to 2018, which provided me with insight into the importance of *umoja* as a tenet of Zanzibari feminism. During that time, coalition members were working to improve the movement of GBV cases through Zanzibar's criminal justice system and advocating for major *kadhi*'s court reforms. The gender coalition often held meetings with criminal justice system stakeholders and citizen activists, where they strategized together to improve GBV case outcomes. These meetings were rife with tension, since gender coalition members often pointed out the inefficiencies and corruption inherent in the criminal justice system. Whenever group tension mounted, however, the gender coalition's leader, veteran women's rights activist Asha Aboud, reminded participants that they were all "building one house."[24] Her frequent mention of "building one house" was an allusion to first Tanzanian president Julius Nyerere's metaphorical use of a shared house to exemplify *umoja* in his political philosophy of *Ujamaa*, or African socialism (Nyerere 1967). Zanzibar's gender coalition has channeled the Swahili cultural tenet and nationalism-tinged language and philosophy of *umoja* since their millennial-era formation, which has helped them in such a politically polarized context.

In addition to their national solidarity as members of Zanzibar's gender coalition, Zanzibari women's rights activists were engaged with a transnational network of Muslim women's rights activists in their recent *kadhi*'s court reform efforts. Zanzibari women's rights activists became enmeshed in a transnational network of Muslim women's rights activists from about 2006 onward, when ZAFELA director Jamila Mahmoud attended the Second International Congress on Islamic Feminism in Barcelona, Spain,[25] under the tutelage of Zanzibari feminist activist and legal scholar Salma Maoulidi. Jamila explained in an interview that she gained insight at the conference on how men strategically interpret Islamic texts to deprive women of their rights.[26] There, Jamila became connected with Malaysia-based Sisters in Islam, which uses feminist interpretations of Islamic scripture and jurisprudence as a foundation for their activism (Basarudin 2016). The seminal First, Second, and Third Congresses on Islamic Feminism in Barcelona marked a mushrooming of new transnational connections and networks between Muslim women's rights activists (Badran 2010). New networks joined the existing Women Living under Muslim Laws (WLUML) and the Sisterhood Is Global Initiative (SIGI), two antifundamentalist networks of Muslim and secular feminists concerned with advancing women's rights in the Muslim world. Both WLUML and SIGI were formed in 1984 and have since been based out of Europe and the United States, respectively (Moghadam 2005).

Sisters in Islam participated actively in the WLUML network from the early 1990s onward (Moghadam 2005), later launching its own transnational Islamic feminist network, *Musawah*, in 2009. *Musawah* describes itself as aiming to apply "Islamic teachings, universal human rights principles, fundamental rights and constitutional guarantees, and the lived realities of women and men today."[27] The most fundamental difference between *Musawah* and both WLUML and SIGI is its deliberate incorporation of an explicitly Islamic approach, among others, for ensuring equality and justice in the Muslim family. The location of its headquarters outside of the West is another notable difference.

Jamila and other ZAFELA leaders leveraged their earlier connection with Sisters in Islam as ZAFELA spearheaded major *kadhi*'s court reform efforts from roughly 2011 onward. By connecting with the influential Malaysia-based Sisters in Islam, ZAFELA leaders were confronting the historical marginalization of African women in international Muslim women's movements. In an article for the Pan-Africanist *Pambazuka* news publication, Jamila's mentor, Salma Maoulidi, attributed African women's marginalization in transnational Muslim women's rights networks to "the perception that they are new converts to Islam and thus not authentic enough when compared to non-Africans. . . . Such a perception has probably prejudiced donors as well as Islamic foundations from giving to independent Muslim women's groups in African countries the way they do in the west or in Southeast Asia" (Maoulidi 2011). Maoulidi suspected that a shift would come soon, upon attending the Muslim Women Leaders at the Frontline of Change Conference in Istanbul, Turkey, in 2011, where there were representatives from twelve African countries among 200 Muslim women leaders in attendance (Maoulidi 2011).

Marking an increased representation of African women in global Muslim women's movements, ZAFELA leaders applied for and received funding in 2011 from the Open Society Initiative for East Africa to support a knowledge exchange with Malaysia-based Sisters in Islam. ZAFELA argued in its funding proposal that a knowledge exchange with Sisters in Islam "would expose [them] to the experiences of other women organizing in Muslim contexts and how they have responded to *kadhi's* court systems and the rights of women in general."[28] ZAFELA members visited Sisters in Islam in Malaysia in 2012, which was followed up with a 2013 visit to Zanzibar by Sisters in Islam and women from peer organizations in Singapore and Indonesia to meet with government and other stakeholders to discuss Islamic legal reform.[29] Gender coalition members employed the strategies they gained from their knowledge exchange with Sisters in Islam in their *kadhi's* court reform efforts, citing the presence of women *kadhis* in other predominantly Muslim contexts and citing Islamic textual support for allowing women to serve as *kadhis*. Commenting on the greater utility for Zanzibari women's rights activists of transnational connections with other Muslim women's rights activists versus with their peers on the predominantly Christian Tanzanian mainland, TAMWA Zanzibar governing board member Shifaa Said Hassan said in a 2018 interview, "But we find something from Malaysia, it really is a little bit sweet meat, you know? There's some sort of a similarity, and similarity in religion is very strong, especially when you want to challenge these *kadhi's* courts, you need to have a very strong argument."[30]

Sisters in Islam and members of Zanzibar's gender coalition actively present themselves as believing Muslims. The gender coalition's religiosity has become an increasingly important part of its public identity, particularly during its advocacy surrounding the right of women to serve as *kadhis*, which Jamila Mahmoud herself described as "a matter of believing."[31] In gender coalition meetings related to *kadhi's* court reform, Zanzibari women's rights activists talked about building *imani* (faith) and *umoja* interchangeably, alluding to an increasingly faith-based unity and solidarity among coalition members.[32] They developed both an instrumental and spiritual solidarity with Sisters in Islam, just as they continue to cultivate *umoja* and now *imani* as a national coalition.

AN OVERVIEW OF WOMEN'S RIGHTS ACTIVISM AND *KADHI'S* COURT REFORM IN ZANZIBAR: 2013–2017

ZAFELA's efforts to reform the *kadhi's* courts picked up speed when their knowledge exchange with Sisters in Islam culminated in a visit by their transnational Muslim women's rights activist peers to Zanzibar in 2013. I imagined the arrival of Malaysian, Singaporean, and Indonesian women's rights activists at Zanzibar's airport, which would have barely evoked notice on a cosmopolitan, Indian Ocean archipelago with deep historical and cultural linkages to Southeast Asia. The Sisters in Islam-led delegation met with Zanzibari stakeholders during their 2013 visit, which included national gender coalition members, the chief justice, magistrates, police officers, and Muslim leaders. The delegation shared *Qur'anic* verses with stakeholders in Zanzibar to highlight why women were permitted to be *kadhis* in Islam.[33]

Jamila remembered her excitement in the lead-up to the meeting and her disappointment when Zanzibari Muslim leaders spoke over the Sisters in Islam-led delegation, insisting, "There's no way women can be *kadhis*, because it's forbidden by the *Qur'an*."[34] A major figure in Zanzibar's judiciary, however, approached Jamila after the meeting to assure her that he would push for legal reform. Soon after the Sisters in Islam-led meeting, the government prepared an amended bill. ZAFELA was invited during the lawmaking process to contribute its recommendations, after which a committee of ministers met to review the new law. Jamila explained:

> Then, a committee of ministers met and said, "No way." They removed so many things, such as the matrimonial division of assets, the right for *kadhi's* court clients to have representation in court, and the right of women to be *kadhis*. After this, we said, "Now we need TAMWA. They're media advocates, so they can publicize, raise awareness, and educate the public about how our proposed recommendations are not counter to Islam."[35]

After the ministers' negative response to ZAFELA's recommendations, Jamila knew that they would need to rely more heavily on their coalition sister organization, TAMWA Zanzibar, which uses the media as a vessel for its activism. Zanzibar's gender coalition would have to anticipate and respond thoughtfully in the media to criticisms of their efforts by local Islamic leaders and by the global Islamist press. For example, in 2014, Hizb ut-Tahrir, a pan-Islamist organization that seeks to reestablish an Islamic Caliphate in the Muslim world, issued a public statement on its blog, calling on Muslim leaders to challenge ZAFELA's efforts to reform Zanzibar's *kadhi's* courts.[36] Like ZAFELA, Sisters in Islam has also faced resistance from the Malaysian chapter of Hizb ut-Tahrir (Basarudin 2016).

The increasingly important role of TAMWA in *kadhi's* court reform was reflected in a 2016 *Zanzibar Leo* article written by TAMWA-affiliated journalist Husna Mohammed.[37] In Mohammed's article, Zanzibar's gender coalition formally called on the government to revisit their stalled efforts to work toward *kadhi's* court reform. The issue of *kadhi's* court reform intensified even more in 2017, soon after I began my fieldwork, when Zanzibar's House of Representatives debated an updated bill that ZAFELA had again contributed its recommendations to. I tried to attend major stakeholder meetings during the gender coalition's *kadhi's* court reform efforts, but ZAFELA lawyers expressed a concern that it would not look very good for them to show up with a white Western woman in tow, since religious leaders often tried to discredit them as being overly influenced by the West and as un-Islamic. I therefore depend most heavily on interview and media data rather than on data collected from participant observation for my analysis in the next few sections.

On September 27, 2017, TAMWA-affiliated *Zanzibar Leo* journalist Husna Mohammed published an extensive article highlighting proposed *kadhi*'s court reforms and the opinions of activists and members of the House of Representatives.[38] Mohammed quoted Jamila Mahmoud in the article, who explained, "All institutions are receiving complaints from women who are going to the *kadhi's* courts and not receiving their rights, such as their right to land that they tended to and maintained while married." Dr. Mzuri Issa, the director of TAMWA Zanzibar and former proponent for *umoja* in her early *Zanzibar Leo* articles, similarly commented on the division of matrimonial property, adding that Singapore had policies within its *kadhi*'s courts to ensure an equitable division of matrimonial property. Mzuri additionally highlighted that many Islamic countries allow women to serve as *kadhis*, *ulama* (Islamic scholars), and *washauri* (advisers) within their Islamic legal structures, such as Malaysia and Indonesia.

In the same two-page spread, Husna Mohammed cited members of the House of Representatives, many of whom were committed to improving the postdivorce allocation of matrimonial property. Elected officials were more conflicted about allowing women to become *kadhis*, which a male member of Zanzibar's gender coalition attributed to their failure to convince members of the house that allowing women to become *kadhis* was consistent with Islam.[39] To illustrate, Panya Ali Abdalla was among several members of the House of Representatives to reflect on the division of matrimonial property. She said, "Many married women are working together with their husbands to tend land and property, but when the marriage ends, these women are getting nothing at all for the land they have tended." Hamza Hassan Juma was the only quoted member of the house to comment on allowing women to become *kadhis*. She said, "Many people abide by a religious attitude that women can't be *kadhis* when in fact Islam has clearly explained, regarding this position, that anyone—man or woman—with a serious religious education is permitted to be a *kadhi*." While there was support among elected representatives for broader *kadhi*'s court reforms, few representatives would publicly vouch for their support of women *kadhis*.

The day after Husna Mohammed's article was published in *Zanzibar Leo*, the House of Representatives issued an official statement that they had voted to cancel the previous *Kadhi*'s Court Act of 1985.[40] In their press release, government leaders were vague about which suggested reforms would eventually become law, explaining that they were trying to simplify the existing legal system and to protect the rights of women and children. The skeletal new law included vague provisions for the division of matrimonial property and a higher education requirement for *kadhis*. On October 4, 2017, a *Zanzibar Leo* illustrator published a cartoon criticizing *kadhi*'s court reforms, in which a male member of the house, dressed in an Islamic *kanzu* (robe) and *kofia* (hat), is painting the exterior of a *kadhi*'s court. The cartoon insinuates that recent *kadhi*'s court reforms represented nothing more to the existing Islamic legal system than a superficial coat of paint.

"PRESIDENT, DON'T SIGN": EXPLORING THE STRATEGIC TEXTS OF ZANZIBAR'S GENDER COALITION

There was a catch after Zanzibar's House of Representatives canceled the existing *Kadhi*'s Court Act of 1985 and created a skeletal new law: the president had yet to officially sign the new bill into law. Members of Zanzibar's gender coalition met in the days following the passage of the revised *Kadhi*'s Court Act of 2017 to strategize. In this section, I analyze a few strategic texts produced by the gender coalition during the period of time between the passage of the law at the end of September and its signing into law by the president in early November: a written press release and two public press conferences published on YouTube. In their strategic texts, activists carefully negotiated growing discontent with their efforts coming from Zanzibar's Organization of Muslim Clerics (JUMAZA) while also citing evidence that women were permitted by Islam to serve as *kadhis*. They additionally highlighted Zanzibar's obligation, as a signatory to major human rights conventions, to ensure "gender sensitivity" in the passage of new laws. In this section, I use strategic texts produced by Zanzibar's gender coalition to guide my analysis. Because I was a participant observer of ZAFELA's work from mid-2017 until mid-2018 and a frequent attendee of gender coalition meetings and events, I have a unique base of complementary knowledge to enhance my analysis.

After the House of Representatives passed new *kadhi*'s court reforms, Zanzibar's national gender coalition met to strategize. The gender coalition made public its first strategic text on October 10, 2017: a press release calling on President Ali Mohamed Shein not to sign the bill until it included a provision for women *kadhis* and *ulama*.[41] The press statement—titled "President, don't sign—activists"—was published in a news blog called "*Zanzibar Yetu*" (Our Zanzibar), produced by prominent Zanzibari woman journalist Salma Said. Since the millennial era, when the archipelago had just one primary state-affiliated newspaper in circulation—*Zanzibar Leo*[42]—Zanzibar has experienced a major influx of private media outlets and news blogs. The gender coalition released several subsequent strategic texts, including a press conference led by TAMWA Zanzibar director Mzuri Issa on October 11, 2017,[43] and another public press conference led by gender coalition member Salma Saadati in October of 2017.[44] In all of these texts, the gender coalition presented three major arguments for why Zanzibar should allow women to serve as *kadhis*. Their first argument was that having women as *kadhis* was not counter to Islam. Their second argument centered on Zanzibar's obligation to ensure gender-equitable governmental policies as a signatory to major transnational human rights conventions. In their third argument, the gender coalition attributed resistance to their efforts to allow women to become *kadhis* to "*mfumo dume*" (patriarchy).

First, in their strategic texts, Zanzibar's gender coalition focused most heavily on producing evidence to prove that having women as *kadhis* was not counter to Islam. To do so, they cited male Islamic authority figures, including the Chief *Kadhis* of Kenya and Malaysia. In their written press release, for example, they cited the Chief *Kadhi* of neighboring Kenya, Sheikh Ahmad Mudhar, who publicly stated in 2011: "There is no rule in Islam preventing a woman from being a *kadhi*. Islamic texts are quiet regarding this issue."[45] The gender coalition tried to appeal to male Islamic authority figures in Zanzibar by citing a male Muslim leader in Kenya.[46] In a press conference published on private Zaima TV's YouTube Channel (and since removed) on October 11, 2017, Mzuri Issa similarly described meeting the Chief *Kadhi* of Malaysia, who personally told her that there was nothing in the *Qur'an* forbidding women from becoming *kadhis*.[47] The gender coalition knew that statements from male Islamic authority figures would carry the most clout for religious leaders in Zanzibar, so they cited the primary argument posed by male Islamic leaders elsewhere that there was nothing in the *Qur'an* against having women serve as *kadhis*. Coalition members presented a simultaneous argument of presence in their official press statement, citing the work of the Prophet Muhammad's wife, Aisha, in recording and preserving Islamic teachings for future generations.[48] Their argument was that women like Aisha have served as authoritative figures in the history of Islam, which supported the notion of having women *kadhis*.

Beyond citing male Islamic authority figures and the historical presence of important Muslim women, the gender coalition cited a precedence of women *kadhis* in other predominantly Muslim countries to support their argument that having women Islamic judges was not counter to Islam. They again referred to the words of Sheikh Ahmad Mudhar from neighboring Kenya that by allowing women *kadhis*, Zanzibar would join the ranks of predominantly Islamic countries like Egypt, Sudan, Tunisia, Kuwait, Turkey, and Palestine.

Reflecting their knowledge exchange with Sisters in Islam, gender coalition members additionally cited the presence of women Islamic judges in Malaysia and Singapore.[49]

The second major argument that activists presented in their strategic texts was Zanzibar's obligation to enact gender-equitable policies as a signatory to major human rights conventions. In their official press statement, Zanzibari women's rights activists wrote, "We believed that Tanzania/Zanzibar, as a country that has signed many international conventions that insist on gender equality, would allow women *kadhis*. . . . But we have discovered as a coalition, to our surprise, that our decision makers seem to be blinded to our human rights obligations."[50] When women's rights activists cited Zanzibar's obligations to international conventions in their official press statement, they insisted that enacting gender-equitable laws would ensure a future of nation building and development. They depended heavily on a postrevolution lexicon of nation building and development from the mid-1960s, which carries powerful linguistic and ideological clout in Zanzibar.

Third, in their strategic documents, coalition members attributed resistance among religious leaders to *mfumo dume*, or patriarchy. To illustrate, in a Zaima TV-published press conference, coalition member Mzuri Issa suggested that while some people were legitimately afraid of going against their religion by allowing women to become *kadhis*, the vast majority of resistors simply wanted to maintain patriarchal rule over religious life in Zanzibar.[51] She called on male religious leaders to look beyond their immediate interests and to consider the interests of future generations. In their official press statement, coalition members suggested that historically, Zanzibaris attended Friday sermons in Arabic, which they could barely understand, yet alone question. They argued that many youth were now gaining a more solid grasp of Islam through their studies abroad, which would eventually result in a reformed, equality-driven Islam in Zanzibar.[52]

Beyond three overarching arguments that they put forth in several strategic texts, coalition members additionally tried, after a new law passed in the House of Representatives but before the president signed it, to establish more peaceful relations with religious leaders, who reflect Zanzibar's enmeshment within a global Islamic revival.[53] Sometime in October, ten activists met with JUMAZA leaders to discuss community-level issues in Zanzibar, strategically designating a male coalition member as their leader in the meeting. In a public press conference held later on the same day,[54] coalition members Salma Saadati and Hawra Shamte sat in front of a group of activists and journalists, each adorned in a traditional, black *bui bui*[55]—a symbol of cultural preservation and women's respectability in Zanzibar. Salma and Hawra departed from their usual choice of colorful dress for the press conference, perhaps to strategically highlight their piety as devout Muslim women. In the press conference, Salma Saadati explained how the meeting with religious leaders and activists unfolded: "Among the social issues we discussed today were moral erosion and the problem of Zanzibaris not protecting their communities."[56] Salma was referring to widespread frustration shared by Muslim leaders and women's rights activists alike that Zanzibaris were not watchful enough of their children's activities, which fueled the major problem of sexual assault.

Salma also explained another topic discussed at the meeting: the issuance of public curses by Zanzibari Muslim leaders against women's rights activists for their efforts to enable women to become *kadhis*. Salma explained that while they did not discuss the issue of women *kadhis* at length in the meeting, all attendees agreed to establish a committee comprised of three religious leaders and four activists to reach consensus regarding the issue of women serving in positions of Islamic authority in Zanzibar.[57] The agreement among activists and JUMAZA religious leaders to establish a committee to reach consensus represented a major step forward in an otherwise tense relationship. In the press conference, Salma continually mentioned the importance of working "*kwa pamoja*," or with unity and togetherness, again reflecting the Zanzibari feminist tenet of *umoja*.

President Shein signed the *Kadhi*'s Court Act of 2017 into law on November 1, 2017,[58] just three weeks after activists called on him to not sign the bill until it included their recommendations. "The president didn't reply," Jamila Mahmoud explained in an interview, "we think he called people who were concerned about what we wanted to add. We heard rumors that some of our recommendations were put in, and he signed it."[59] In the final *Kadhi*'s Court Act, women were not permitted to be *kadhis*, but "the division of matrimonial assets was there," Jamila described, "and he agreed to have women as *ulama* in the courts, because we have women scholars of Islamic law here in Zanzibar." Women will hold new roles as authoritative purveyors of Islamic legal knowledge within the *kadhi*'s courts, even if they are not permitted to adjudicate Islamic legal cases as judges.

In a surprising turn of events, soon after the final passage of the *Kadhi*'s Court Act of 2017, JUMAZA's Sheikh Muhidin issued a vitriolic press statement condemning Zanzibar's gender coalition, perhaps because of the controversial reforms that they succeeded in passing. A private television station, KTV Tanzania, published Sheikh Muhidin's statement on its YouTube channel.[60] In his statement, Sheikh Muhidin said:

> The committee that we promised to establish with women's rights activists concerning the challenges that they face, this committee will not materialize. . . . We cannot agree to engage with this hypocrisy, with these two-faced activists. . . . Our communities should take every step to fight these activists, because they are dangerous in our Zanzibari communities. They are plucking ideologies

from other places[61] that are tearing apart our communities, causing us to become mentally confused, and taking away our awareness. . . . There is nothing in the *Qur'an* that allows a woman to be a *kadhi*, so we cannot join hands with them in their efforts.[62]

Zanzibar's gender coalition was devastated by Sheikh Muhidin's public statement. The disappointment of Halima, a lawyer, was especially palpable when I saw her at ZAFELA's office on November 21, 2017. "It would have been better if he had told us to our face! This is patriarchy, not religion," she lamented. Women's rights activists nearly succeeded in cultivating some degree of *umoja* with religious leaders, through their joint agreement to form a committee in order to establish consensus on the issue of women *kadhis*. But just as quickly as the possibility of a committee came to fruition, it disappeared with the condemnation of Zanzibari women's rights activists by JUMAZA leader Sheikh Muhidin. JUMAZA counteracted an argument posed by the Chief *Kadhis* of Kenya and Malaysia that there was nothing in the *Qur'an* against allowing women to become *kadhis* with the opposite argument, that there was nothing in the *Qur'an* supporting women *kadhis*.

Moving forward, Zanzibari women's rights activists realized that it would be difficult to cultivate any degree of solidarity with JUMAZA in their continuing efforts to ensure that women would someday become *kadhis*. They had successfully developed *umoja* with the media and to some extent with the government, in part because of the membership structures of coalition organizations TAMWA and ZAFELA, whose feminist members occupied every media outlet and ministry on the archipelago. When it came to the question of women *kadhis*, however, government leaders were reticent to challenge JUMAZA's public proclamations. In planning for the future, Zanzibari women's rights activists returned to an argument from their official press statement: that it would be young Zanzibari scholars of Islam who would sow the seeds of change.

"LET'S CONTINUE TO BUILD *IMANI*": STRATEGIZING FOR THE FUTURE

During my fieldwork in Zanzibar, I was able to talk with two central members of the gender coalition—Jamila Mahmoud and Hawra Shamte—about how they envisioned moving forward in their quest to continue to reform the *kadhi*'s courts. When I visited Hawra at TAMWA Zanzibar's rural Tunguu offices during the height of the rainy season in April of 2018, she was focusing on a new law regarding the division of matrimonial property after a divorce. She explained to me that the law had yet to be fully defined in terms of what would be recognized as a contribution by women in marriage and that women's rights lawyers should be involved in ironing out the law's *kanuni* (rules).[63] In late 2018, TAMWA published another strategic text to exert influence over what would count as a woman's contribution toward marital property.[64] In it, TAMWA outlined diverse understandings of matrimonial property from different legal frameworks around the world. They argued in the report that Zanzibar's courts should recognize the labor that women have injected into the upkeep of a home when matrimonial property is allocated between divorced spouses. TAMWA Zanzibar sought a departure from mainland Tanzania's Law of Marriage Act, which usually requires monetary receipts from women to prove their contributions.

Reflecting its engagement with a transnational network of Muslim women's rights activists, who have been engaged in a feminist exegesis of the *Qur'an*, TAMWA began its report with a quote from medieval Islamic juridical scholar Ibn Qayyim: "The *shari'a* is all about justice, kindness, common good, and wisdom. Any rule that departs from justice to injustice . . . or departs from common good to harm . . . is not part of the *shari'a*, even if it is arrived at by literal translation."[65] Zanzibari women's rights activists are equipped with a deep knowledge of Islamic jurisprudence as they seek to influence the ironing out of the new *Kadhi*'s Court Act of 2017. In their citation of Qayyim's quote, TAMWA anticipated and foreclosed the ability of religious leaders to put forth their predictable argument that the *Qur'an* did not permit an equitable division of matrimonial property. TAMWA's implied argument was that an inequitable division of matrimonial property was inherently unjust and could therefore not be considered *shari'a*, since divine law must by definition ensure the common good.

In her explanation of their next steps, Jamila Mahmoud talked about building public solidarity with Islamic leaders who quietly supported them, lamenting, "There are some *shehe* [Islamic leaders] inside there, they say, 'We are supporting you, but since we are men, we can't say anything in front of our colleagues.'"[66] Jamila was especially disappointed by the lack of support she received from a prominent Zanzibari woman Islamic scholar. Jamila tried to involve her in their advocacy surrounding the right of women to become *kadhis*, but the woman declined, not wanting to upset her male peers. Jamila lamented, "There are so many people that are afraid to speak in public, and for me, it's like, why are you afraid? Who are you afraid of? Because if you are a Muslim and believe in God, it's still loyal, how you are doing it. So why are you two-faced? You have to decide to believe or not to believe."[67] For Jamila, enabling women to serve as *kadhis* was an enactment of her faith.

Just as Jamila was dedicated to cultivating public support among religious leaders who secretly supported them, she was committed to fostering a separate women and youth-centered Islamic solidarity. She spoke excitedly about the gender coalition's goal of supporting a cadre of young women to study Islamic jurisprudence so that women are prepared to assume the post of *kadhi* when the law changes. She envisioned social change as stemming from young women, who would invest themselves in Islamic education abroad before returning home to assume positions of Islamic authority in Zanzibar.[68] They would feel more of a sense of obligation to their faith—an Islam that promoted equitable gender relations—than they would to the male-dominated status quo. The law would eventually change, and women would be equipped with higher Islamic education when it did.

Soon before I left Zanzibar, on April 25, 2017, I attended a gender coalition meeting at the offices of ANGOZA, a coalition organization in the energetic, peri-urban neighborhood of Mombasa. When I arrived, coalition members were in the midst of reflecting on their efforts to reform the *kadhi*'s courts. They had ideas about how they could have done better. One activist suggested that they needed more *uvulimu* (perseverance) and *ushirikiano* (sharing, participation). Others voiced their agreement, suggesting that TAMWA should not serve alone as the public face of the coalition. Suleiman,* a male coalition member whom I had seen at several other meetings, interjected, insisting, "As activists, we have built *imani*. Let's continue to build *imani*." Most meeting attendees voiced their agreement with Suleiman's statement. His words reminded me of Asha Aboud's insistence at meetings of diverse stakeholders on the importance of *umoja*, which she exemplified with the metaphor of building a shared house. Suleiman was using the word *imani* not in its literal meaning as faith, but to refer to a faith-based *umoja*, or solidarity, that the coalition had cultivated in their efforts to reform the *kadhi*'s courts.

In her foundational book about gender and Islam in Africa, Margot Badran (2011) posed the question, "How can women [in Nigeria] construct a functioning, depatriarchalized Islam . . . in the arena of the community and society at large, and not in the restricted atmosphere of the *shari'a* courts?" (207). In the context of Zanzibar, would the presence of women *kadhis* simply reflect depatriarchalized *kadhi*'s courts or a depatriarchalized Islam in society at large? It is unclear, but for now, Zanzibari women's rights activists like Rahma, Jamila Mahmoud, and Hawra Shamte are driven by the divine vision of a woman *kadhi*; the image of a cadre of young women Islamic scholars; a deep knowledge of Islamic jurisprudence; and national and transnational faith-inspired *umoja* in their divinely ordained work.

NOTES

1. An asterisk denotes the changing of a name to protect confidentiality.
2. Between January and August of 2017, the *kadhi*'s court of Kwerekwe opened 394 divorce cases, while the next busiest court of Mkokotoni opened fifty-seven

divorce cases. Zanzibar's most populous island of Unguja, where I conducted my field research, has seven *kadhi*'s courts. *"Takwimu za Kesi, Mahakama ya Kadhi Unguja,"* January–August 2017.

3. Rahma's interpretation of verse 4:128 from the *Qur'an*.

4. Rahma's interpretation of verse 65:2 from the *Qur'an*.

5. Religion has become increasingly politicized in Zanzibar. Islamic reformists often aligned themselves with the opposition party, CUF, and perceived the establishment of the state-affiliated *mufti*'s office in 2001 as an attempt by the ruling CCM party to claim undue religious authority in Zanzibar (Stiles 2009; Loimeier 2009).

6. Personal conversation on September 19, 2017. Loimeier (2009) has commented on the increasingly expansive Islamic education provided by Zanzibari *madrasas*.

7. Mahmoud, Jamila. June 5, 2018. Interview with Jessica Ott. English. New Jang'ombe, Zanzibar.

8. "Jamii yatakiwa kujiepusha na migogoro ya kifamilia," *Zanzibar Leo*, October 13, 2002, 1–3.

9. Ibid.

10. Mohammed, Husna, "TAMWA yataka marekebisho sheria mahakama ya kadhi Zanzibar," *Zanzibari Leo*, June 16, 2016, 1–2.

11. Mahmoud, Jamila. June 5, 2018. Interview with Jessica Ott. English. New Jang'ombe, Zanzibar.

12. Stiles (2009) detailed the phenomenon of *kadhis* forcing women to pay back their dowers even in instances when their husbands misbehaved in marriage. She described *kadhis* as being concerned with men's ability to remarry postdivorce, in a setting of increasing economic insecurity.

13. Shamte, Hawra. April 24, 2018. Interview with Jessica Ott. English. Tunguu, Zanzibar.

14. This may change, since 2017 legal reforms vested *kadhis* with more power over the allocation of matrimonial property after a divorce.

15. Generally, cases involving smaller amounts of property are handled by ZAFELA lawyers, *kadhis* courts, district courts, or the *mufti*'s office, while cases involving larger amounts of property are handled by ZAFELA lawyers, regional courts, the high court, or the *mufti*'s office. Appealed cases move upward through the high courts of Zanzibar and Tanzania.

16. Shamte, Hawra. April 24, 2018. Interview with Jessica Ott. English. Tunguu, Zanzibar. Mahmoud, Jamila. June 5, 2018. Interview with Jessica Ott. English. New Jang'ombe, Zanzibar.

17. Mohammed, Husna, "Serikali kutafuta makadhi wenye taaluma kubwa," *Zanzibar Leo*, November 17, 2003, 1–3.

18. Shamte, Hawra. April 24, 2018. Interview with Jessica Ott. English. Tunguu, Zanzibar. Mahmoud, Jamila. June 5, 2018. Interview with Jessica Ott. English. New Jang'ombe, Zanzibar.

19. I use the word "national" in quotes, because while Zanzibar technically maintains a controversial union government with Tanzania and is a part of the Tanzanian nation, it has for the most part maintained a distinct civil society from the mainland.

20. Mohamed, Husna, "NGOs za wanawake zaanzisha mtandao maalum wa kijinsia," *Zanzibar Leo*, December 19, 2002, 6.

21. Issa, Mzuri, "NGOs zifanye kazi kwa pamoja kutatua matatizo yanayowak-abili," *Zanzibar Leo*, March 25, 2003, 8.

22. Hassan, Shifaa Said, "Nafasi zaidi za uongozi wa kitaifa zitolewe kwa wan-awake," *Zanzibar Leo*, October 9, 2002, 5.

23. Abdi, Mwanajuma, "Wanawake wa vyama mbali mbali wataka wawe na umoja," *Zanzibar Leo*, July 29, 2005, 1–3.

24. I observed two coalition-led meetings with criminal justice stakeholders in which Asha Aboud and others appealed to group *umoja* by reminding attendees that they were all "building one house"—on March 30, 2018, at the offices of Zanzibar's organization for disability rights, and on April 21, 2018, at a building called "Malaria" in Kwa Mchina.

25. Jamila described the conference as having occurred in Europe in 2006. Based on her description of the conference attendees and theme, I believe she was referring to the Second International Congress on Islamic Feminism held in Barcelona in 2006.

26. Ousseina Alidou (2013) described a similar networking of Muslim women legal experts from Kenya and India, which she referred to as "legal transnationalism."

27. "Musawah Framework for Action," *Musawah*, last modified November, 2018, http://www.musawah.org/wp-content/uploads/2018/11/MusawahFrameworkf orAction_En.pdf.

28. "Learning Exchange ZAFELA," *Scribd*, https://www.scribd.com/document /238149996/Learning-Exchange-ZAFELA, accessed October 19, 2018.

29. Mahmoud, Jamila. June 4, 2018. Interview with Jessica Ott. English. New Jang'ombe, Zanzibar.

30. Hassan, Shifaa Said. March 14, 2018. Interview with Jessica Ott. English. Zanzibar Town, Tanzania.

31. Mahmoud, Jamila. June 5, 2018. Interview with Jessica Ott. English. New Jang'ombe, Zanzibar.

32. I observed the interchangeable use of *imani* and *umoja* at a coalition meeting held at the offices of ANGOZA in Zanzibar's Mombasa neighborhood on April 25, 2018. It was also visible in a coalition press release from late 2017: "Rais Usisaini—Wanaharakati," *Zanzibar Yetu*, last modified October 10, 2017, https://zanzibariyetu .wordpress.com/2017/10/10/rais-usisaini-wanaharakati/, accessed October 12, 2018.

33. Mahmoud, Jamila. June 5, 2018. Interview with Jessica Ott. English. New Jang'ombe, Zanzibar.

34. Ibid.

35. Ibid.

36. "Hizb uh Tahrir Wataka Waislamu Zanzibar Kupinga Muswada wa Sheria ya 'Kuimega' Mahakama ya Kadhi," *Ahbaabur Rasul*, last modified August 2014, http: //ahbaabur.blogspot.com/2014/08/hizb-uh-tahrir-wataka-waislamu.html, accessed October 12, 2018.

37. Mohammed, Husna, "TAMWA yataka marekehisho sheria mahakama ya kadhi Zanzibar," *Zanzibar Leo*, June 16, 2016, 1–2.

38. Mohammed, Husna, "Wanaharakati watoa mswaada pendekezi wa mahakama ya kadhi," *Zanzibar Leo*, September 27, 2017, 12–13.

39. He said this at a gender coalition meeting held on April 25, 2018, at the offices of ANGOZA.

40. Abdallah, Khamisuu, and Amina Haruna, "Gavu: Sheria kadhi kumaliza changamoto," *Zanzibar Leo*, September 28, 2017, 2.

41. "Rais Usisiani – Wanaharakati," *Zanzibar Yetu*, https://zanzibariyetu.worpress.com/2017/10/10/rais-usisaini-wanaharakati/, accessed October 12, 2018.

42. Mussa, Ussi, "Vyombo vya habari binafsi bado vinahitajika," *Zanzibar Leo*, December 5, 2002, 5.

43. "Mswada mpya wa mahakama ya kadhi wapingwa Zanzibar," posted by "Zaima TV," October 11, 2017, https://m.youtube.com/watch?v=jlhjiuMxAbY, accessed May 21, 2018.

44. "Kadhia ya Mahakama ya Kadhi," posted by "TAMWA Zanzibar," January 18, 2018, https://m.youtube.com/watch?v=ZRROa-Ozc0, accessed May 21, 2018.

45. "Rais Usisiani – Wanaharakati," *Zanzibar Yetu*, https://zanzibariyetu.worpress.com/2017/10/10/rais-usisaini-wanaharakati/, accessed October 12, 2018.

46. When he made a public proclamation supporting women *kadhis*, Sheikh Ahmad Mudhar was in a tough bargaining position to retain Kenya's *kadhi*'s courts in light of major constitutional reforms and so eventually conceded to the demands of many Kenyan human rights activists that Muslim women be allowed to serve as *kadhis*. He used an argument that was circulating in Kenya at the time, that the post of *kadhi* was ultimately a judicial rather than a religious position and should therefore be open to women, who were permitted to participate as leaders in other parts of Kenya's judiciary (Alidou 2013).

47. "Mswada mpya wa mahakama ya kadhi wapingwa Zanzibar," posted by "Zaima TV," October 11, 2017, https://m.youtube.com/watch?v=jlhjiuMxAbY, accessed May 21, 2018.

48. "Rais Usisiani – Wanaharakati," *Zanzibar Yetu*, https://zanzibariyetu.worpress.com/2017/10/10/rais-usisaini-wanaharakati/, accessed October 12, 2018.

49. Ibid.

50. Ibid.

51. "Mswada mpya wa mahakama ya kadhi wapingwa Zanzibar," posted by "Zaima TV," October 11, 2017, https://m.youtube.com/watch?v=jlhjiuMxAbY, accessed May 21, 2018.

52. "Rais Usisiani – Wanaharakati," *Zanzibar Yetu*, https://zanzibariyetu.worpress.com/2017/10/10/rais-usisaini-wanaharakati/, accessed October 12, 2018.

53. Islamic revivalists in Zanzibar ascribe to heterogeneous beliefs but broadly focus on returning to a "pure" Islam, unencumbered by external threats (Turner 2009).

54. "Kadhia ya Mahakama ya Kadhi," posted by "TAMWA Zanzibar," January 18, 2018, https://m.youtube.com/watch?v=ZRROa-Ozc0, accessed May 21, 2018.

55. A *bui bui* is a conservative, black, cape-like garment worn by Swahili women.

56. "Kadhia ya Mahakama ya Kadhi," posted by "TAMWA Zanzibar," January 18, 2018, https://m.youtube.com/watch?v=ZRROa-Ozc0, accessed May 21, 2018.

57. Ibid.

58. Revolutionary Government of Zanzibar, "An Act to Repeal the Kadhi's Courts Act No. 3 of 1985 and to Provide for the Re-establishment of Kadhi's court, to

Prescribe Certain Matters Relating to Kadhi's Court and Matters Incidental Thereto," last modified November 2017, http://www.zanzibarassembly.go.tz/act_2017/act_9.p df, accessed January 8, 2019.

59. Mahmoud, Jamila. June 5, 2018. Interview with Jessica Ott. English. New Jang'ombe, Zanzibar.

60. "WANAWAKE WA ZNZ WATAKA UKADHI KTK MAHAKAMA YA KADHI," published by "KTV TZ," November 14, 2017, https://m.youtube.com/wat ch?v=HLSjD_DqxHE, accessed May 21, 2018.

61. Malaysia-based Sisters in Islam similarly describes accusations of adhering to "Western" ideas as one of their main challenges (Basarudin 2016).

62. "WANAWAKE WA ZNZ WATAKA UKADHI KTK MAHAKAMA YA KADHI," published by "KTV TZ," November 14, 2017, https://m.youtube.com/wat ch?v=HLSjD_DqxHE, accessed May 21, 2018.

63. Shamte, Hawra. April 24, 2018. Interview with Jessica Ott. English. Tunguu, Zanzibar.

64. TAMWA Zanzibar, "Analysis of Section 5 of the Kadhi's Court Act (No. 9 of 2017) on Prescriptions Related to Actual Contribution to Matrimonial Assets," https://www.tamwaznz.org/reports/b0cade82e7685dc8419e2e90.pdf, accessed January 10, 2019.

65. Ibid.

66. Mahmoud, Jamila. June 5, 2018. Interview with Jessica Ott. English. New Jang'ombe, Zanzibar.

67. Ibid.

68. Ibid.

REFERENCES

Alidou, Ousseina D. 2013. *Muslim Women in Postcolonial Kenya: Leadership, Representation, and Social Change*. Madison: University of Wisconsin Press.

Badran, Margot. 2010. "An Historical Overview of Conferences on Islamic Feminism: Circulations and New Challenges." *Revue Des Mondes Musulmans et de La Méditerranée* 128. http://journals.openedition.org/remmm/6824.

———. 2011. "Shari'a Activism and Zina in Nigeria in the Era of Hudud." In *Gender and Islam in Africa: Rights, Sexuality, and Law*, edited by Margot Badran. Washington, DC: Woodrow Wilson Center Press.

Basarudin, Azza. 2016. *Humanizing the Sacred: Sisters in Islam and the Struggle for Gender Justice in Malaysia*. Decolonizing Feminisms. Seattle and London: University of Washington Press.

Bissell, William Cunningham, and Marie-Aude Fouere. 2018. "Memory, Media, and Mapinduzi: Alternative Voices and Visions of Revolution, Fifty Years Later." In *Social Memory, Silenced Voices, and Political Struggle: Remembering the Revolution in Zanzibar*, 1–36. Dar es Salaam, Tanzania: Mkuki na Nyota.

Calaguas, Mark J, Cristina M Drost, and Edward R Fluet. 2007. "Legal Pluralism and Women's Rights: A Study in Postcolonial Tanzania." *Columbia Journal of Gender and Law* 16(2): 471–549.

Hirsch, Susan F. 1998. *Pronouncing and Persevering: Gender and the Discourses of Disputing in an African Islamic Court*. Language and Legal Discourse. Chicago: University of Chicago Press.

Loimeier, Roman. 2009. *Between Social Skills and Marketable Skills: The Politics of Islamic Education in 20th Century Zanzibar*. Vol. 10. Islam in Africa. Leiden: Brill.

Maoulidi, Salma. 2011. "The Face and Challenge of Muslim Women's Movements." *Pambazuka News: Voices for Freedom and Justice*, October. https://www.pam bazuka.org/gender-minorities/face-and-challenge-muslim-women%E2%80%99s -movements.

Moghadam, Valentine M. 2005. *Globalizing Women: Transnational Feminist Networks*. Baltimore and London: The Johns Hopkins University Press.

Nyerere, Julius K. 1967. *Uhuru Na Umoja: A Selection from Writings and Speeches, 1952–65*. London: Oxford University Press.

Stiles, Erin E. 2009. *An Islamic Court in Context: An Ethnographic Study of Judicial Reasoning*. New York: Palgrave Macmillan.

Stockreiter, Elke E. 2015. *Islamic Law, Gender, and Social Change in Post-Abolition Zanzibar*. New York: Cambridge University Press.

Tripp, Aili Mari, Isabel Casimiro, Joy Kwesiga, and Alice Mungwa. 2009. *African Women's Movements: Transforming Political Landscapes*. Cambridge: Cambridge University Press.

Turner, Simon. 2009. "'These Young Men Show No Respect for Local Customs'— Globalisation and Islamic Revival in Zanzibar." *Journal of Religion in Africa* 39(3): 237–261.

Chapter 3

"Instant Interventioning"

Digital Networks, Visibility, and Support against Gender-Based Violence in South Africa

Elene Cloete

INVISIBLE CONNECTIONS

GIRLS(ICE), a network of WhatsApp[1] groups and roughly 3,000 women, emerged in 2017 after the gruesome murder of twenty-one-year-old University of Stellenbosch student Hannah Cornelius. The first group was started by Jenna Beebee, a fellow University of Stellenbosch student. She explains: "After Hannah's murder, I immediately felt threatened as a woman living not only in Stellenbosch but also in South Africa. I realized that as a community we could not rely only on emergency services to save us from or support us during violent incidents. We need to face these problems front on, and as a community, support one another" (email exchange with author, November 2018). Jenna's personal proximity to the victim not only brought the realities of gender-based violence (GBV) into sharp focus but also motivated her to seek immediate, even if short-term, solutions to such realities. There are options like tasers, pepper spray, and actual emergency buttons and services. But as Jenna argued, these things are not as readily available as one's smartphone, its push notifications, and immediately reactive applications.[2] What is also missing, Jenna sensed, was a community support group from which women can draw support, comfort, and even help. WhatsApp became Jenna's platform of choice, providing readily available social networking opportunities and push notifications.

It took less than an hour for Jenna's first GIRLS(ICE)—*Girls In Case of Emergency*—group to reach its capacity of 265 users. When this happened, her friend started the second group, and within three days an estimated

3,000 women were actively networking in sixteen different WhatsApp groups. Unlike other informal WhatsApp groups, GIRLS(ICE) groups act as emergency buttons, instantly notifying fellow group members about danger. When panicked, one does not necessarily remember local emergency numbers or have time to think about who to contact, Jenna shared. But with an application like WhatsApp, users can instantaneously share pictures, location, messages, and voice notes, and if shared with up to 265 members, the chances of getting the attention of at least one person increases.

GIRLS(ICE) members are protective of their closed networks. To join the groups, you have to be added by an existing member.[3] GIRLS(ICE) is also reserved for those who identify as women.[4] At the start of the group, Jenna added only women, because "as supportive as men are, there are many that are not." She further added that "It was important for me to make sure that every single woman participating in the group chat felt safe enough to message the group when they felt vulnerable. And if this meant excluding men, it will be what I do" (email exchange with author, November 2018).

VISIBLE ACTION

On Wednesday, August 1, 2018, the #TheTotalShutDown campaign, led by women and gender nonconforming people,[5] made itself visible to the broader South African public and state. It gained such visibility by organizing nineteen marches in the country's major cities, and in the capitals of neighboring Botswana, Lesotho, and Namibia, during which thousands of women united against GBV. Through these marches and accompanying social media campaigns, #TheTotalShutDown communicated at least three messages. First, that women's frustration around ongoing GBV is felt nationwide. While several protests and campaigns have emerged during preceding years, #TheTotalShutDown was the first campaign since the famous 1956 Women's March and Women's Coalition marches during the 1990–1994 transition period to focus on rallying and subsequently gaining nationwide support to address violence against women (Gouws 2018a). This meant that women in different parts of the country rallied in solidarity against GBV, visualizing their discontent via posters and verbalizing their anger through slogans and chants. Second, #TheTotalShutDown wanted to make an economic point. By rallying women to partake in marches on a normal working day, and in the middle of the week, the campaign signaled that women's discontent has economic implications, at least for a couple of hours. #TheTotalShutDown also communicated these intentions during their premarch communication. For example, via different online sources event organizers sent the following message to women who could not attend the march in person and men who are supportive of their cause (but were asked to stay away):

> If you do want to contribute to the action, organizers advise that you refuse to buy anything at all on Wednesday. Their goal is to shut down the economy for a day—or at least put a significant dent in it—so, we'd suggest you get your food shops and errands done by Tuesday evening. (The South African, July 31, 2018)

A third message was aimed directly at the South African government and political leaders, demanding structural change around violence against women. The campaign did this by delivering a concrete list of twenty-four demands to government officials, stipulating the legal and administrative changes needed to make women feel safer in their own country. The movement's actions continued after the 2018 marches, with an ongoing social media presence, frequent local marches, a close watch on the government's actions in addressing GBV, and online awareness campaigns that bring attention to GBV incidents and court cases.

SOUTH AFRICA'S EPIDEMIC OF GBV

The emergence of GIRLS(ICE) and presence of #TheTotalShutDown evidence the persistence of GBV[6] and its impact on South African women. A 2018 Africa Check survey indicates that South Africa's rate of femicide is five times higher than the global average and nationwide statistics predict that one in two women will experience some form of violence within their lifetimes (Naidoo 2018). Additionally, a 2013 report by the United Nations World Health Organization described violence against women as a global health problem of "epidemic proportions" and considering figures from South Africa, this epidemic takes on alarming proportions.

Women are not passively accepting this "war on their bodies" (Moletsane 2018), nor do they accept the lackluster response of organizations, institutions, and governmental entities responsible for rectifying such violence. Instead, they seek solutions to intervene not only where help is needed but also to disrupt the state's limited approach to addressing the violence. Women's solutions emerge on at least two fronts. First, they are demanding substantial structural changes, with such efforts manifesting through the #TheTotalShutDown marches and ongoing campaigns. These actions are targeted at achieving faster progress in implementation of institutional and government policies that can institute gender equality and eradicate violence against women (Moosa 2018b; Naidoo 2018; Gouws 2018a). Since such structural changes often require time, women also have to consider the immediate and ongoing needs arising from GBV. A second level of solutions therefore involves networks of immediate support. GIRLS(ICE), for example, use invisible online spaces to protect women against sexual violence, in both the preventative and the reactive sense of the word. When women feel threatened, they can share such feelings on their WhatsApp group and a network of other women will immediately be aware of such danger, and if need be, come to their rescue in whatever form necessary. While temporary, and hopefully a precursor to deeper structural change, these online networks have some immediate value. They are instrumental in providing women with support structures helpful in negotiating the challenging reality of GBV.

In this chapter, I situate women's networks such as GIRLS(ICE) and #TheTotalShutDown and their responses to violence against women in broader conversations about GBV in South Africa. My objective is not to gauge whether such networks are effective or not, nor to analyze the composition and content of their online and offline activities, postings, or conversations. Instead, I argue that these networking efforts, as they present themselves in GIRLS(ICE) and #TheTotalShutDown, contribute to three conversations about GBV. The first conversation involves women's online networking efforts and accompanying proactive mobilizing strategies in dealing with the threat of GBV. By considering such efforts, including those beyond the South African contexts, I argue that online networks provide women with alternative spaces and options to deal with the realities of GBV. But, these spaces differ in order to serve the needs of their users. The second conversation concerns women's responses to GBV, differentiating between at least two types of solution-seeking initiatives: those that are reactive and thus responsive to the immediate needs of women facing violence, and those initiatives concerned with seeking deeper structural change. Feminism is not one movement, and the same can be said about online feminist initiatives. In this case, Fotopoulou (2016) warns us against thinking about online feminist activism as one "unified identity." I do, however, argue that while not identical, many initiatives actively working toward gender equality can be mutually reinforcing, especially when considering the overarching epidemic of GBV. In their different ways, and appreciative of different context and varying needs, the online support networks I describe in this chapter seek solutions to persistently high levels of GBV. The third conversation takes into consideration the variations in women's support networks and their position on public visibility. While some choose to remain more *invisible*, only active within closed-off online spaces, others tap into the power of *visibility*, both online and offline, to actively engage with the public sphere. The extent of such visibility, I argue, is, however, directly related to the needs of the social network in question. Ashley Currier's (2012) interpretation of visibility provides a productive vantage point to consider women's actions around GBV.

TO BE OR NOT TO BE VISIBLE:
STRATEGIES OF BEING SEEN

Social movements use visibility and invisibility as tactics when networking around social justice issues. In the contexts of nonprofits advocating for LGBTQ+[7] rights in Southern Africa, Ashley Currier's (2012) research found that these organizations' advocacy efforts and the work done to support the rights of the LGBTQ+ community are closely linked to how much they preferred to be in the public eye or not. Some organizations, Currier found, remain invisible by choice, not only to protect the interest of their nonprofit but also their constituents, who in many cases might be vulnerable to public humiliation, stigmatization, and the violence that stems from gender discrimination. Other nonprofits, however, use visibility to promote gender rights. By publicly and visibly advocating for gender equality, these nonprofits work toward greater public awareness and, in turn, state and political support. Arguably, such visibility, to borrow from Audrey Lorde, makes the personal public, and highlights the discrimination endured by the LGBTQ+ community. While some nonprofits use *invisibility* as a tactic to protect their constituencies and in such a way provide the support needed, other nonprofits use *visibility* not only to empower their organizations' operations but also to strengthen the support they provide to the LGBTQ+ community. Both groups of nonprofits Currier refers to therefore see invisibility and visibility as strategies rather than eventual end goals.

When considering visibility and invisibility, especially in the context of social movements, two things are of note. First, visibility and invisibility are not polar opposites nor mutually exclusive. Instead, these concepts are "complementary and simultaneously coexisting" (Currier 2012, 10), and thus responsive to the varying opinions of different audiences and actors social movements might engage with. Second, positions around visibility and invisibility are not static nor are they indefinite. On the contrary, as Currier (2012) notes, individuals, groups, or social movements' visibility are "fluctuating conditions that correspond to changes in the sociopolitical fields in which individuals, social groups, and social movements are embedded" (7). Depending on the situations, organizations move fluidly between states of visibility and invisibility, all depending on their needs, their immediate social contexts, and the more general political conditions under which they function. For example, a change in political power can translate into sudden changes in gender rights' legislation, and if such changes are to reinstate more conservative norms, gender advocates might reconsider how visible their actions should be. In contexts where visibility can mean legal or even life-threatening consequences, invisibility may be the safer option. Whether to be visible or not is therefore a choice people make based upon their sociopolitical environments.

Visibility: Social Movements and ICTs

Social movements rely increasingly on social media to communicate their social justice advocacy efforts, raise their visibility, and set in motion their targeted structural changes (Manual Castells 2011, 2015; Fotopoulou 2016). As Thompson (2005) reminds us, "The making visible of actions and events is not just the outcome of leakages in systems of communication and information flow . . . but also a strategy of individuals who know very well that mediated visibility can be a weapon in the struggles they wage in their day-to-day lives" (31). For many social movements, information and communications technology (ICTs) and social media platforms are just the tools they need to bolster their social justice advocacy efforts. ICTs have therefore become a popular choice for movements to strengthen their operations. Such popularity, as Pavan (2015, 2017) argues, and which I will explain further below, resides in the networking *infrastructure* social media platforms provide and their *sociotechnical* characteristics.

In terms of networking infrastructure, social media provides users with the technical and "baseline infrastructure" that enables them to develop connections that are quick, yet personal, and communication networks that are multiuser, multitasker, and managed by more than one individual (Pavan 2017, 435). A WhatsApp group, for example, can provide users with the required infrastructure. Additionally, communication via such platforms is in most cases cheaper and thus lowers the overall cost of participation, with people being able to participate in social actions without having to travel or be present at specific locations (Clark-Parsons 2019). This is not to say that social movements did not already have networking capabilities prior to the rise of the "network society" (Castells 2011), but the emergence of social media platforms such as Twitter and Facebook has significantly bolstered social movements' ability to network and achieve greater visibility.

However, the networking opportunities that social media platforms provide as well as their ability to enable varying degrees of visibility are not enough to initiate social change. The true change agents remain the activists who drive such social change, participate in social movements, and deploy different strategies to mobilize their objectives. It is this combination between the technical (the social media platform) and the social (represented by the individuals using the social media platform) that constitute the sociotechnical characteristics of social media (Pavan 2017).

ICTs and social media platforms are not without their shortcomings. On the contrary, these technologies and accompanying online spaces can replicate offline gender hierarchies and patriarchal control, as illustrated in the work of scholars like Lori Kendall (2002) and Judy Wajcman (2004). Such gender discrimination manifests itself through online sexual harassment, cyberstalking, and image-based sexual exploitation[8] (Henry and Powell 2018). Equally so, when governments and community development practitioners introduce ICTs into social, political, and cultural contexts, it happens within existing gender hierarchies (Webb 2016). In many cases, these hierarchies will stamp their control and ownership onto such new technologies. Rather than providing women the opportunity to escape gender discrimination, ICTs run the risk of reifying unequal power distribution that fosters discrimination. This means that while ICTs and social media can empower women, these spaces can also make women even more vulnerable to male subjugation (Fotopoulou 2016). The availability of and access to ICTs is not a magical solution to gender discrimination. Women using ICTs and social media platforms therefore have to consider strategies to protect themselves and their actions.

Despite this disclaimer, feminist scholars and activists continue to see the value of ICTs and related social media platforms in buttressing resistance against, and critique of, the status quo. In these online networks, one can recognize how the marginalized creates what Nancy Fraser (1990) labels *subaltern counterpublic spaces*. These online platforms provide the spaces where women's voices are audible and where they engage in visible resistance and political activism (Salter 2013). As I illustrate below, such online activism of individuals and wider social movements are often in direct conversations with more traditional forms of street protests. Things are accelerated online, and this translates to increased offline organizing and awareness raising around social justice issues. But Fotopoulou's argument about the dialectic relationship between media institutions and social life holds true: in the case of social movements, the "slower ways of experiencing the world" (2016, 157) remain important and cannot be overlooked.

Hashtag Feminism and Intentional Visibility

Strategies to make sexual abuse visible are political. In addition to making the *personal public*, strategies around visibility also entails making the *personal political*. Clark-Parsons (2019) unpacks the confluence of social media, visibility, and political performance. Nowhere has this been more prominent than in hashtag feminism: "Feminist activism that appropriates Twitter's metadata tags for organizing posts and public-by-default nature to draw visibility to a particular cause or experience" (Clark-Parsons 2019). An example of such feminism is the #MeToo movement, which has brought global attention to the impact of gender harassment and sexual violence on women's well-being. Social media platforms such as Twitter are providing women a space to "document their suffering in personalized ways" while making their experiences of sexual assault public (Mendes et al. 2018; Wood et al. 2018).

The power of hashtag feminism is nestled in both its use of visibility and the integration of social media and offline collective action. These actions, as Khoja-Moolji (2015, 348) argues, produce a form of "intimate publics" wherein complete strangers end up forming online communities based upon close affection. As a result, hashtag feminism, and its insistence that the experiences of women enduring sexual violence should be made public, has spurred on greater public awareness of GBV. A second equally important characteristic of hashtag feminism as represented by the #MeToo movement is the public naming of perpetrators. This "call-out culture" is a fairly recent societal phenomenon defined as the tendency within activist spaces to "highlight instances or patterns of oppressive policy, behavior, and language used by others" (Jenkins 2019). As a kind of informal online justice-seeking mechanism, the use of "call-out culture" not only adds to the public visibility of the movement but also gives a sense of restorative justice to the victims of sexual assault (Powell 2015; Wood et al. 2019). Clark-Parsons (2019) appropriately recognizes a politics of visibility in the processes associated with hashtag feminism, since it is activism "focused on shifting how we represent, interpret, and respond to social injustices through public performance" (3). An overarching goal of these processes is therefore to enable change and encourage "a transformative politics of visibility" (Clark-Parsons 2019, 3). It is by insisting on making issues visible through the performative actions housed by online spaces that feminists are not only creating awareness but also demanding deep structural change.

The #MeToo movement also took to South Africa's social media in October 2017, with the powerful testimony of Jennifer Ferguson, artist and former African National Congress Member of Parliament, as one of the more prominent cases.[9] But, as many scholars and activists argue, the movement did not enjoy the same traction in the South African contexts as compared to those in the United States and Europe (Gouws 2019; Ajayi 2019). This is not due to a lack of agency on behalf of South African women. Rather, the #MeToo movement's limited traction has more to do with the Western origins of the #MeToo movement and the reality of it being a movement largely dominated by white women. Additionally, as gender activists such as Pumla Gqola (2015) assert, South African society is deeply informed by patriarchy and the "female fear factory." It is this fear, produced and reproduced by patriarchy's control over women's bodies, that might discourage women from openly sharing intimate details of their domestic lives, let alone their experiences of GBV (Moore 2019). Instead, invisibility is the safer option, not only to protect victims of sexual assault from becoming victimized but also to save them from the scourge of public shaming. Such invisibility and individual anonymity, for both victim and perpetrator, stand in stark contrast to the intentions of the #MeToo movement, which operates primarily in the public arena.

This is not to say that South African women are not speaking out against GBV or engaging in initiatives to support each other in such situations. On the contrary, as Gouws (2019) reminds us, numerous South African women's networks have emerged in the last few years, all committed to seeking solutions for the country's GBV crisis. Many of the recent campaigns used ICTs and social media to communicate their objectives and motivations to a broader public. How these recent networks present themselves and utilize online spaces, however, depends on the needs their network wishes to address, and the subsequent level of visibility required by the group. Visibility deployed in both online and offline spaces therefore becomes a resource South African women deploy in a very strategic manner to deal with the realities of GBV.

Before elaborating more on the South African–based #TheTotalShutDown, I discuss below a few regional examples of women's strategic use of visibility and ICTs when addressing violence against women. I maintain that these regional examples exemplify the same underlying claim: the extent to which women deploy visibility and the integrative power that comes from social media and political activism is dependent on their group's needs and ultimate goals.

ICTs and Visible Activism against GBV

GIRLS(ICE)'s use of ICTs to develop their community of support is similar to other women-led online networks across the African continent. In South Africa, the Western Cape Anti-Eviction Campaign used mobile phones to strengthen their mobilization efforts around land rights and insufficient municipal service delivery (Chiumbu 2012). On a wider level, scholars have recognized African women's application of ICT in responding to their specific social, political, and economic needs (Tripp et al. 2009; Buskens and Webb 2008, 2014). To name but a few, this includes women's use of ICTs to promote their small-scale businesses (Sow 2014), increase access to education (Zelezny-Green 2018), and mobilization around political issues, with #BringBackOurGirls in Nigeria being a prime example (Morse 2014).

There are also those women networks that, similar to GIRLS(ICE), use ICTs in response to sexual violence and harassment. Three examples come to mind. In Zambia the country's Planned Parenthood Association teaches young women to use Twitter in situations where they feel vulnerable to sexual violence (Banda 2013). Access to such a platform, as is also the case with GIRLS(ICE), provides women with an immediate emergency button to request help from other WhatsApp group members: at the very least, to share their location. While somewhat different in their approach, Kenya's women-led *Flone Initiative* also uses ICTs to bring awareness to sexual violence as it manifests within the realm of public transport (O'Donnell and Sweetman 2018). With the goal of training public transport operators on sexual violence, the Flone Initiative encourages women to use a crowd-mapping platform to report when and where they have experienced sexual harassment and assault. The data collected via this platform not only informs the Flone Initiatives' interventions but also provides the evidence the organization's activists need to demand political attention and legislative changes.

The *Harissa* campaign in Cairo, Egypt, is another Africa-based women's network that uses online crowd-mapping in response to GBV. Founded in 2010, Harissa operates under the premise that if more people take action against GBV, rather than looking away, more can be done to eradicate such violence. To bring such awareness to light, the organization encourages people to map out unsafe zones and shed light on places where GBV takes place frequently. Such mapping happens on an interactive online application, with HarassMap activists asking bystanders to intervene if they witness sexual assault. The application also provides users a place where they can describe their experiences and pinpoint the exact locality of GBV incidents on GoogleMaps. In the process they hope to not only create awareness of the breadth of sexual harassment but also motivate witnesses to speak out rather than remain bystanders. In their analysis of Harissa, Abdelmonem and Galan (2017) use the concept *action-oriented* to capture the activists' "urge to organize against sexual violence." They found that HarrassMap's activists insist that societal change is only possible if "women react against sexual intrusions and support each other in such endeavors" (163). In this case, actions taken to curb sexual violence entail direct street intervention followed by deeper structural change.

ICTs have also provided fertile soil for the recent rise of hashtag feminism in Africa. The combination of feminism and action-oriented activism, as seen among Egyptian organizations aligns with GIRLS(ICE)'s networking efforts in that they encourage women to remain supportive of each other through direct intervention. The biggest difference, however, resides in what such intervention entails. While GIRLS(ICE)'s intervention is invisible, "behind the scenes," and supportive in case women need immediate support, HarassMap encourages outspokenness within the public sphere, seeing such visibility as an important means toward structural change. In this case, HarassMap's insistence on public awareness, public actions, and subsequent structural changes exemplifies a kind of visibility politics around GBV, not that different from the activism encouraged by hashtag feminism.

Feminist visibility politics is surely present in South Africa, with women using both online and offline spaces to make their outrage about persistent sexual violence visible. Such outrage is aimed directly at policy makers, with activists insisting on transformative change. Setting the scene of such discontent was the 2016 #EndRapeCulture movement, followed by the nationwide #TheTotalShutDown movement that started in 2018. Both these movements gained participant and logistical support through online spaces, with social media providing these social movements with the technological infrastructure to communicate and operationalize their objectives. Similarly, the social movements' offline presence has been equally impactful in shedding light on women's frustrations regarding GBV. Their offline activism creates a foundation for more successful ways of using visibility, through marches and streetside protests. Arguably, the combination of both online and offline activism is mutually reinforcing in pushing the needle toward structural change.

"ENOUGH IS ENOUGH": STRUCTURAL CHANGE USING ONLINE NETWORKING AND STREETSIDE ACTIVISM

#EndRapeCulture

Similar to women's protests during South Africa's democratization, #TheTotalShutDown "represented an historic moment for women working to bring GBV to an end" (Naidoo 2019). It made women's frustrations with the status quo visible through public displays of discontent. Among many precursors, the 2016 #EndRapeCulture campaign deserves attention. As Gouws (2016a, 2016b) argues, this campaign rewrote the script on public activism against GBV in South Africa, including public performances of frustration, with some participants being topless and others using whips to demonstrate their anger. The #EndRapeCulture campaign, which started on South African university campuses and took shape alongside the #FeesMustFall movement, drew heavily from intersectionality (Crenshaw 1991), with black women students arguing that oppression refers not only to race but also to gender, sexuality, sexual orientation, and able-bodiedness. #EndRapeCulture was significant for at least two more reasons: First, the campaign, as Gouws asserts, acted as a powerful South African version of the #MeToo movement, even before the #MeToo movement happened. It bravely encouraged young women to openly name perpetrators of sexual violence. In doing so, women exposed men's entitlement even while they continued to live in constant fear of being raped or sexually brutalized. Second, the #EndRapeCulture campaign acted as a powerful unifying tool to bring women together—"a feminist solidarity with their sisters all over the country" (Gouws 2016a). Such a sense of sisterhood, also present in Namibia, as Ndakalako-Bannikov argues in chapter 4, provides not only the support and accompanying networks to make women feel noticed and accepted, but also pushes for the enablement of deep structural change.

Solidarity is also present in the sense of community sought by the GIRLS(ICE) group. The difference, however, lies first in the spaces in which such solidarity exists, and second, in the groups' use of visibility. The WhatsApp groups' communities function in hidden spaces seeking immediate relief in the face of GBV. In contrast, the hashtag movements' solidarity resides in women's combined actions toward speaking out against violence in public and working in visible ways toward structural change. An example of such structural change comes with the #EndRapeCulture campaign, which not only provided greater public awareness by shedding light on the vulnerability of younger women on university campuses but also led to the establishment of a university task force at the University of Stellenbosch in March 2016, aimed at achieving policy design to improve women's safety. This included a report, circulated in July 2017 that recommends ways rape on the university's campus can be addressed.

#TheTotalShutDown

While the #EndRapeCulture mostly took place on university campuses and demanded attention from higher education institutions' administrators and governance, the #TheTotalShutDown Intersectional Women's Movement moved GBV onto the national stage. Organized by an alliance of feminist and gender activists, the movement intends to shed light not only on the prevalence of GBV but also on women's frustrations with the state's limited responses. The movement seeks to raise such awareness using online as well as public spaces, as was the case in 2018 with its nationwide marches. A July 31, 2018, press release succinctly captures the movement's goals:

> On 1 August [2018] we will all say "Enough!" We will not work; we will not contribute to the country's bottom line. Instead we will take our bodies onto the streets and join marches in Johannesburg, Cape Town and Bloemfontein. We will do what is necessary to get the attention of politicians, business and decision makers. (Sonke Gender Justice, July 31, 2018)

The marches turned the movement's listed objectives into actions. With slogans such as "my body, not your crime scene," "enough is enough," "tired of silence," and shouting, "enough violence, enough campaigning, enough lip-service!" thousands of women across the country forced the realities of GBV loudly into the public sphere. At the marches in Cape Town, Pretoria, and Bloemfontein, women formally submitted the movement's demands to government officials. Such demands included a review of existing developments of a National Action Plan, the reestablishment of a Joint Monitoring Committee on the Quality of Life and the Status of Women, providing more support for and monitoring of the Commission for Gender Equality, the implementation of structures that will prevent secondary victimization, better and increased support for Thuthuzela Care Centres (TCCs),[10] the sentencing of GBV perpetrators, and a National Gender Summit to address GBV (Moosa 2018b). At a minimum, these are some of the things #TheTotalShutDown insisted on following the August 2018 marches.

If reactions by the South African government, including the president, are indicators of successful marches, the #TheTotalShutDown movement's August 1, 2018, marches surely were. A noteworthy response was the government's commitment and eventual organizing of a National Gender Summit, one of the movement's twenty-four demands. The government, including President Ramaphosa, convened this two-day National Gender Summit in early November 2018. The event brought together academic, activist, governmental, and NGO representatives. #TheTotalShutDown leadership played a central role in the structuring of this summit, insisting that summit attendees develop five thematic areas, including prevention, accountability, laws and policies, coordination, and support and response (Moosa 2018a). One of the summit's outcomes includes President Ramaphosa's signing of the declaration against GBV and femicide, which he did at the launch of the country's 84th Sexual Offences Court in March 2019. The declaration outlines the government's plans to not only fix the criminal justice system and provide better legal protection but also to work with community leaders and civil society to alter patriarchal sentiments, and fixing the criminal justice system (Mogoatlhe 2019). While structural changes like these take time, the president's recognition of the problem is a step in the right direction.

The #TheTotalShutDown Movement's success has and continues to depend on extensive online and offline networking. This was not only when organizing the 2018 marches but also in managing their continued efforts toward addressing GBV. The movement uses platforms like Facebook and Twitter, which allow organizers to communicate the movements' intentions and subsequently develop a strong audience and participant base. These online platforms also act as a vocal notice board, encouraging women to share news, events, and photos of past and upcoming events. Following the marches, such networking also includes a detailed description of the different demands the campaign presented to government officials.

The August 2018 marches were not the end of #TheTotalShutDown, nor the subsequent National Gender Summit. On the contrary, using their online platforms, the movement continues to provide visible spaces for its followers to take action on GBV-related issues. These spaces are especially helpful in providing followers information about related events, such as the 2019 anniversary of the first marches and local vigils for victims of GBV. Then another visible role of these online spaces relates to accountability, with followers posing questions about the government's progress toward addressing the movement's demands, as well as political actors' promises toward eradicating GBV. These acts of accountability, particularly comments made on Twitter, are visible; this in turn keeps the responsibilities and actions of the government within the public eye, and thus subject to public scrutiny. The movement's use of visibility is however selective. Its Facebook page, for example, is a closed group and thus requires prospective members to submit a request for access. Such selective invisibility, similar to the GIRLS(ICE), can act as a type of protection against potential stalkers.

Visible Demands for Change

The #TheTotalShutDown movement brings three considerations to the forefront. First, the movement, in combination with the #EndRapeCulture, energized South African women to voice their concerns and demand gender equality. This determination is reminiscent of the country's historic movements toward political and social change (Gouws 2018b). This includes the Soweto Uprising in 1976 (see Nieftagodien 2015), the iconic 1956 Women's March (see Brooks 2008), and the country's women's movements of the 1980s and 1990s (see Hassim 2006). One can attribute this reenergizing of earlier forms of women's movements to the networking potential embedded in online spaces, where communication, agitation, and monitoring becomes easier to do. Second, continuous efforts of women to bring their frustrations about GBV to the public sphere are especially visible in younger spaces such as university campuses, where young women actively participate in making their voices heard. In South Africa, the #FeesMustFall movement invigorated such mobilizations and inspired young women to engage with gender-related concerns. Moreover, within the #FeesMustFall Movement, as Langa et al. (2017) found, several questions about gender inequality and violence emerged encouraging renewed conversations on these important topics.

A third point concerns the connection between women's public advocacy efforts and real structural change. We are starting to see hopeful change transpiring from the National Gender Summit. This is primarily due to women activists' insistence on raising public awareness around GBV and pressuring policy makers to operationalize policies designed to address sexual violence and eventually guarantee greater gender equality. Yet, at a local level, the fear and vulnerability women face on a daily basis remains a pressing concern. These efforts of engaging the law, monitoring implementation, and raising consciousness are "slow strategies" that do not necessarily deliver immediate results (Gouws 2016b, 411). In the meantime, women still have to consider how they can live with and live through the realities of GBV. Many of them, as we have learned from the #EndRapeCulture campaign are young women (ages fifteen to twenty-four), who are particularly vulnerable to violence and are thus seeking immediate assistance. Online support groups such as GIRLS(ICE) can fill this intermediate space, by providing temporary assurance to women who remain vulnerable to sexual violence. In this case, the GIRLS(ICE) groups exemplify women's networks that are not necessarily accessible via websites, blogs, or public Facebook pages, nor visible on the streets demanding the attention of policy makers. Instead, they operate in invisible spaces, providing support to those not yet ready to be in public.

CONCLUSION

Talking about a society free of GBV as impossible will do injustice to the agency of gender advocates and activists, both inside and outside of state institutions. As Britton's (2006) work suggests, such agency needs to be harnessed as a joint effort, tackled collectively by the nonprofit sector, coalitions between the state and the civil society, and grassroots organizations. Such collective approaches to addressing GBV should not only be in the way of reactive support but also involve deep structural change, ranging from operationalizing policies to implementing legislation in support of women's rights. Additionally, we should consider more ontological ways of thinking about GBV. Du Toit (2014) convincingly argues that historic, economic, and patriarchal reasons might underwrite South Africa's high levels of violence against women but by only considering such reasons, we take agency away from perpetrators and instead blame their violent actions primarily on psychological or extraordinary processes. What is overlooked in the process, Du Toit further argues, are the temptations accompanying sexual violence. Perpetrators run little to no *punitive* risk when committing such violence, especially considering slow police work and the relatively few convictions made against such offenses. Similarly, perpetrators face little *social* risks from their communities, with people more frequently blaming victims than perpetrators. At the core remains an even bigger temptation: the authority and accompanying power to completely alter, if not destroy, the victim's world. The power embedded in such control, as Du Toit (2014) argues, is a temptation many perpetrators find hard to resist.

Only when considering these temptations and the subsequent impacts on women's lives, can we start holding men accountable for their actions. When this happens, Naidoo (2018) argues, we will start empowering survivors of abuse. Such empowerment should not come from women themselves, but should be nested in forms of state and government support. Active courts and quick prosecution, supported by strong legislative systems and supportive political actors, will surely contribute to such empowerment. But instituting and operationalizing these structures takes time and in the meanwhile, women remain vulnerable to violence. They therefore have no other option but to develop their own networks of support, or *instant interventions*, either for immediate resolve in the face of danger or for enabling activism against GBV. In many instances, and increasingly so, women look toward ICTs as a productive medium to enable such networking and accompanying support.

In this chapter, I considered how online networks provide women with different kinds of support in light of GBV and the "war on women" (Van Allen 2015). I argued that women's networks seek interventions against GBV, and also work in tandem with existing advocacy efforts. Such interventions are not necessarily prominent in the public sphere. In contrast with the #TheTotalShutDown movement and the #EndRapeCulture campaigns, women engage in less visible structures such as GIRLS(ICE) and use a behind-the-scenes approach to support each other. These interventions, in combination with more visible forms of activism, add to a wider framework of networking support against GBV and rising femicide. In this case, Ashley Currier's description of nonprofit organizations' LGBTQ+ advocacy in Southern Africa provides a productive entry point in our approach to both visible and invisible forms of networking support. In this case whether women choose to be either visible or invisible becomes a conscious and strategic choice. This choice is not due to a lack of willpower to fight for change, but rather to speak to immediate challenges accompanying GBV. In combination with other online networks, groups like GIRLS(ICE) participate in a digital sisterhood that is not immediately obvious nor visible, yet which provides the networking support and connections women need when facing persistent sexual violence. And as is obvious from the #TheTotalShutDown slogan, women's public frustration in combination with their actions in addressing GBV confirms that women have had enough—"enough is enough." Whether through publicly noticeable activism or more invisible online networks, women take action to intervene.

NOTES

1. WhatsApp, a mobile instant messaging application and subsidiary of Facebook, is tied to a user's telephone number and works on Android, iOS, and Windows mobile platforms. Users can send instant messages, voice notes, images, and videos to other users, and also partake in group chats, which allows users to communicate with up

to 256 people simultaneously. With approximately 1.3 billion users, one billion daily users, and support for sixty languages, the application's current popularity increasingly equals that of Facebook Messenger and outshines other instant messaging applications such as *WeChat* and *Viber* (Latif Dahir 2018).

2. 2019 figures on South African mobile phone users support this logic, stating that approximately twenty-three million users or more than a third of the country's total population are smartphone users (Business Insider 2019). Of this population, eighteen million frequently use social media applications, with WhatsApp being a popular option (Kemp 2018; Muzenda 2018).

3. GIRLS(ICE) is a closed group, which means that unless you receive an invitation to join, you will not have access to their conversational board, the participants, or their profiles. Such privacy is an intentional strategy to keep users safe and I therefore had no intentions to join the group or to ask questions specific to the group's membership, content, or conversational style. I thought this would be intrusive and ignorant of the group's objectives, that is, to keep their users safe. Instead, I used published articles describing the group's activities and conversations with the group's founder to develop a basic understanding of their existence and operations.

4. In an effort to respect the group's privacy and composition, I refrained from asking about members identifying as trans women.

5. Gender nonconformity refers to gender expression that does not necessarily identify with masculine or feminine gender norms.

6. GBV has become a collective term, representing the concepts of heteropatriarchal violence, domestic violence, and sexual violence (McFadden 2018).

7. Currier chose LGBT as acronym to refer to the organizations she worked with in Namibia and South Africa (Currier 2012, 175).

8. Also known as revenge pornography, this involves the "creation, distribution, or threat of distribution, of intimate or sexually explicit images of another person without their consent" (Henry and Powell 2018, 201).

9. On March 20, 2018, Ferguson officially pressed charges against South African Football Association president Danny Jordaan.

10. TCCs are one-stop facilities developed to provide immediate support to victims of GBV and aim to reduce secondary victimization while building an immediate case ready for successful prosecution. These centers are placed in hospitals and communities with highest reported instance of rape (Britton 2006).

REFERENCES

Abdelmonem, Angie, and Susana Galán. 2017. "Action-Oriented Responses to Sexual Harassment in Egypt." *Journal of Middle East Women's Studies*13(1): 154–67.

Ajayi, Titilope F. 2018. "#MeToo, Africa and the Politics of Transnational Activism." *Africa Is a Country*. Accessed August 13, 2019.

Banda, Lillian. 2013. "Zambia Teens Learn Twitter and Facebook to Stop Violence Against Women." *Women's News Network*, April 12, 2013. https://womennesnetwork.net/2013/04/12/zambian-teens-twitter-and-facebook/

Britton, Hannah. 2006. "Organising Against Gender Violence in South Africa." *Journal of Southern African Studies* 32(1): 145–63.

Brooks, Pamela E. 2008. *Boycotts, Buses, and Passes Black Women's Resistance in the US South and South Africa*. Amherst, MA: University of Massachusetts Press.

Business Insider. 2019. "More Than 13 Million New Smartphones Were Sold in South Africa Last Year—And Almost Two-Thirds Cost Less Than R1,500." *Tech*, February 21, 2019. https://www.businessinsider.co.za/more-than-13-million-new -smartphones-were-sold-in-south-africa-last-year-and-almost-two-thirds-cost-less -than-r1500-2019-2

Buskens, Ineke, and Anne Webb. 2008. *Creating New Realities?: African Women Using ICT's for Empowerment*. London: Zed.

Buskens, Ineke, and Anne Webb. 2014. *Women and ICT in Africa and the Middle East: Changing Selves, Changing Societies*. London: Zed Books.

Castells, Manual. 2011. *The Rise of the Network Society*. Hoboken, NJ: Wiley and Sons.

Castells, Manual. 2015. *Networks of Outrage and Hope: Social Movements in the Internet Age*. Hoboken, NJ: John Wiley and Sons.

Chiumbu, Sarah. 2012. "Exploring Mobile Phone Practices in Social Movements in South Africa: The Western Cape Anti-Eviction Campaign." *African Identities* 10(2): 193–206.

Clark-Parsons, Rosemary. 2019. "'I See You, I Believe You, I Stand With You': #MeToo and the Performance of Networked Feminist Visibility." *Feminist Media Studies*, June, 1–19.

Crenshaw, Kimberle. 1991. "Mapping the Margins: Intersectionality, Identity Politics, and Violence Against Women of Color." *Stanford Law Review* 43(6): 1241–99.

Currier, Ashley. 2012. *Out in Africa: LGBT Organizing in Namibia and South Africa*. Minneapolis: University of Minnesota Press.

Du Toit, Louise. 2014. "Shifting Meanings of Postconflict Sexual Violence in South Africa." *Signs: Journal of Women in Culture and Society* 40(1): 101–23.

Flone Initiative. n.d. "Report It, Stop It." Accessed August 1, 2019. https://floneinitiat ive.org/index.php/report-it-stop-it/

Fotopoulou, Aristea. 2016. *Feminist Activism and Digital Networks: Between Empowerment and Vulnerability*. London: Palgrave Macmillan UK.

Fraser, Nancy. 1990. "Rethinking the Public Sphere: A Contribution to the Critique of Actually Existing Democracy." *Social Text* (25–26): 56–80.

Gouws, Amanda. 2016a. "How South Africa's Young Women Activists Are Rewriting the Script." *The Conversation*, June 15, 2016. https://theconversation. com/how-south-africas-young-women-activists-are-rewriting-the-script-60980

Gouws, Amanda. 2016b. "Women's Activism Around Gender-Based Violence in South Africa: Recognition, Redistribution and Representation." *Review of African Political Economy* 43(149): 400–415.

Gouws, Amanda. 2018a. "#EndRapeCulture Campaign in South Africa: Resisting Sexual Violence Through Protest and the Politics of Experience." *Politikon* 45(1): 3–15.

Gouws, Amanda. 2018b. "South Africa May Finally Be Marching toward Solutions to Sexual Violence." *The Conversation*, August 8, 2018. https://theconversation

.com/south-africa-may-finally-be-marching-towards-solutions-to-sexual-violence-101261

Gouws, Amanda. 2019. "#MeToo Isn't Big in Africa. But Women Have Launched Their Own Versions." *The Conversation*, March 7, 2019. https://theconversation.com/metoo-isnt-big-in-africa-but-women-have-launched-their-own-versions-112328

Gqola, Pumla Dineo. 2015. *Rape: A South African Nightmare*. Johannesburg: Jacana Media. Kindle.

Hassim, Shireen. 2006. *Women's Organizations and Democracy in South Africa: Contesting Authority*. Madison: University of Wisconsin Press.

Henry, Nicola, and Anastasia Powell. 2018. "Technology-Facilitated Sexual Violence: A Literature Review of Empirical Research." *Trauma, Violence, and Abuse* 19(2): 195–208.

Jenkins, Cerian. "Calling Out Call-Out Culture." *cerianjenkins.com* (blog), June 11, 2019. www.cerianjenkins.com/2019/06/11/calling-out-call-out-culture/

Kemp, Simon. 2018. "Digital in 2018: 'World's Internet Users Pass the 4 Million Mark.'" *We Are Social*, January 30, 2018. https://wearesocial.com/uk/blog/2018/01/global-digital-report-2018

Kendall, Lori. 2002. *Hanging Out in the Virtual Pub: Masculinities and Relationships Online*. Berkeley: University of California Press.

Khoja-Moolji, Shenila. 2015. "Becoming an 'Intimate Publics': Exploring the Affective Intensities of Hashtag Feminism." *Feminist Media Studies* 15(2): 347–50.

KPMG. 2014. *Too Costly to Ignore: The Economic Impact of Gender-Based Violence in South Africa*. https://assets.kpmg/content/dam/kpmg/za/pdf/2017/01/za-Too-costly-to-ignore.pdf

Langa, Malose. 2017. *#Hashtag: An Analysis of the #FeesMustFall Movement at South African Universities*. Johannesburg/Cape Town: Centre for the Study of Violence and Reconciliation.

Latif Dahir, Abdi. 2018. "WhatsApp Is the Most Popular Messaging App in Africa." *Quartz Africa*, February 14, 2018. https://qz.com/africa/1206935/whatsapp-is-the-most-popular-messaging-app-in-africa/

McFadden, Patricia. 2018. "Contemporarity: Sufficiency in a Radical African Feminist Life." *Meridians: Feminism, Race, Transnationalism* 17(2): 415–31.

Mendes, Kaitlynn, Jessica Ringrose, and Jessalynn Keller. 2018. "#MeToo and the Promise and Pitfalls of Challenging Rape Culture through Digital Feminist Activism." *European Journal of Women's Studies* 25(2): 236–46.

Mogoatlhe, Lerato. 2019. "South Africa Just Signed a Declaration to End 'National Crisis' of Gender-Based Violence." *Global Citizen*, April 1, 2019. https://www.globalcitizen.org/en/content/gender-based-violence-declaration-south-africa/

Moletsane, Relebohile. 2018. "'Stop the War on Women's Bodies': Facilitating a Girl-Led March Against Sexual Violence in a Rural Community in South Africa." *Studies in Social Justice* 12(2): 235–50.

Moore, Elena. 2019. "'My Husband Has to Stop Beating Me and I Shouldn't Go to the Police': Family Meetings, Patriarchal Bargains, and Marital Violence in the Eastern Cape Province, South Africa." *Violence Against Women*. https://doi.org/10.1177/1077801219840440

Moosa, Fatima. 2018a. "Gender Summit Concludes with Declaration Adopted." *The Daily Vox*, November 2, 2018. https://www.thedailyvox.co.za/gender-summit-concludes-with-declaration-adopted-fatima-moosa/

Moosa, Fatima. 2018b. "Here's What #TheTotalShutdown Movement Is Demanding." *The Daily Vox*, August 13, 2018. https://www.thedailyvox.co.za/heres-what-thetotal-shutdown-movement-is-demanding-fatima-moosa/

Morse, Felicity. 2014. "The Bring Back Our Girls Campaign Is Working: Boko Haram Should Be Scared of a Hashtag." *Independent*, May 13, 2014. https://www.independent.co.uk/voices/comment/the-bring-back-our-girls-campaign-is-working-boko-haram-should-be-scared-of-a-hashtag-9360830.html

Muzenda, Mako. 2018. "A Messaging App with Data-Free Texts Is Targeting WhatsApp in South Africa." *Quartz Africa*, August 18, 2018. https://qz.com/africa/1361692/a-messaging-app-with-data-free-texts-is-targeting-whatsapp-in-south-africa/

Naidoo, Kammila. 2018. "Confronting the Scourge of Violence Against South Africa's Women." *New Agenda: South African Journal of Social and Economic Policy* (71): 40–44.

Naidoo, Kamilla. 2019. "The War on Women and Children in South Africa." *Africa Is a Country*, January 30, 2019. https://africasacountry.com/2019/01/the-war-on-women-and-children-in-south-africa

Nieftagodien, Noor. 2015. *The Soweto Uprising*. Athens: Ohio University Press.

O'Donnell, Amy, and Caroline Sweetman. 2018. "Introduction: Gender, Development and ICTs." *Gender and Development* 26(2): 217–29.

Pavan, Elena. 2015. "#Takebackthetech and #WhatAreYouDoingAboutVAW. Reclaiming ICTs and Soliciting Stakeholders' Responsibility to End Violence Against Women." *Feminist Media Studies* 15(1): 159–62.

Pavan, Elena. 2017. "The Integrative Power of Online Collective Action Networks Beyond Protest: Exploring Social Media Use in the Process of Institutionalization." *Social Movement Studies* 16(4): 433–46.

Powell, Anastasia. 2015. "Seeking Rape Justice: Formal and Informal Responses to Sexual Violence Through Technosocial Counter-Publics." *Theoretical Criminology* 19(4): 571–88.

Salter, Michael. 2013. "Justice and Revenge in Online Counter-Publics: Emerging Responses to Sexual Violence in the Age of Social Media." *Crime, Media, Culture* 9(3): 225–42.

Sonke Gender Justice. 2018. "Sonke Gender Justice Will March in the #TheTotalShutDown—Will You?" July 31, 2018. Accessed August 1, 2019. https://genderjustice.org.za/article/sonke-gender-justice-will-march-in-the-thetotalshutdown-will-you/

Sow, Rainatou. 2014. "Women and ICT in Africa: A New Digital Gap." *Al Jazeera*, May 28, 2014. https://www.aljazeera.com/indepth/opinion/2014/05/women-ict-africa-new-digital-ga-201452210244121558.html

Thompson, John B. 2005. "The New Visibility." *Theory, Culture & Society* 22(6): 31–51.

Tripp, Aili Mari, Isabel Casimiro, Joy C Kwesiga, Alice Mungwa, and Oxford University Press. 2009. *African Women's Movements: Transforming Political Landscapes*. New York: Cambridge University Press.

University of Stellenbosch. 2017. "Report: Recommendations on Addressing EndRapeCulture at SU." https://www.sun.ac.za/english/Documents/Stellenbosch%20University%20EndRapeCulture%20Report%202017.pdf

Van Allen, Judith. 2015. "What Are Women's Rights Good For? Contesting and Negotiating Gender Cultures in Southern Africa." *African Studies Review* 58(3): 97–128.

Wajcman, Judy. 2004. *Techno Feminism*. Cambridge: Polity.

Webb, Anne. 2016. "Information and Communication Technology and Contesting Gender Hierarchies." *Journal of Information Policy* 6: 460–74.

Wood, Mark, Evelyn Rose, and Chrissy Thompson. 2019. "Viral Justice? Online Justice-Seeking, Intimate Partner Violence and Affective Contagion." *Theoretical Criminology Theoretical Criminology* 23(3): 375–93.

World Health Organization. 2013. "Violence Against Women: A Global Health Problem of Epidemic Proportion." *Media Centre*, June 20, 2013. https://www.who.int/mediacentre/news/releases/2013/violence_against_women_20130620/en/

Zelezny-Green, Ronda. 2018. "'Now I Want to Use It to Learn More': Using Mobile Phones to Further the Educational Rights of the Girl Child in Kenya." *Gender and Development* 26(2): 299–311. https://doi.org/10.1080/13552074.2018.1473226

Chapter 4

"All This Drama"

Intervening Narratives and Precarious Performances in the Namibian Online Fictional Diary The Dream of a Kwanyama Girl

Martha Ndakalako-Bannikov

On July 4, 2014, the first chapter of the online fictional diary[1] named the *Dream of a Kwanyama Girl Season One* was posted anonymously on Facebook on a page with the same name. At the end of this chapter, the author[2] added, "Comments are welcome." What then unfolded was a twenty-nine chapter first-person narrative posted over a period of fifty-seven days in which the author continually invited commentary and interacted with their readership concerning elements of the story told. The narrative speaks to a dominant discourse in Namibia referring to "*Kandeshi*" behavior—a word ascribed to women who obtain boyfriends for monetary gain. This discourse was initiated by music group PDK's release of their song "Dirty Kandeshi" in 2012. *The Dream of a Kwanyama Girl*'s author used the Facebook platform and a fictional narrative to facilitate a dialog with their readership concerning the Kandeshi lifestyle of the characters and the direction of the story. This chapter explores the intervention this literary work makes in Namibian social discourses. In portraying the precariously performed lives of Kandeshis, *The Dream of a Kwanyama Girl* problematizes the simplistic definition of "gold-digger" commonly applied to these women. Further, it implicates broader society and the failure of traditional values to assist young, ambitious Namibian women in a changing world. This chapter argues that *The Dream of a Kwanyama Girl* offers a nuanced intervention to the commonly held perceptions of the Kandeshi lifestyle. In its interactive form, the narrative affects the popular discourse surrounding Kandeshis, thus allowing for the possibilities of considering positive change within Namibian society.

FRAMEWORKS: THE COUNTERPUBLIC
SPHERE AND SOCIAL DRAMA

This chapter analyzes *The Dream of a Kwanyama Girl* within the societal context in which it was produced and in dialog with a song released by the Namibian kwaito[3] music group PDK, in which the neologism "Kandeshi" was coined. To consider how it functions as an intervention, I frame *The Dream*[4] within the theoretical contexts of *the counterpublic sphere* and *social drama*. Robert Asen (2000) explains that as a critical term, counterpublic foregrounds the way in which normative discussions in a public sphere hide alternative discourses and in turn how people work to make these excluded discourses visible (426). Counterpublics also highlight the varying power relations among the many diverse groups that constitute the public sphere (425).[5] Asen explores Nancy Fraser's framework of counterpublics in which Fraser argues that members of marginalized groups circulate counterdiscourses to allow for oppositional understandings of their own identities, interests, and needs, and in this way expand the "discursive space" (428). The Facebook narrative is not merely oppositional, however. Its effectiveness lies in complicating the simplicity of the dominant narratives, and in doing so it expands discursive space. Also significant is that the narrative uses fiction to create its discursive space and shape alternative interpretations of Kandeshi identities. While this counterpublic may offset the discursive privilege that the dominant narrative holds, it will not entirely overcome it because, as will become apparent, both the Kandeshis that the narrative depicts and the medium of Facebook which allows for this discursive space are subordinate in mainstream society and media. *The Dream* uses the Facebook platform to create a discursive counterpublic sphere, fostering debate concerning the Kandeshi lifestyle that is alternative to the dominant reading of these identities. This counterpublic sphere is unique in that the community does not form with a particular agenda in mind, that is, to address a common concern. Rather, the counterdiscourse emerges in the comments made by the readers and their engagement with the author concerning the nuances of the narrative. This happens, however, in constellation with *social drama*.

Social drama allows us to see what *The Dream*'s narrative counters. Victor Turner (1987) defines social drama as "aharmonic or disharmonic social process[es] arising in conflict situations" (74). These processes are initiated and performed in the public sphere and disrupt the quotidian flow of life.[6] Thus, they unveil the tensions in a social structure normally concealed by habitual day-to-day activities. Furthermore, they make visible the way a society thinks, what it values, and its inequalities in any given historical moment (90). Social dramas occur in four phases: breach, crisis, redressive action, and reintegration. The "breach" is the act which disrupts regular, norm-governed social relations and initiates the social drama, and during "crisis" the breach may widen. "Redressive action" occurs when the offense is addressed, and this can range to include personal advice and informal mediation or arbitration, formal juridical and legal action, or the performance of "symbolic acts" (75) to appease the conflicting parties. In the final phase—"reintegration"— the disturbed social group is reintegrated, or there is recognition of the irreparable schism between the contesting parties.[7] The Kandeshi social drama that *The Dream* participates in involves a social critique of the sexual behavior of young women, behavior that is traditionally judged as deviant, immoral, and a blight on the societal landscape. The theory of social drama allows us to circumvent this type of argument as it is an approach that considers human societies as produced out of "human processes"—acts or performances—that transform the cultural landscape, rather than as harmonious constructs or groups aimed toward a pure ideal culture that must be attained. In this case, society is governed by rules and customs that dictate behavior, but that are often incompatible with each other in particular situations (Turner 1987, 74). Therefore, acts typically considered as discrepant or flaws are in fact clues to social process, and furthermore, are able to make visible the genuine novelty and creativeness that can emerge in the performance situation as individuals navigate the intersections of contradictory social expectations (77). This perception of culture not only refrains from applying value judgments to particular acts or behaviors, but regards these as revelatory, and as holding transformative potential within their cultural context.

In considering the behavior of young women in Windhoek as deviant, PDK's song and music video release initiated a social drama in Windhoek society, in which *The Dream* participates as a form of redress by creating a counterpublic sphere where an alternative narrative to PDK's song is discussed. However, while *The Dream* participates as redressive action, it also occurs in a marginalized space and deals with a subordinated social group. This does not suggest that this space or social group is without agency. Netta Kornberg (2018), while acknowledging the power of oppressive systems, challenges "the notion of total powerlessness" commonly assumed in discussions of marginality (245). As a socioeconomic and political position, marginality is generally defined as "lack (of participation, reciprocation, capital or choice, among other things) and belonging (fulfilling a role in society by being exploited)" (Kornberg 2018, 244). However, power is diffused rather than monopolized at the center, and therefore, despite the "asymmetrical binds" that define the marginalized in a society, this position also allows for some independence (244). It is a position and space inherent with contradictions that are instructive (245). Both the narrative space of a Facebook page and the subordinated position of Kandeshis are marginal to the mainstream. But both hold transformative possibilities, and thus address, complicate, and challenge the Namibian social drama.

THE NAMIBIAN SOCIAL DRAMA

On March 23, 2012, all-male Namibian kwaito music group PDK released their single "Dirty Kandeshi" on YouTube. The song is about a young woman named Kandeshi who, in the chorus, is described in the following manner: "Dirty Kandeshi, seduce someone 'cause she want his money / Dirty Kandeshi, breaking my heart 'cause she want my money / [Wakaka, wakaka, wakaka, ye] you're dirty, dirty, dirty / [Montwe woye kamunend-unge ye] in your brain there is no intelligence" (PDK 2012). In the song and video Kandeshi is depicted and described as a single-minded, unintelligent seductress who preys on men for their money, and the men—the victims in this scenario—are heartbroken. Thus, PDK capitalized on the tension within Windhoek society surrounding the behavior of women like Kandeshi, and simultaneously initiated a social drama. The song was a hit, eliciting social commentary from Namibia's many media sources. Two weeks after the release, an article in *The Villager* newspaper described the music video in the following manner:

> The flick is simple: they are strangers who meet in a restaurant; drag each other home to bed; play and the guy leaves for the toilet while she ransacks his drawers and wallet. When he returns from the loo, she asks for money to do her nails and hair; he surrenders his bank card; she hugs the guy and fishes out his wallet from the back pocket. That's Dirty Kandeshi—the hottest and most played music video these days. In the video, PDK portrays the hustle of a wallet miner, who uses her pout and curves to dive into the pockets of most [*sic*] naive men to look in her direction. (Halwoodi 2012)

The article continues with PDK-member Patrick Mwashindange outlining the band's motive for making the video: "We want to give a different perspective of a woman's hustle [. . .] The video is not explicit. We wanted something fun with a message and a story of survival" (2012). Yet the song's lyrics belie this seeming-benevolent motive, and while the music is upbeat and the video is colorful and well filmed, "a woman's hustle" is portrayed in a derogatory manner that is nothing new. Perhaps the only difference is that this "hustle" is specific to Namibia.

Namibians confirmed this societal specificity as the video continued to gain popularity and discursive traction. A month after its release, radio station Energy 100FM asked their audience on Facebook: "What is your definition of Dirty Kandeshi and do they exist in Namibia?" (2012). This question elicited a string of comments, many calling "Dirty Kandeshis" Namibia's version of "gold-diggers." Also of note is that within a month of the song's release, the term "Dirty Kandeshi" had become a descriptor for the type of woman portrayed in the video. And while many of the responses to the radio station's questions protested the term "gold-digger" and the descriptor "dirty" (one respondent asked: "who makes them dirty after all"), these were drowned out in preference for the "gold-digger" signifier. This preference became further evident in January 2013 when, almost a year after the video's release, *the Namibian* newspaper announced that comedian Lazarus Jacobs would return to the stage with a new show: "Keeping Up with the Kandeshis" (Kaulinge 2013). When interviewed by the National Theatre of Namibia to promote his show he was asked "What defines a Kandeshi to you and what is your take on them?" Jacobs responded, "I don't define who a Kandeshi is, it has already been defined by society as a gold-digger." The interviewer went on to state that "[T]he show will clearly leave the audience with the expression: 'A Sista has got to get paid. By any means necessary!'" (NTN Namibia 2013). The term's entrenchment in Namibian society and its vocabulary was further demonstrated a month after Jacobs's show (a year after the song's release) when a front-page column in *the Namibian* read, "Perhaps your girlfriend is nothing more than a Kandeshi. Hope she's not a dirty Kandeshi. When kwaito group PDK produced the song 'Dirty Kandeshi' they would never have thought that it would become such an iconic song, about girls just chopping guys' money" ("Pulling a Woody" 2013).[8] Clearly this song speaks to a situation in Namibia that resonates with popular unease concerning women's behavior which deviates from normative societal expectations.

It is also evident that the music video, a modern product with a conservative message, reflects the nation's discourse concerning Namibian identity which highlights modernity and progress, as well as respect for tradition and patriarchy as some of its defining features.[9] This intersection of notions of conservatism and progressive modernity makes navigating the resultant contradictions in Namibian national identity a complicated process, particularly for young women. PDK's music video, on the one hand, highlights Windhoek modernity in its various upscale locations, yet, on the other, it conceals a gendered discourse which holds the song's Kandeshi—and women in general—to an impossible standard of behavior. Such unrealistic expectations do not consider socioeconomic disadvantages such as Namibia's high unemployment rate and the enduring effects of apartheid that continue to limit black Namibians' educational opportunities, particularly for women.

This denigration of female sexuality is a product of "male models of power" (Lorde 1984). It is therefore no surprise that the expectation of chaste behavior is not applied to Kandeshi's sexual partners. *The Dream* complicates the oversimplified assessment the music video gives by highlighting the tensions between notions of tradition, modernity, and gender inequality that the young women in the narrative navigate. Using the Facebook platform, *The Dream* acts as the "redressive action" phase of the social drama. Not only does it speak back to the message the video and the media disseminate, but in the nuanced perspective it provides, it transforms perceptions of these women.

NARRATIVE INTERVENTION: *THE DREAM OF A KWANYAMA GIRL*

The Dream complicates the situation of young women caught at the intersection of gendered traditions and popular progressive notions of modernity. Like other online fictional diaries, the story is about young women who use sex to gain access to money and power; and similar to other works in the genre, *The Dream* is sympathetic to the plight of these young city women (Bosch Santana 2018, 94). Of note is that while the narrative's melodrama and hypersexuality highlight the easy victimization of these young women by men and at times their inadvertent mistreatment by older women in Namibian society, they also reveal the women's strong desire for independence. The Kandeshis in the narrative are, after all, ambitious education-seeking women. Such storytelling as a means of envisioning other subjectivities and possibilities for liberatory thought aligns with the themes of decoloniality inherent to the African literary tradition (Irele 2001). *The Dream* exemplifies a recent trend in contemporary African women's fiction, which highlights the intimacies of bodily violence in order to reframe patriarchal violence and women's agency. Chilozona Eze (2016) describes these contemporary novels as foregrounding the woman's body, but not as a symbol of something else (the nation, or tradition, for instance) but rather "as homes to their individual selves . . . as exclusively theirs, not as belonging to society or their culture" (3). In this female body-conscious context, they also foreground the relationship between African men and women, thus interrogating the devastating implications of the African patriarchal gaze for the female body (3, 9). Eze reads this body consciousness and insistence on self-possession as "a call for a moral reappraisal of society's relation to the personhood of women who suffer gender discrimination" (6). In line with this tradition, *The Dream* shows how Kandeshi behavior emerges out of a complex melding of ideologies that constrain and obscure the women's own desire for independence and frames their self-assertion and acts for agency as deviance. While the narrative imagines the possible lived conditions of negotiating patriarchy and the frequently resultant sexual violence, the narrative also contextualizes this behavior within generational relationships between women, exploring tensions regarding traditional expectations for women in the context of city life and highlighting the themes of motherhood and sisterhood.

Analysis of *The Dream*

The Dream, publicized on Facebook two years after the release of "Dirty Kandeshi," tells of the experiences of the protagonist Nangula. After graduating from high school, Nangula leaves her village in northern Namibia and goes to live with her aunt Lahja in Windhoek, the capital city, to attend the University of Namibia. There, Nangula is drawn into the lifestyle of a Kandeshi, and her life becomes a series of precarious performances in which she must navigate her aunt Lahja's suspicions and expectations of conservative behavior, struggle to keep a clear head in the face of the glamorous life her cousin Blackberry introduces her to, and manage the frequently unwelcome attention of the men who prey on her.

Nangula's introduction to Windhoek life is a rough one that immediately positions her relationship with her cousin Blackberry as a sisterhood, and the relationship with her aunt Lahja, who Nangula lives with, as an antagonistic mother-daughter relationship. The bus that transports her from her home village to Windhoek arrives at the station late at night, and Nangula has no means of contacting her aunt who was supposed to meet her. Borrowing the bus driver's cellphone, she calls aunt Lahja, gets no response, and leaves a message. She then calls Blackberry and leaves another message. The impatient bus driver eventually leaves her to wait at the dark bus station alone. A well-dressed man—who Nangula refers to as Mr. Leather Jacket—appears and kindly offers to loan her his cellphone. When no one answers, he leaves, reassuring her that if anyone calls back, he will let them know where she is. He returns two hours later in his expensive car—"a 320i BMW"—and tells her "['inavadenga natango shiveli'] 'They haven't called yet, dear, but just come with me I will get you home'" (*The Dream* 2014, Chapter 2).[10] Afraid of the suspicious characters lurking around the bus station, and feeling out of options, Nangula gets into the car. The man takes her to a bar and drugs her, but before he can carry her out to his car, Blackberry, who happens to be at the same bar, recognizes her cousin and, making a scene, wrests Nangula away from Mr. Leather Jacket.

The following day, Blackberry takes Nangula to their aunt's house. Blackberry and aunt Lahja do not get along. When Blackberry moved from the village to Windhoek three years ago, she lived with aunt Lahja, but their relationship became strained as Blackberry became increasingly socially active. Eventually aunt Lahja evicted Blackberry, accusing her of prostitution. For this reason, Lahja is suspicious when Nangula appears at her door a day late, and in Blackberry's company. When Nangula tells her of her encounter, her aunt does not believe her:

> I could see the disgrace directed to me on my aunt's face as she looked at me in disgust, ["Meumbo omu hamo totameke kukala hopopi iifundja nande, ngenge osho ngaho tokakala hokala nokakumbu oko takekulongo uumbudi"] "You won't start your life here by telling lies in this house, if this is the case you can go live with this prostitute here [Blackberry] who will teach you her thieving ways, your mother sent you here to go to school not to sleep around." (Chapter 3)

Nangula is then told to sleep on a mattress in the garage, as her aunt "would not allow liars and whores to sleep in her house" (Chapter 3). While the relationship between Nangula and her aunt improves the following day, it remains strained. Much of the tension between aunt Lahja and Nangula arises from Lahja's own hostility to Blackberry and her influence on Nangula. Nangula's careful navigation of her aunt's demand for chaste behavior reveals the unequal gender ideologies that structure these young women's social realities.

This becomes evident one evening when Nangula has dinner with aunt Lahja and her friend Aunt Helena, where the two older women attempt to determine the implications of Nangula's glamorized appearance—what Helena refers to as "swagga."

> We ate with her friend Aunty Helena in the dining room [. . .] "So Nangula, you surely look like a city girl now, I could hardly recognise you the day I brought your aunt from the airport, [o swagga ne ndishi vati,] apparently you have swagga now, it's not a bad thing but be careful of the boys they like to take advantage of the pretty girls," said Aunty Helena [. . .] I told her that I was just interested in my school books, I also told her about my makeover just so I get her off my case, "Well my cousin has been kind to me, she bought me Brazilian hair and gave me her old clothes and shoes, I just couldn't say no and she insisted, apart from that I really just keep myself busy with school," I said, "But surely the boys come up to you don't they, with a beautiful face and body like that, these boys are not blind," said Aunty Helena [. . .] "Helena [otopopi iikwashike ano, ef' okaana kiilonge omambo ako,] what are you going on about, leave the child to her studies and books, Nangula [. . .] finish school before you start dating," said my aunt. (Chapter 25)

Nangula's response to this not-so-subtle interrogation is "I was suspecting they wanted me to tell them whether I'm seeing anyone . . . but I later realised they were just trying to get me talking, I pretended to be innocent" (Chapter

25). This pretense at innocence is crucial to understanding the tension surrounding the Kandeshi social drama. As the passage indicates, the "innocent" behavior that is prized is a focus on education (rather than appearance and "boys"), abstinence, and respect for one's elders demonstrated through obedience. Any indication of contrary behavior implies guilt. While the "swagga" of a city girl is not inherently bad, it attracts men who "take advantage of the pretty girls." And where the pretty girls here are victims, also implied is that these young women are complicit in their own victimization. Therefore, the Kandeshi esthetic—the basis of Helena and Lahja's concern—signifies not only a lack of innocence but also an admission of guilt on some level, and the burden remains on Nangula to prove her innocence.[11] She must explain that her makeover is not a result of Kandeshi behavior. Nevertheless, the possibility of her guilt is because of her associations—to Blackberry and to the Kandeshi esthetic. As the narrative continues, Blackberry draws Nangula further into the lifestyle of a Kandeshi and Nangula must navigate this precarious and complex new identity. In turn, the readers respond to the storyline with critique, advice, and a range of emotions, shifting the Facebook page from that of a merely narrative space to a discursive space.

The Dream Team: Creating a Facebook Counterpublic Sphere

While Facebook affords *The Dream* a public platform, the narrative circulates and facilitates a discursive environment by inviting reader engagement. In this way, *The Dream* performs very much in the way Wendy Willems (2011) speaks of informal media and popular culture in Africa: as an "essential means through which ordinary people have sought to engage, debate and contest the state" (48). Willems further states that research on popular culture usually emphasizes "dissensus and conflict," the various forms of popular culture allowing ordinary Africans to raise and discuss issues of importance to them (49). Similarly, *The Dream* becomes a counterpublic sphere in that the narrative intervenes in the popular discourse initiated by PDK's song, and by inviting reader engagement the author facilitates discourse regarding the narrative. At the end of Chapter 3, for example, after Nangula climbs into Mr. Leather Jacket's car, Nangula ends her first-person narrative by asking the readers "[W]hat would you have done if you were in my shoes?" This is a frequent question at the end of chapters, which both the readers and the author take seriously, discussing alternative possibilities or solutions to Nangula's problems in the comment section. Furthermore, between chapter releases the author frequently posts encouragements on the page admonishing the readers to stay engaged, to "read on" and "watch out" for the following chapters. In responses to readers' comments, they frequently ask readers to "like" and "share" the page, stating in one response to a reader: "[D]o invite friends to

the page though. We have to keep it running" (*The Dream* 2014, Chapter 3).
To a new reader's comments at the end of Chapter 1, the author responds,
"[M]y dear we are at Chapter 8 now, please don't get left behind [. . .]
Welcome aboard." The author's approach to this work, therefore, is that it is
deeply interactive and collaborative. Implied is that the writer and the readers are working together to make Nangula's dream of becoming a chartered
accountant come true. The author refers to this collaboration as "The Dream
Team." The Dream Team is important because it is not merely that the author
shares the story on Facebook, but in creating a collaboration—a mission—the
space of this Facebook page becomes a discursive space.

Because of the Dream Team's familiarity with Windhoek, the discussion
is simultaneously about the narrative and real gender concerns in Windhoek
and wider Namibia. Some readers frequent the upscale locations mentioned
in the text, or at least are familiar with them. One reader states, for example:
"I swear I saw Nangula that night at Monaco" (Chapter 7). Such familiarity
with both the locations and the behaviors of these women gives the narrative
plausibility. In fact, while this fictional narrative is told in first person, both
the author and the readers comfortably conflate fiction with biography, storytelling with reality.

Readers frequently assume this narrative is a biography, and the author does
not dissuade them. For instance, after reading about Nangula's initial encounter with her aunt described above, a reader stated: "mem your aunt is cruel
. . . wasn't it cold in the garage??" The author responded: "Eish, you can only
imagine. A welcome in the city," to which someone else wrote: "the way city
life is . . . it always has a way of welcoming people with a hard slap" (Chapter
3). Other readers do not call the narrative a biography, but nevertheless relate
it to Windhoek's day-to-day. One reader writes: "haaha this is a true story"
(Chapter 1). Another comments: "[. . .] I'm sure many Windhoek city girls can
relate" (Chapter 7), and "[. . .] a true experience of a lot of our girls" (Chapter
3). Another states: "[. . .] this is really what is happening in Namibia" (Chapter
18). One reader goes further and specifies the storyline to someone she knows.
In the comments for Chapter 18, a reader named Penny asks: "Queen??? is
this you" to which another reader responds: "which Queen, Penny?" Penny
responds with "this other gal . . . my sister's cousin." It is evident, then, that
this work is more than just a far-fetched fictional tale for the readers. It allows
them to consider and discuss subject matter in the narrative that corresponds
to very real conditions in Windhoek society. The narrative's relation to lived
experience is confirmed by the author. Early on they make it clear that *The
Dream* is "all just based on Windhoek experiences, plus a little creativity,"
using the blurry line between fiction and reality to inform and elicit discussion
regarding the nature of these "Windhoek experiences" (Chapter 14). When a
reader commented, "you are telling the story of many young girls in that city,"

the author responded with "Yep. It is indeed a very informative story" (Chapter 3). Another reader described the narrative as both an "educating and captivating storyline" (Chapter 13). Thus, through the narrative, the readers are able to contemplate the implications of the narrative's affinity to the everyday experiences of many members of this community as they participate in Nangula's precarious navigations of patriarchal and traditional societal expectations.

These navigations bring into view the unpleasant and violent undercurrents in Namibian society that simplifications obscure. For instance, while readers frequently disapprove of Blackberry's (and her close friends, a group of Kandeshis called the Divas') behavior, ambivalence surfaces in their comments when the narrative presents the details that lead to this behavior. The conversation that occurs after Chapter 18 demonstrates this. In this chapter, after her suicide attempt Angie, a member of the Divas, confesses that she has contracted HIV from her stepfather, who had been sexually abusing her for years. Upon this revelation, Blackberry panics and confesses that one night at a party at Angie's house, she got drunk and went to lie down in the guest bedroom. Angie's stepfather, upon entering the room, mistook her for Angie and raped her. Afterward, when he realized his error, he paid Blackberry to "keep [her] mouth shut and [they] agreed it would never happen again," and that they would keep it from Angie. Blackberry was concerned that she had contracted the virus too. Nangula, upon hearing this, was concerned that Blackberry may have been the one to inadvertently pass it on to her friend. In the comments following this chapter, a reader states: "It is a very nice interesting story, but sad at the same time. Blackberry is not right in the head, she barely thinks straight. Well, I Don't want to think that we have such girls in Windhoek." While clearly disapproving of Blackberry, the reader demonstrates discomfort at the thought that such "girls" exist in Windhoek. Also, for the reader, Blackberry bears the fault—not Angie's stepfather. The judgment is, however, accompanied with a sense of ambivalence, evident in the fact that the reader does not deny that these girls exist, but rather that (s)he does not "want to think" that they exist in Windhoek. Nevertheless, the narrative creates a space in which to think through such situations and their consequences. Another reader posted: "Shit like this happened to my friend *real life*" to which the author responded: "True hey . . . it's all about the real story" (*The Dream* 2014, Chapter 18). This narrative suggests that the "real story" behind the life of a Kandeshi is far more complicated and precarious than a simple matter of greed.

Intervening Narratives and Transformation

Another way in which *The Dream* functions as a counterpublic sphere is in the readers' interventions in the narrative proper. The collaborative, interactive nature of *The Dream* goes beyond the Dream Team's commenting on, sharing and liking the page, and extends to the narrative itself. The question "what would you do in my shoes" that frequently concludes each chapter elicits discussion that not only transforms readers' perception of Kandeshis but affects how the narrative unfolds. *The Dream* performs as a communal text that survives, thrives, and shifts through the interaction. The narrative itself becomes a space of communal contemplation of Kandeshi lifestyle in Windhoek as the author addresses readers' concerns in the comments or incorporates their suggestions in subsequent chapters. This happens, for example, after Chapter 4 in which a Mr. Police Officer blackmailed Nangula. After bringing her home from a party, he takes a picture of her in her party clothes, threatening to tell aunt Lahja unless Nangula agrees to a sexual relationship with him. "What would you do in my shoes?" asks Nangula at the end of the chapter. One of the reader advises: say that "anty doesnt want her to leave the house or you on your periods, . . . or else let him tell anty [sic]." Another reader concurs: "i would be on my periods everyday till the police officer gve up [sic]." And another advises: "I would rather let him tell my aunt cause even if you sleep with him you not guaranteed that he wouldn't tell her and maybe he could have a camera somewhere and take a video while having sex and later tell your aunt you a prostitute!!!dressing like a prostitute is not proof enough but sex video is!!!!" In Chapter 6, Nangula takes the advice of the readers: "So I told him I'm a virgin and that I wasn't ready to have sex with anyone . . . I also told him that I was on my periods and that if he gave me more time I would consider it when I get ready." This does not work and only angers the policeman, and Nangula is coerced into a sexual act. After this traumatic incident, Nangula goes out with her cousin, wanting to get drunk to forget what happened. In response to this chapter, a reader commented: "how on earth u go drink to forgot ur problems if u just started? i wont fuck dat evil officer i would rather accuse him dat he took d advantg of me being home alone n he wanted to rape me [sic]," to which the author replied: "But he threatened her, or maybe he was just bluffing, it's a tough call." This narrative incident and the interactions between the author and readers highlight the text's communal narrative structure that shapes the story. Equally significant, however, is that in including the readers' suggestions (and their failure in the narrative) the author challenges the frequently uncomplicated and easy readings of these women's lives and solutions to their behavior and calling attention to the socially embedded nature of Kandeshi lives.

"ALL THIS DRAMA": THE REALITY OF PASSION KILLINGS AND TRADITIONAL EXPECTATIONS

How, therefore, does the counterdiscourse offered in *The Dream* map onto real conditions in Namibian society? What needs to be redressed in light of this narrative? Along with being at risk for contracting HIV and other sexually transmitted diseases, the gender-based violence the young women in the narrative continually face reflects the situation many women encounter in Namibia and throughout southern Africa. This gender-based violence is, as Patricia McFadden explains, both bodily and discursive; it is "heteropatriarchal violence, domestic violence, and sexual violence" but also includes "the more powerful notions of patriarchal impunity and violation in discussions regarding women's bodies and their integrity" (McFadden 2018, 421).[12] In Namibia, gender-based violence has been frequently and problematically referred to as passion killings, femicide which stems from "sudden bursts of rage" and which occur between intimate partners (Sevenzo 2016). These murders are frequently committed between young couples but affect older couples as well, and women are usually the victims (Sevenzo 2016).[13] In *The Dream*, this kind of murder haunts the Divas.

Maria, one of Blackberry's friends, is murdered by her wealthy boyfriend. This murder is described as a "passion killing" (*The Dream* 2014, Chapter 12), positioning the violence directed to Kandeshis within the wider concerns related to these ongoing murders of women in Namibian society. As Farai Sevenzo (2016) finds, at the heart of some discussions surrounding solutions to passion killings is the assumption that the underlying reason for these murders is resources. For instance, a man may be enraged at the amount of money he has spent on a partner and, feeling robbed, murders her (Sevenzo 2016). However, Mary Hikumuah (2014) complicates this perspective and critiques the discourses perpetuated in the media regarding these murders. After discussing the media's problematic sensationalistic reporting of these murders, Hikumuah states:

> Another factor I believe has escalated these brutal murders is our music industry and media. Now we talk non-chalantly [*sic*] about dirty Kandeshi and "chopping" my money. These very words are used to describe the brutally murdered women, mothers, daughters and sisters [. . .] It appears we have a society that has cultivated a culture of the barter system where women give their bodies in exchange for material goods. This sort of environment breeds distrust, dishonesty, selfishness and unfaithfulness. I guess what runs through my mind now is "how do we stop this epidemic?" . . . Perhaps we can start by making a conscious decision to see the brutal murders as deviations from normal behaviour [*sic*] rather than as the norm.

Beyond the simplistic perspective of Kandeshi behavior perpetuated in the media, Hikumuah both highlights and critiques the "barter system" at the heart of these relationships as a reason for such murders. However, while Hikumuah describes this system as "women [giving] their bodies in exchange for material goods," *The Dream* adds a layer of nuance to what is occurring in these barter relationships, which shifts the weight of responsibility suggested in the assumption that women simply "give" their bodies. What also occurs in these barter relationships is that men expect sex in exchange for material goods; men barter their material goods for the pleasure of a woman's body. Women are not the only ones getting something out of these relationships, but the derogatory simplification of Kandeshi behavior labels them as greedy and promiscuous, assumes male innocence—naïveté—and subsequently justifies violence toward these women. Also apparent in *The Dream* is that these exchanges are frequently coerced, widening the implications of these relationships even further. Sevenzo also suggests that along with easy access to lethal weapons, alcohol and drug abuse, and crushing social inequalities, Namibia's violent colonial past continues to haunt the present, having left deep psychological scars that the nation has yet to reckon with (2016). What this discussion regarding resources and social inequality must also reckon with is that underlying these relationships—this system—is a deeply unequal gendered system of interaction that, on the one hand, undergirds male privilege and easy access to women's bodies yet at the same time demands their chastity. Therefore, while redressive action is required in the perspectives regarding gendered behavior and gender-based violence, *The Dream* also makes visible concerns regarding perceptions of tradition and the way that traditional expectations exert pressure on young women.

There is a clear opposition in the narrative between older and younger women, in which the older women are in positions of power and expect traditional behavior from their subordinated juniors. While this is not the case in all such relationships in the narrative, frequently the older women hold younger women to strict standards of conservative behavior, reading any behavior that deviates from their expectations as implying sexual misconduct. This is evident in Nangula's arrival to aunt Lahja's house recounted above, and a similar dynamic is also implied in the events leading up to Maria's death:

> Blackberry told me how [Maria's] sister chased her out of the house a year ago . . . Maria's sister once came to [Blackberry's] flat in Khomasdal with Maria's bags and her clothes hanging out, telling her not to come back home because she always went out and stayed out all weekend and her apparent words were that Maria ["okwiininga oshikumbu shomo Venduka"] "has become one of Windhoek's prostitutes." After that Maria started dating rich guys and one could well assume that she did it for survival . . . unfortunately she ended up dating Roberto, the one man who now took her precious life away. (Chapter 13)

In both cases, the conservative expectations applied to Maria and Nangula have to do with patriarchal, traditional expectations regarding young women's behavior which are taken as a given—as an indigenous component of Namibian societies. However, Heike Becker (2007) argues that "patriarchal social and cultural features commonly presented as indigenous ('traditional') in contemporary Namibia" came about as a result of "colonialism, Christianity and local elites in the reconstruction of gender and tradition during the colonial period" (26) so that "rather than being a remnant of the past, what is today presented as tradition, in fact, reflects more the impact of the Christian missions and the complex and often contradictory interaction of the colonial administration's ideas about 'proper' gender relations with those of a conservative male elite among the indigenous communities" (30).[14] These influences have had long-lasting effects and have shaped postindependence views on gender equality and tradition. Furthermore, in Namibian debates regarding tradition, those for and against tradition both assume that indigenous cultural traditions have always been inherently patriarchal, and Becker argues that these traditions need to be historicized (Becker 2007, 23, 26). *The Dream* invites a reassessment of these traditions as they continue to structure and support an unequal Namibian society. A noted generational divide in approaches to gender means that "on one hand, there seems to be a reconfiguring of sexual morality due to desire by the young to be 'modern.' On the other hand, their parents and the elders emphasise [*sic*] constraint and the importance of 'tradition'" (LaFont 2007, 5). As we will see in *The Dream*, this tension between youthful performances of perceived modernity and conservative notions of traditional behavior can lead to many misjudgments.

One such misjudgment in *The Dream* poignantly reveals the consequences of hegemonic patriarchy on culturally valued traditional ideals. The night after rescuing Nangula from Mr. Leather Jacket, Blackberry dragged her to a party, which quickly got out of control. Nangula felt unsafe, and Blackberry was too drunk to protect either of them. The police arrive and Nangula states:

> I was rejuvenated and my spirit refreshed when I saw the cop lights outside [. . .] I pleaded with the cops to take us home, I begged them, one lady cop told us to go home the same way we came here, ["Omuli née niiAngola tamukolwa mwadjala mwafa ee prostituta, oshili epipi lo paife tamulengifa aanu man"] "Here you are hanging out with these Angolans getting drunk and dressed like prostitutes, honestly today's generation embarrasses us," she said. I never hated a cop until today, surely she would take her own daughter home. (*The Dream* 2014, Chapter 4)

The female police officer takes it for granted that Nangula arrived at the party willingly and refuses to help them. Her accusations and "embarrassment" at the behavior she infers mirror aunt Lahja's attitude to Blackberry, and Maria's sister to Maria. But most telling is Nangula's own disillusionment at the policewoman's attitude when she states: "surely she would take her own daughter home." In many Namibian cultures, the proper relationship between older and younger women is conceptualized and enacted in the manner of a mother/daughter relationship. Thus, "traditionally," it is right that the policewomen and aunt Lahja should be concerned and even embarrassed when their "daughters" misbehave. But Nangula's mentioning of it at this moment suggests that the policewoman, in refusing her help, has failed—both as an officer of the law and traditionally as a mother to them. But perhaps this failure is connected to the corrosive environment of city life that the novel suggests, and signals deep-seated tensions that emerge in the process of balancing Westernization and African "traditional" ways of life—a tension that the African city frequently represents. What is clear, however, is that Nangula implicates "mothers" in Kandeshi behavior and suggests that perhaps commonly held traditional values have failed to provide support and practical assistance for many of Namibia's young ambitious women.

Thus, the narrative highlights the difficulty of feminist practices of solidarity among its younger and older women in this context. Rather, the Divas form a sisterhood of collaborative solidarity that includes some older women and that stands in contrast to motherhood. This framing is important because in the context of third-world feminist discourse it seems to deviate from African women's continued concerns regarding feminism. Historically, the concept of feminism has been contested by many African women writers and theorists (and other women of color) because of its Western origins and patriarchal concerns rooted in the nuclear family structure that has been a source of oppression for women.[15] For African women, patriarchal oppressions have not manifested in the family in the same way. Furthermore, for many African societies, motherhood is an important institution around which women find solidarity and a great measure of agency—whether or not they are mothers.[16] While this is the case in Namibia as well, in many instances, the narrative reveals a motherhood tied to colonially influenced tradition that manifests in "gendered nationalist conservatism" (McFadden 2018, 423) so that feminist practice toward younger women from the context of this motherhood is difficult, if not impossible. Aniko Imre's definition of nationalism suggests why this is the case: "It has been well established that the we of nationalism implies a homosocial form of male bonding that includes women only symbolically, most prominently in the trope of the mother . . . Nationalist discourses are especially eager to reassert the 'natural' division of labour [*sic*] between the sexes and to relegate women to traditional reproductive roles" (quoted in McFadden 2018, 424). Such a definition reminds us of nationalism's "masculinist ideology and identity" (425) underpinnings. In contrast, McFadden offers a framework that will allow women to "build a bridge of solidarity . . . based on a sense of integrity and self-exploration" (428). The radical feminism she describes means cultivating a way of life that is transformative in its day-to-day, for one's own life and those around you through seemingly small changes that make women's lives livable[17] and gives them some measure of freedom. These changes may in turn become the ground on which to eventually build larger reforms (2018, 425–428). McFadden's discussion of this kind of activism does not diminish the difficulty women encounter when having to form bonds across different racial and class categories, but it is necessary. It asks women to caringly collaborate across their differences and inequalities (428). In *The Dream*, feminist solidarity is enacted beyond the confines of nationalism, ethnic differences, and the constraints of cultural tradition.

In contrast to *The Dream*'s problematic motherhood, the "sisterhood" that defines the solidarity among Blackberry, Nangula, and their Kandeshi friends, as well as other supportive older women, is practical; it is a means of survival. Therefore, I do not wish in any way to romanticize the alliance that forms between the Divas. These characters, in their subordinated and precarious positions, take patriarchy as a given, and while they infrequently challenge it, they also define the parameters of their alliance in order to determine how to gain measures of agency and freedom. Their desire is not to change society, but rather their own circumstances, and this is what their sisterhood is directed toward. While in the novel older women hold the younger ones to a standard of behavior that does not help them navigate the complex hegemony of patriarchal society, these Kandeshis help each other, and sisterhood steps in where motherhood falters. For instance, it is Blackberry who assists Nangula in her social adjustment to Windhoek. Blackberry's care for Nangula is practical, nuanced. She asks Nangula:

> "Is our aunty giving you money [. . .] a girl needs to be financially independent you know," [. . .] I just told her that as long as I had a roof on top of my head and I did not need to go to bed hungry that was all that mattered to me, then my cousin asked if I even had a bank account so I told her "NO" [. . .] "Og Nangula ano how do you survive oshili?, this is the new millennium you should have your own digits in your own bank account, it shows independence [. . .] Some of us are planning ahead my dear, you never know what tomorrow brings for you [. . .] tomorrow first things first, I want to take you to the bank so that I open a bank account for you, I will deposit $5000 for you but after that it's up to you to keep the money flowing." (*The Dream* 2014, Chapter 23)

Despite the tensions and difficulties the Divas face, they demonstrate a strong desire for independence and security that is founded on the ability to care for oneself, and these are achieved through the help of friends: "The Divas were so loyal to each other," states Nangula. "[T]hey did not take their sisterhood for granted." Patriarchal social structures typically deem men the providers and protectors of women, but this is not the case in *The Dream*, and frequently neither is it the case in the lived conditions of Namibian society. In a reflective moment, Nangula summarizes this precarious social position that many young women find themselves in: "All this drama that has been going on has exposed me to a lot of secrets, it has exposed me to the life of dangers and social evils we always read about in the newspapers back at home, it has exposed me to the life of the party in Windhoek, it has exposed me to men who did not like me for me but for how I walked, talked and looked" (*The Dream* 2014, Chapter 13). These are secrets, dangers, and social evils that she now intimately exposes to the narrative's readers, speaking back to Windhoek society's perception of Kandeshis, and thus advocating for a change in the conversation. The women in *The Dream* (and, as the readers infer, in Windhoek's day-to-day) must navigate hegemonic patriarchal structures that idealize the appearance of innocence and chaste behavior for young women, but perhaps do not take into account the changed and changing social climate. The narrative demonstrates the tension between these ideals and lived experience, and makes visible where and how these ideals falter and fail—for both women and men. But as patriarchal structure privileges men, women—and, in the case of *The Dream*, young women—bear the weight of these tensions.

CONCLUSION: TRANSFORMATION AT THE MARGINS

This chapter considers how a social media platform allows for the interrogation of existing norms and the development of a discursive "counterpublic sphere." I argue that a discursive network that involves the readers, author, and the narrative develops, reflects, dissects, and critiques gender norms. When PDK released "Dirty Kandeshi" they tapped into Namibian society's gendered and patriarchal tensions regarding the behavior of young women in Windhoek, initiating a social drama. *The Dream of a Kwanyama Girl* in turn allows for an engaging conversation that critiques the existing social systems and reevaluates our perceptions of Kandeshis. While on the surface these women live carefree, partying lives, simultaneously envied and disliked by many of their peers, *The Dream* makes visible that their public social lives conceal the complexity of navigating a patriarchal society that holds women to an impossible level of moral behavior. And in a society where older women are held in higher esteem in traditional and nationalistic ideology, younger women bear the heavyweight of morality. In this narrative, they are judged harshly when they falter. *The Dream* offers a perspective that holds transformative possibilities for both the readers' perceptions and the dialog surrounding Kandeshis. In this way it begins the process of redressive action—advocating for social change. However, the platform that allows for the narrative to circulate also makes it difficult to access, as each chapter gets buried by previous chapters. The new reader must then spend much time scrolling back through twenty-eight chapters and comments to read the first chapter—a literal subordination of the text. Also, apart from comments by the readers that highlight their own ambivalence to the mainstream dominant narrative, change is difficult to track, but perhaps it is evident in that communal contemplation is happening.

Finally, I conclude with consideration regarding the resilience and creativity of people in the face of difficulty. There are inequalities inherent to Namibia's social systems, and Kandeshis navigate them, but not merely as victims, because patriarchy leaves "in its wake untold destruction and dread, as well as the often unintended possibilities of transformation and renewal" (McFadden 2008, 19). Perhaps a reader best sums up the precarious performances these women enact in a description of Blackberry: "Weiyuuuu . . . [nge kuna enghono, kala wuna endunge] if you don't have strength, you'd better have intelligence . . . that's Blackberry for you right there" (*The Dream* 2014, Chapter 14). Throughout the narrative Nangula asks: "what would you do if you were in my shoes?" The question is an invitation heavy with context, not easily answered and full of transformative possibility.

NOTES

1. *The Dream of a Kwanyama Girl* is part of a southern African genre of digital fiction which Stephanie Bosch Santana defines as online fictional diaries (2018). My dissertation considers the place of *The Dream of a Kwanyama* girl in this network of regional fiction. This chapter, however, is limited to a more localized analysis of the relationship between this narrative and its Namibian social context.

2. The author remains anonymous while posting the narrative on Facebook. While I am aware of the author's identity, I choose to respect their choice to remain anonymous and will refer to this person with the pronouns "they, their, theirs."

3. A genre of southern African music.

4. I will be using this abridged title going forward.

5. Peter Dahlgren (2005) sets out a framework for understanding political discussion online and argues that rather than allowing for effective deliberative democracy, the internet is better understood as allowing for "the development of new ['extraparlamentarian'] democratic politics" (160). Habermasian deliberative democracy privileges "the procedures of open discussion aimed at achieving rationally motivated consensus." However, the rational biases of deliberative democracy tend to overlook other important means of communication that influence democracy, including "the affective, the poetic, the humorous, the ironic, and so forth" (156).

6. Examples of social dramas can range from a public dispute between two people to a court case.

7. Daniel Avorgbedor (2004) critiques this model of social drama, arguing that Turner's final phase—"reintegration"—suggests normalization (34). Thus, in Avorgbedor's model of social drama, three things can occur after a group or individual acts to redress the social drama. Firstly, the conflict may continue until the groups exhaust themselves. Secondly, mediation may work and resolve the conflict; or, thirdly, mediation fails and conflict continues and/or escalates in a violent loop between the groups. Whatever the outcome, the society participating in the social drama is transformed (Avorgbedor 2004, 35). Avorgbedor's reading of social drama as transformative no matter the outcome is a productive way to interpret the discursive intervention *The Dream* affords.

8. The term "chopping" is slang for lavish spending.

9. As Suzanne LaFont (2007) points out, despite Namibia's very progressive constitution regarding gender equality, national identity is understood in very conservative terms, and "a reverence for 'traditions,' including those that deny gender equality and sexual self-determination, is defended under the auspices of nationalism" (1). Also, Henning Melber (2014) discusses how the ruling political party after independence in 1990—the South West Africa People's Organization (SWAPO; now referred to as Swapo Party)—went about outlining a Namibian nationalism founded on patriarchy and the valorization of the liberation movement. This ideology was an extension of their politics during the liberation movement, as the foremost party agitating for Namibian liberation.

10. I have chosen to leave my quotes from the narrative and the comments from the readers in their original form, grammatically for the sake of authenticity. Elsewhere I explore the use of language and grammar in this narrative as it pertains to literary form, and as it contributes to our understanding of global anglophone as a literary field and critical lens (Ndakalako-Bannikov 2021).

11. This is very much associated with victim blaming, a feature of rape culture where women are blamed for eliciting the sexual violence committed against them.

12. McFadden warns that the term "gender-based violence" (and its acronym "GBV") is disempowering for women because it does not allow us to name the particular violences and violations we experience and in turn formulate particular plans of actions as a means of address. In other words, it can be counter to radical feminism. Also, for a reading on the gendered concerns South African young women face, see Cloete's discussion of femicide and gender-based violence in South Africa in this volume (Chapter 3).

13. These cases are also frequently characterized by the suicide of the perpetrators, although this is not always the case (Sevenzo 2016).

14. Meredith McKittrick (2002) discusses extensively how Christianity functioned as social reform in Owambo communities in the North beginning in the late nineteenth century and its afterlives in post-independence Owambo society. See Kwame Gyekye's (1997) consideration of the relationship between the modern and the traditional in forming contemporary society. Also see Terence Ranger's (1983, 1993)

discussion of the way in which traditions in colonial and postcolonial Africa were invented, modified or evolved to suit contemporary needs.

15. See Oyèrónké Oyěwùmí's (1997, 2016) careful exploration of the implications of feminism's western origins. Also see Buchi Emecheta (2007) and Molara Ogundipe-Leslie (1994).

16. See Oyèrónké Oyěwùmí (2003) for a description of the importance of motherhood in many African cultures and families. She state that

> mother-derived ties are the most culturally significant, and that mothers have agency and power. Fundamentally, motherhood is not usually constructed in relation to or in opposition to fatherhood; it is conceived in its own right. Mothers are perceived as especially powerful-literally and mystically, in regard to the well being of the child. They are therefore the pivot around which family life is structured and the child's life rotates. In this family system, unlike in the nuclear family, motherhood is the most important source and model of solidarity, and being a mother is perceived as an attractive and desirable goal to achieve (12).

17. Judith Butler's (2004) concept of livability also applies here. Livability considers how some lives are considered of more value than others. In the context of "socially vulnerable" peoples (18), these can easily be subject to dehumanization leads to physical violence toward them (25). McFadden describes an approach to life that may be considered as a model of, and in conjunction with, Butler's challenging yet necessary call for "ethical and social transformation" (38) required to render all human lives as valuable and respectable.

REFERENCES

"Pulling a Woody on Kandeshi." 2013. *The Namibian*, April 12, 2013. https://www.namibian.com.na/107087/archive-read/Pulling-a-Woody-on-Kandeshi.

Asen, Robert. 2000. "Seeking the 'Counter' in Counterpublics." *Communication Theory* 10(4): 424–446.

Avorgbedor, Daniel. 2004. "The Turner-Schechner Model of Performance as Social Drama: A Reexamination in Light of Anlo-Ewe *Halo*." In *African Drama and Performance*, edited by John Conteh-Morgan and Tejumola Olaniyan, 227–236. Bloomington: Indiana University Press.

Becker, Heike. 2007. "Making Tradition: A Historical Perspective on Gender in Namibia." In *Unraveling Taboos: Gender and Sexuality in Namibia*, edited by Suzanne LaFont and Diane Hubbard, 21–38. Windhoek: Gender Research and Advocacy Project, Legal Assistance Center.

Bosch Santana, Stephanie. 2018. "From Nation to Network: Blog and Facebook Fiction from Southern Africa." *Research in African Literatures* 49(1): 187–208.

Butler, Judith. 2004. *Undoing Gender*. New York: Routledge.

Dahlgren, Peter. 2005. "The Internet, Public Spheres, and Political Communication: Dispersion and Deliberation." *Political Communication* 22(2): 147–162.

Emecheta, Buchi. 2007. "Feminism with a Small 'f.'" In *African Literature: An Anthology of Criticism and Theory*, edited by Tejumola Olaniyan and Ato Quayson, 551–557. Malden: Blackwell Publishing.

Energy 100FM. 2012. "What Is Your Definition of Dirty Kandeshi and Do They Exist in Namibia?" *Facebook*, August 29, 2012. https://www.facebook.com/Energy100f m/posts/367754593259726.

Eze, Chilozona. 2016. *Ethics and Human Rights in Anglophone African Women's Literature: Feminist Empathy*. Cham: Palgrave Macmillan.

Gyekye, Kwame. 1997. *Tradition and Modernity: Philosophical Reflections on the African Experience*. Oxford: Oxford University Press.

Hailonga-van Dijk, Panduleni. 2007. "Adolescent Sexuality: Negotiating Between Tradition and Modernity." In *Unraveling Taboos: Gender and Sexuality in Namibia*, edited by Suzanne Lafont and Dianne Hubbard, 130–147. Windhoek: Gender Research and Advocacy Project, Legal Assistance Center.

Halwoodi, Linekela. 2012. "PDK's 'Dirty Kandeshi' Flick Damn Good." *The Villager*, April 1, 2012. http://www.thevillager.com.na/articles/1328/PDK-s--Dirt y-Kandeshi--flick-damn-good/.

Hikumuah, Mary. 2014. "How Do We Stop the 'Passion Killing' Epidemic." *The Namibian*, February 14, 2014. http://www.namibian.com.na/index.php?id=11980 6&page=archive-read.

Irele, F Abiola. 2001. *The African Imagination: Literature in Africa and the Black Diaspora*. New York: Oxford University Press.

Kaulinge, Selma. 2013. "Lazarus Jacobs Is 'Keeping up with the Kandeshis.'" *The Namibian*, January 18, 2013. https://www.namibian.com.na/index.php?id=104326 &page=archive-read.

Kornberg, Netta. 2018. "Power at the Margins: Black Female Agency in Two Namibian Novels." In *Writing Namibia: Literature in Transition*, edited by Sarala Krishnamurthy and Helen Vale, 241–261. Windhoek: Unam Press.

LaFont, Suzanne. 2007. "An Overview of Gender and Sexuality in Namibia." In *Unraveling Taboos: Gender and Sexuality in Namibia*, edited by Suzanne LaFont and Diane Hubbard, 1–19. Windhoek: Gender Research and Advocacy Project, Legal Assistance Center.

Lorde, Audre. 1984. "Uses of the Erotic: The Erotic as Power." In *Sister Outsider: Essays and Speeches*. Berkeley: Crossing Press. Ebook.

McFadden, Patricia. 2008. "Globalizing Resistance: Crafting and Strengthening African Feminist Solidarities." *The Black Scholar: Journal of Black Studies and Research* 38(2–3): 19–20.

———. 2018. "Contemporarity: Sufficiency in a Radical African Feminist Life." *Meridians: Feminism, Race, Transnationalism* 17(2): 415–431.

McKittrick, Meredith. 2002. *To Dwell Secure: Generation, Christianity, and Colonialism in Ovamboland*. Portsmouth: Heinneman.

Melber, Henning. 2014. *Understanding Namibia: The Trials of Independence*. New York: Oxford University Press.

Ndakalako-Bannikov. Forthcoming, 2021. "Authors, Readers, and the Virtualscapes of Namibian Digital Literature: 'The Dream of a Kwanyama Girl' and other Facebook Serial Fictions." *Postcolonial Text*, Special Issue *Digital Africas*.

NTN Namibia. 2013. "Kandeshi Interview." *Facebook*, March 7, 2013. https://www.facebook.com/events/538771146154145/permalink/551250351572891/.

Ogundipe-Leslie, Molara. 1994. *Recreating Ourselves: African Women and Critical Transformations*. Trenton: Africa World Press, Inc.

Oyěwùmí, Oyèrónké. 1997. *The Invention of Women: Making an African Sense of Western Gender Discourses*. Minneapolis: University of Minnesota Press.

———. 2003. "Introduction: Feminism, Sisterhood and *Other* Foreign Relations." In *African Women and Feminism: Reflecting on the Politics of Sisterhood*, edited by Oyèrónké Oyěwùmí, 1–24. Trenton: Africa World Press, Inc.

———. 2016. *What Gender Is Motherhood? Changing Yorùbá Ideals of Power, Procreation, and Identity in the Age of Modernity*. New York: Palgrave.

PDK. 2012. "Dirty Kandeshi." *YouTube Video, 4:30*, March 23, 2012. https://www.youtube.com/watch?v=V_fDYv60zhE.

Ranger, Terence. 1983. "The Invention of Tradition in Colonial Africa." In *The Invention of Tradition*, edited by Eric Hobsbawm and Terence Ranger, 211–262. Cambridge: Cambridge University Press.

———. 1993. "The Invention of Tradition Revisited: The Case of Colonial Africa." In *Legitimacy and the State in Twentieth-Century Africa: Essays in Honour of A. H. M. Kirk-Greene*, edited by Terence Ranger and Olufemi Vaughan, 62–111. Houndmills, Basingstoke, Hampshire: Macmillan, in association with St. Antony's College, Oxford.

Sevenzo, Farai. 2016. "Letter from Africa: Namibia's Battle with Passion Killings." *BBC News*, March 3, 2016. https://www.bbc.com/news/world-africa-35705739.

The Dream of a Kwanyama Girl. 2014. "Read On..Chapter One." *Facebook*, July 4, 2014. https://www.facebook.com/permalink.php?story_fbid=735274683195667&id=720699087986560.

Turner, Victor. 1987. "The Anthropology of Performance." In *The Anthropology of Performance*, 72–98. New York: PAJ Publications.

Willems, Wendy. 2011. "At the Crossroads of the Formal and Popular: Convergence Culture and New Publics in Zimbabwe." In *Popular Media, Democracy and Development in Africa*, edited by Herman Wasserman, 46–62. New York: Routledge.

Wilson-Tagoe, Nana. 2007. "Representing Culture and Identity: African Women Writers and National Cultures." In *Africa After Gender?* edited by Catherine M Cole, Takyiwaa Manuh, and Stephan F Miescher, 223–241. Bloomington: Indiana University Press.

Chapter 5

Caribbean Women Writers

Forging a New Frontier in the Regional Literary Tradition

Lafleur Cockburn

INTRODUCTION

The exclusion of women writers from the initial Caribbean literary canon traces back to early nineteenth-century slave narratives. However, with the publication of Mary Prince's 1831 autobiographical slave narrative,[1] *The History of Mary Prince, A West Indian Slave*, and Mary Seacole's 1857 autobiography,[2] *The Wonderful Adventures of Mrs. Seacole in Many Lands*, the work of Caribbean women writers became available for public consumption. Moreover, although the British slave trade was abolished in 1807, slavery was still legal in the colonies. Abolitionists used both slave narratives as political tools to engage the moral compass of their predominantly white target audience. Despite the emotional experiences linked to these early narratives, they lacked subjectivity, identity, and an authentic sense of self. Robert Levine (2007) argues that "slave narratives cannot creatively work with language and narrative to portray an individual self" (99), because the enslaved Caribbean woman was viewed as chattel. She was degendered (treated as male laborers), sexually violated (available to whomever her master deemed fit), and intentionally kept illiterate. Nevertheless, she was able to keep her history and culture alive through oral tradition passed down through generations. Indeed, slaves were like walking repositories of African folklore and proverbs. After slavery, once education became available to women, orality was transcribed to oral literature. This literature confronted issues of identity and migration, two of the Caribbean's most defining characteristics, as Caribbean women writers disrupted the existing literary dialog in the region, revamped it to reflect their presence and reimagined a Caribbean space from the female perspective.

Gareth Griffith (1992) suggests that the birth of the Caribbean novel inter-twines with the writer's identity as person and artist. Griffith matches the novel's growth with the movement for political autonomy within the region. In his view, imperialism influences both the structure and the content of the Caribbean novel. Griffith posits that "the [Caribbean] novel was born out of the need to indicate the presence in what had been constructed as absence, and the absence in what had been represented as full presence" (129). The lit-erary evolution from early slave narratives to imagined futures is dominated by a patriarchal and European presence. I submit that black female autonomy, as represented in early twentieth-century literary works, is "constructed as absence" and I recognize the absence of the female voice, though it has been "represented as full presence" in later works. Caribbean women writers insert themselves in this literary transition by adopting orality as a main construct in their work. This is an effective strategy that not only highlights their agency but also points toward the region's connection to the African diaspora.

This chapter traces the way women's literature has intervened in the canon of Caribbean literature in the past, their interventions both transforming the canon and making space for women writers to further innovate Caribbean literature. I map the interventions of four authors—Olive Senior, Michelle Cliff, Jamaica Kincaid, and Nalo Hopkinson—through close analysis of selected short stories and novels. I consider how each author employs orality to analyze gender, identity, and migration before locating them in the broader movements of conceptual decolonization and Afrocentricity. Caribbean women are, without a doubt, contributors to the ever-evolving face of world literature. They challenge postcolonial and Eurocentric notions of gender by directly addressing various forms of patriarchy. The impact of their efforts on the dynamic global movement of female interventions should not be taken lightly.

ANGLOPHONE CARIBBEAN: GEOGRAPHY AND LITERARY HISTORICAL CONTEXT

The Caribbean refers to an archipelago located in the Caribbean Sea between North and South America, and southeast of Central America. The region is predominantly English. Sixty-two percent of the islands are former British colonies and overseas territories, and currently form the Commonwealth Caribbean. The remaining 38 percent of the islands are divided among the Spanish, French, and Dutch. Some islands either changed hands or were divided between different colonial powers.[3] The Caribbean region, therefore, offers an eclectic blend of Anglophone, Hispanophone, Francophone, and Dutch-speaking literature. The islands share close geographical space and a common colonial history of slavery, yet different cultural influences shape their literature, as illustrated in the St. Lucian French creole, the indigenous Garifuna influence in St. Vincent and the Grenadines, or the vibrant Indian culture in Trinidad and Tobago.

I use the term "Caribbean" to refer to literature from the Anglophone Caribbean: the islands ranging from The Bahamas in the North, and Trinidad in the South—to the British mainland territories of Belize in Central America and Guyana in South America, whose coastlines border the Caribbean Sea. Caribbean literature, influenced and shaped by European literature, is described as a "twentieth-century phenomenon" (Stewart Brown 1999). Although a British linguistic insularity inundated early Caribbean literature, writers such as Derek Walcott and Kamau Brathwaite led the way with cultural interchange across the region. Brown (1999) speaks about Derek Walcott's respect for Martiniquian Aimé Césaire, and Kamau Brathwaite's admiration for that of Cuban Nicholás Guillén.

The short story plays a significant role in the formation of the Caribbean literary tradition. Some of the most important Caribbean fiction, particularly by women, has appeared in short story form. According to the *Encyclopedia of African-American Culture and History*, it is within the short story form that Caribbean writers have shown most awareness of formal innovations existing elsewhere in the world. Short story collections have the potential to unite different genres and create dialog between stories with contrasting perspectives of the world. It is an effective medium to embody the complex realities of Caribbean existence through the intervening connections of women writers. These connections may not be as explicit as direct collaborations, but they are present nonetheless. Antonio Benitez Rojo (1996) considers the Caribbean space to be so saturated with messages and codes that it is suspended in a soup of signs. Chaos is averted when certain repeated regularities, discernable only to the trained eye, are identified. I consider the women writers as trained eyes; their work adds insight into the region's landscape, making it more than just a sea (Mary Gallagher 2002). Edouard Glissant (1992) introduces the premise of the region as a rhizomatic root system with an esoteric cohesiveness. He describes a connectivity beneath the surface, like the interlocking, subterranean roots of a rhizome, which link each island, transforming the regional space into a fluid, open area. This is representative of the achievements of the Caribbean women writers. The women writers I discuss below lend constant reassurance to other writers and women in general through their presence at conferences, symposiums, and seminars. They are continually giving workshops, interviews, and keynote addresses, and they partake in discussions and interviews that give them the opportunity to express themselves verbally and develop their ideas, further illuminating the oral component to their written work. These writers[4] are staples in the regional circuit of literary festivals. Their involvement in the regional literary landscape has resulted in the inevitable realignment of postcolonial theories and criticisms to accommodate feminist discourse. It has also led to innovation in terms of new themes and presenters at conferences, symposiums, and seminars, and has elicited the engagement of scholars, researchers, and students alike with the work of women writers. Interventions, then, are the ongoing domino effect that has created a movement and legitimized women's literary work.

Public access to literary works in the region became a reality when literary journals such as *Kyk-Over-Al* in Guyana, *Focus* in Jamaica, and *Bim* in Barbados began to publish short pieces in the 1930s and 1940s. By mid-century, with the "Windrush" era[5] (a period characterized by an influx of Caribbean migrants to postwar England), the Caribbean experienced a boost to its literary growth. Una Marson, a Jamaican immigrant writer, spearheaded *Caribbean Voices*,[6] a BBC radio program which ran from 1943 to 1958. It featured the work of pioneering Caribbean writers such as Samuel Selvon, George Lamming, V. S. Naipaul, Michael Anthony, and Derek Walcott. *Caribbean Voices* offered a space for the dissemination of Caribbean writing in London, while exposing the writers to a wider audience within the region. Marson finally returned to Jamaica, and though conflicting sources make her direct connection to other women writers vague, her advocacy for national literature and her focus on female confidence and beauty in her own work secure her contribution to the dynamic women writers' movement. Brown and Rosenberg in *Beyond Windrush: Rethinking Postwar Anglophone Caribbean Literature* view the "Windrush" era as a major signifier in the perception of Anglophone Caribbean cultural history. The Caribbean Artist Movement (CAM) became known as a literary and cultural movement. CAM followed the BBC radio program with conferences in 1967 and 1969, which also became significant hubs and social centers for the major writers in the region. Some of the most renowned names from this cross section of writers include Claude McKay, C. L. R. James, Victor Reid, Roger Mais, Martin Carter, and Wilson Harris. The formation of the Caribbean literary canon is credited to these male writers.

Despite the apparent silence of the female voice during the formation of the Caribbean literary canon, women writers such as Jean Rhys and Paule Marshall championed its existence by challenging the dominant patriarchal narratives of both the European and the Caribbean literary institutions. They began a thematic revolution by inserting the Caribbean female perspective and voice on issues of identity and migration/exile. Rhys's work chronicles the life of the mad woman stuck in the attic in Charlotte Bronte's 1847 *Jane Eyre*,[7] and Marshall narrates the life of a female migrant in New York.[8]

Both women present migration through a fresh viewpoint, examining its emotional cost to family relations and its link to identity. *Wide Sargasso Sea* and *Brown Girl, Brownstones* have become primary examples of pioneer work that writes back to the empire. Rhys and Marshall fanned the initial embers of awareness, prompting women to be conscious of their own power through representation of autonomous vocal female characters. By 1988, at the inaugural "Caribbean Women Writers International Conference," Marshall was present to usher in a new era in literature led by women writers, and though Rhys had passed on, her work was included in the presentations.[9] As more women became aware of the capacity of literature, the initial embers of awareness ignited into flames of creativity as women writers from across the Caribbean and its diaspora produced literature that inserted the female perspective into the regional literary canonic discourse, altering the predominantly patriarchal and Eurocentric view to reflect a more balanced perspective.

The period during and following independence (1962–1983) was marked by activism and social consciousness as the colonies sought to become autonomous, independent states.[10] The literature of the period reflects this social consciousness as writers such as Pauline Melville, Opal Palmer Adisa, Merle Collins, Christine Craig, Velma Pollard, Lorna Goodison, Olive Senior, and Michelle Cliff led the way for contemporary female voices, who unapologetically told their stories in their own way. They set the pace and paved the way for contemporary writers such as Jamaica Kincaid and Nalo Hopkinson, who took the female voice into new territories of the abstract and speculative. Caribbean women writers discuss similar issues and themes as their male counterparts, but they offer fresh insight into common concerns that stem from race, gender, migration, and identity.

The recent recognition that Caribbean women writers have received from international and regional writing competitions attests to the significance of their intervention and contributions to the Caribbean literary tradition. Women writers won 65 percent of the regional leg of The Commonwealth Short Story Prize since its inception in 2012,[11] with Sharon Millar[12] and Ingrid Persaud[13] of Trinidad and Tobago winning the overall award in 2013 and 2017, respectively. Women are well represented in The Bocas Lit Fest,[14] subdivided into: The One Caribbean Media (OCM) Bocas Prize for Caribbean Literature,[15] The CODE Burt Award for Caribbean Young Adult Literature,[16] and The Johnson and Amoy Achong Caribbean Writers Prize (JAAWP).[17] Since the inception of the prize in 2011, three women, including Olive Senior, won the OCM prize. Women writers dominate The Code Burt and Johnson and Amoy Achong prizes. They also represent well in the leading literary award in Barbados—The Frank Collymore Literary Endowment Award.[18]

TOWARD DECOLONIZATION

Caribbean societies are a multiethnic, multicultured pepperpots with descendants from European colonizers, slaves, indentured workers, and indigenous peoples. Caribbean households have always been predominantly matrifocal, yet women were rarely included in formal power structures in the community. Errol Miller (1988) in "The Rise of Matriarchy in the Caribbean," suggests that the matrifocal forms present in Caribbean societies are unintended consequences of the power struggles between men. Furthermore, the role of teaching the younger generations through oral traditions is credited to family matriarchs. According to Brown (1999), oral traditions include songs, stories, prayers and performances, and versions of history and mythology. These evolved into forms of preaching (the sermon), calypso, political and religious speech, and storytelling (folktales). After slavery, grandmothers took on the task of educating their immediate descendants, particularly girls, about their culture and heritage. The women of the Anglophone Caribbean, like African griots,[19] passed on knowledge to their children and grandchildren through folktales and legends. This oral custom later morphed into other oral forms such as calypso, preaching, and contemporary performance readings. Their main tools consist of what Carolyn Cooper (1993) refers to as core features of orality: proverbs, riddles, and the repetitiveness found in folktales and songs. Boys, on the other hand, either received formal education, or learned from the men of the household, who focused mainly on physical labor. Formal education in Caribbean societies followed a colonial syllabus, and only became widely available for women around mid-twentieth century. Even so, it was rare for girls to access education beyond the secondary level, and despite their education, women were socialized along the traditional patriarchal lines of ultimately managing a home. The four main writers in this discussion present female characters who are all connected to their matrilineal ancestry, whether through their mothers, grandmothers, or female guardians. The resistance, reinterpretations, rebellion, redefinitions, and revisions that come from the fictitious world of each story dismantle the colonial culture that renders matrilineal relationships dormant. The potential of these influences to reshape how females view themselves in relation to each other, their communities, and their histories in the real world is significant. Moreover, as part of the African diaspora, the intervening connections established in the literary works of Caribbean women writers transcend regional borders to intersect with global literature, thereby commanding a collective approach to the reclamation of matrilineal history.

Colonialism involves both physical conquest and psychological attacks on the social system of a colonized land and its people, where indigenous traditions, cultural practices, and language are gradually modified, and sometimes replaced by the colonizer. Kwasi Wiredu (2009) believes that the superimposition of Western categories of thought may be fairly described as a *conceptually colonized mentality* (9). Consequently, the physical departure of the colonizer does not guarantee the end of colonialism. The gradual and subtle process of mental conditioning takes centuries, and therefore it is only fair to assume that a reversed process would require just as much, if not more time. Fortunately, Wiredu concedes that a colonized mentality can be corrected with *conceptual decolonization* (9), the reversal of colonized mentality. Nelson Maldonado-Torres (2007) supplements Wiredu's optimism with his view that long-standing patterns of power that emerged as a result of colonialism can be broken with decolonization: a straightforward approach of self-evaluation without the obscurity of European perceptions or violence.

The Caribbean islands gained autonomous self-governance after more than 400 years of European colonialism. The first generation of twentieth-century African Caribbean women writers emerged from the islands at the forefront of this decolonization movement. In Jamaica, Una Marson and Louise Bennett[20] used *nation language* and oral tradition to reflect Jamaica's Africa-derived culture. Wole Ogundele (2002) believes, "A people's language is their history at the linguistic level, its use a largely unconscious but constant expression of their historical being and identity" (130), but Alison Donnell and Sarah Lawson-Welsh (1996) deem nation language as a culturally specific term, which affirms a positive status for Caribbean nonstandard linguistic forms. According to Kamau Brathwaite (1995), the African aspect of our Caribbean heritage strongly influences nation language. It exists in the region's oral tradition, a significant strand of orality that emphasizes humor (Brathwaite 1984). Though nation language shares some lexical features with English, it differs "in its contours, its rhythms and timbre, its sound explosions" (Brathwaite 1995, 311) and includes signifiers of the oral tradition inherited from our African ancestors. Ngũgĩ wa Thiong'o (2008) considers African-language literatures decolonial, since they carry African culture. For Brathwaite (1995), the culture gleaned from these signifiers exists in the traditions of the spoken word. English is forced to articulate the oral traditions in the presence of nation language, therefore the use of oral lore in Caribbean women's writing is a calculated maneuver in connection with their bid for recognition and inclusivity. They recognize literature as one of the greatest tools of decolonization.

Olive Senior's *Summer Lightning*

Olive Senior is a Jamaican writer based in Canada. Her collection of short stories, *Summer Lightning*, exposes orality's strength as an adhesive agent for identity within the Caribbean space, particularly for female selfhood. According to Philippe Denis (2000, 2) oral history aims to improve knowledge of the past by documenting the destinies of otherwise ignored actors. While Marjorie Thorpe (1998) identifies these "actors" as ordinary people, I venture to call them *women*. Thorpe recognizes folktales, a main feature of orality, as the form of oral tradition that best expresses concerns for ordinary people (35). Similarly, Samuel Oliroch Imbo (2002) proposes that folktales are "the regular mode of maintaining and explaining connections between the past and the present" (47). Imbo believes that European colonization and the resulting contact between Western scholarship and African traditions set in motion a chain reaction that continues today (xi), a reaction described by Ismail S. Talib (2002) as a "subtler kind of colonialism, which now lives, virtually unnoticed in the minds of the native population" (105). Olive Senior uses orality to lead a discourse into identity, particularly that of the female in the Caribbean society, and experiments with Wiredu's theory of "conceptual decolonization." Through her adolescent protagonists, she aims to subvert unsavory aspects of African and Caribbean culture derived from Eurocentric ideas of religion and women.[21]

In the short stories "Do Angels Wear Brassieres?" and "Confirmation Day," Olive Senior (1986) uses female child protagonists to challenge and defy existing societal values and beliefs embedded in religion. Senior's approach shows her involvement as a postcolonial writer who is determined to develop "viable cultural identities" to replace those "inevitably thrusted on the society via the culture of former colonial masters" (Keith Booker 1996, 149). Senior's two protagonists, Beccka[22] and the unnamed character in "Confirmation Day," subvert the expectations of female subjugation to become mouthpieces critiquing religion. Senior's work confronts the doctrines passed down from the colonial era and registers disapproval at the results. She uses folklore and imagery to effectively share her concerns with the reader.

"Do Angels Wear Brassieres?" embodies brash critique wrapped in innocence. Beccka is likable and humorous in her childish guiltlessness; nevertheless, the intimidation of the adult world and its forceful intrusion into her playful space is a significant key to the messages hidden behind her character. She is introduced at the beginning of the narrative as her mother unsuccessfully tries to convince her to pray for her aunt:

> "And Ask God to bless Auntie Mary." Beccka vex that anybody could interrupt her private conversation with God so, say loud loud, "No. Not praying for nobody that tek weh mi glassy eye marble."
>
> "Shhhhh! She wi hear you!"

"A hear her already . . . but I sure that God is not listening to the like of she. Blasphemous little Wretch."

Beccka just stick out her tongue at the world, wink at God who she know right now in the shape of a big fat anansi in a corner of the roof. (67)

According to Mervyn Morris (1993), Beccka uses the "language of feeling" to express herself. Morris refers to Creole as the most intimate language for most Caribbean societies. As such, it may be regarded as another significant feature of orality, acting as a conduit between the protagonist and the reader. Beccka's reaction reveals friction between postcolonial religious discourse shaped by a Western ideology and Caribbean traditional beliefs molded from an African heritage. She refuses to entertain praying for her aunt who took away her toy, thereby opposing the concept of forgiveness, a key Christian principle. Yet, she winks at her idea of God, who is an "Anansi." *Anansi* is one of the most important characters of Caribbean folklore. He takes the shape of a spider whose cleverness knows no limit as he tricks his way out of difficult situations. The Ashanti people, brought to the Caribbean as slaves from West Africa, passed down the Anansi myths through their descendants. This friction between the religious beliefs inherited from the colonial masters and the traditional folklores that are kept alive through orality illustrates Senior's engagement with Wiredu's conceptual decolonization.

Using the mind of a female child protagonist, Senior directly challenges the value system of the adult world, and by extension, the Eurocentric perceptions of deity. Aunty Mary depicts God as an unforgiving being who will not listen to an errant child. The phrase "the like of she" implies scorn and suggests that Beccka is not worthy of his attention. On the other hand, Beccka presents her perception of a deity, one that is easily identifiable and less imposing to her. Her God is a spider on the wall and not just any spider. He is an Anansi, a popular figure in Caribbean folklore known for his trickery and cunning. Helen Tiffin (1992) suggests that the figure of Anansi represents the negative aspects of slave society. Anansi's adventures are therefore prescriptive measures aimed at rising above cultural and social barriers hindering growth in the postslave society. Tiffin explains that Anansi has the ability both to contain the past and yet convert it into a creative future, thus he is associated with the creative artist. Senior's female protagonists dismantle and then personalize the original belief system, reinforcing the notion of the assimilation of different ideas while retaining one's core identity; effectively containing the past, while converting it into a creative future. In effect, using the Anansi trope challenges colonial art forms and esthetic standards that reflect *self-representation*, a concept linked to self-definition and identity (Renu Juneja 1996, 3).

The adult world, in the form of Aunt Mary's rules, threatens Beccka's childish realm of curiosity and intrigue. She reacts by deliberately stepping across the prohibited threshold of her aunt's room and trying on her clothes: "Beccka in Auntie Mary room-which is forbidden-dress up in Auntie Mary bead, Auntie Mary high heel shoes, Auntie Mary shawl, and Auntie Mary big floppy hat . . . all forbidden" (71). The recurrence of "Auntie Mary" and "forbidden" invokes the repetitive feature of orality. Senior uses the technique to underline the rebellious attitude of a young female actively pushing back against a culture inundated with colonial and patriarchal ideology. Playing dress-up, Beccka pushes past the reality of her aunt's room to the world of her childish imagination, where she methodically defies several decrees, a testament to her psychological maturity.

> Beccka seeing herself as a beautiful lady on the arms of a handsome gentleman. . . . They about to enter a nightclub . . . Beccka know this is the second wickedest thing a woman can do. At a corner table . . . Beccka do the wickedest thing a woman can do—she take a drink. . . . She take the story in her head to the room next door . . . as she does the third wickedest thing a woman can do which is dance all night. (70–71)

Senior highlights the absurdity of placing specific regulations on the female body. She uses a woman to lay down the rules, and then enters the imagination of her young protagonist to break each one. Beccka not only addresses the tangible areas of these conventions by stepping into her aunt's forbidden room but also illustrates the capacity of the female to reverse a colonized mentality. Beccka's inquisitiveness is a direct attack on values imposed on women by society. She demonstrates an uncanny ability, reminiscent of her Anansi God, to outwit the adults, even if only in the make-believe realm of a child. Beccka's attitude reiterates Carole Boyce-Davies's (1999) views on *unicentricity*. Boyce-Davies challenges the imagination to pursue other paradigms that move away from the perception of Eurocentric views as the core of logic in unicentricity. Senior offers a *variable approach*, which is a new space in Beccka's imagination within which she is free to break rules and do what makes her happy.

Senior draws further attention to the tensions between the playful world of the child and the stark domain of adults through Beccka's encounter with the archdeacon and her aunt's reaction to her innocent question.

> "Now Rebecca. Hm. You are a very clever very entertaining little girl. Very. . . . Your aunt tells me you are being prepared for confirmation. Surely you must have some questions about doctrine hm, religion, that puzzle you. No serious questions?"

Beccka look at Archdeacon long and hard.

"Yes," she say at long last in a small voice. Right away Archdeacon sit up straighter. . . . "Sir, what I want to know is this for I can't find it in the Bible. Please Sir, do angels wear brassieres?" (75)

This question is simple and straightforward, yet it mortifies her aunt, her mother, and the archdeacon. There is pandemonium as her aunt spills refreshments meant for her pious guest, and he is grateful to have a reason to leave. He has no answer for Beccka's question. Beccka's encounter with the archdeacon unveils the hilarity in the "enigmatic indirection of riddle" (Cooper 1993, 2)—a major element of orality. Beccka's fun riddles are a way of commenting on the solemn mode reserved for religious issues. This moment also exposes the forced seriousness that adults place on simple matters. Senior challenges the reader to observe a new way of looking at and reacting to religious discussions, particularly when it comes to the female body. This is illustrated by the practical response of Beccka's friend, Mr. O'Connor, to the same question that baffled the Archdeacon. "'Well Beccka, as far as I know only the lady angels need to.' Beccka laugh cant done. Wasn't that the answer she was waiting for?" (79). Beccka is motivated to read the Bible with the goal of challenging the archdeacon. This is decolonization of the mind in action: women familiarize themselves with the patriarchal regulations hidden within all institutions (religious, legal, educational) and actively interrogate society using the philosophies of their oppressors as catalysts.

Senior uses a child protagonist such as Beccka because it is easier to expose such issues with humor. Sam Vazquez (2012), in the introduction of *Humor in the Caribbean Literary Canon*, talks about taking "bad something make laugh" (1). He quotes Patricia Mohammed (2012) "A Blueprint for Gender in Creole Trinidad," expressing how humor allows the unpalatable to be evoked and easily digested (1). The repetitive feature of the oral tradition enables Beccka to not only challenge religious codes but also affirm her identity. She is engaging a narrative device whose purpose involves deconstructing the ideals of patriarchy by refusing to be controlled—directly or indirectly—by the codes presented in her environment. Indeed, Beccka, according to Olive Senior,[23] is speaking directly to the reader. She is telling her own story in her own mother tongue (qtd. in Nasta 1992, 245).

In "Confirmation Day," an unnamed female narrator heads to church to be initiated into her grandmother's faith through a confirmation ritual. The narrative is framed by a solemn tone, illustrated by the use of the intensely religious first line of the *Duino Elegies* by Rainer Maria Rilke[24] that reads: "Who, if I cried, would hear me among the angelic orders?" This question echoes the thoughts of the protagonist who solemnly contemplates the concept of

Christianity. Her approach, though childlike, is very philosophical. She paints a vivid picture with a synchronized assault on the visual, olfactory, and auditory senses, easily transferring her perception of the church to the reader: "It rained the day of my confirmation. I went into the damp mildewed vestry. The mildew mingled with the smell of bats' dropping . . . [and competed] with the squeak of the old pipe organ" (80). The gloomy and depressing imagery creates an ominous atmosphere heightened by the continuous use of stream of consciousness throughout the story. The constant flow of feelings mirrors the litany of the Catholic Church, but it also accentuates the repetitive nature of orality and the protagonist's skilled conveyance of discomfort in her physical and emotional environment. She is definitely not fond of the church nor the confirmation ritual.

Senior continues to interrogate colonially influenced religious ideologies through the juxtaposition of child and adult, and colony and crown. She uses the uncertainty of her young unnamed protagonist to highlight the mystification associated with the doctrines of the colonial masters: "Today I will become a child of god yet I do not know what they mean" (81). She contemplates her situation and wonders if she will lose herself in the confirmation ritual—"Maybe becoming a child of God and dying were the same thing" (82)—equating the unknown with death. She addresses the Christian deity as "Him" and where others see a loving God, she perceives a threatening presence: "His judgment was swift and terrible" (82). The protagonist finally has an epiphany before the end of the ritual: "The cup is too hard against my teeth it is too large and I want to cry out and the bishop gently forces my head back and I hardly taste wine at all and it does not taste like the Blood of Christ" (84). She is conscious that her grandmother's beliefs and affiliations are not her own, and she rejects them: "I know instinctively that not . . . the blood of Christ nor the Book of Common Prayer can conquer me" (84). This is a moment of self-affirmation. Her identity does not have to be a copy of her grandmother's. The setting of the church for this realization sends a powerful message, since, as Joycelin Massiah (1986) explains, "Even a passing knowledge of Caribbean culture shows what a potent force religion is and always has been on the everyday lives of women, especially on their socialization and behavior" (185). The narrator's internal conflict captures her fear of disappointing her grandmother, the bishop or their God. Her rejection despite all her fears reflects the mindset of a new generation of Caribbean women who are able to boldly face their truths, even if it means disappointing those who are not able to do the same. This direct engagement with patriarchal structures imbedded in Caribbean spirituality is a counterdiscursive attempt to reverse the detrimental effects of indoctrination in a male-dominated society. Moreover, although this confrontation takes place in the fictional world of a story, the words are meant to spark awareness in the consciousness of its readers. Such a catalyst is needed to help light fires of epiphany that will invoke real girls to question their own reality.

The male figures in both "Do Angels Wear Brassieres?" and "Confirmation Day" are background characters. Yet Senior's juxtaposition of formal positions of power (Archdeacon, King George, the bishop) with domestic status highlights the powerlessness of the main female characters. The absolute acceptance of church doctrines by older women clashes with the open interrogation and rejection of these teachings from the girls under their care. According to Velma Pollard (2013) in "An Introduction to the Poetry and Fiction of Olive Senior," the child's eye used by Senior is not childlike. It is a clear vision through which the irrationalities of adults and the inequalities in society are expressed. Senior's focus on issues rather than characters signals a shift in how women view the institution of the church and paves the way for female empowerment as the new generation embraces alternative actions in their quest for self-sufficiency. It is no longer enough to obey instructions without questioning motives. The concept of patriarchal rejection is not new, but it is one of many links in the chain of resistance being reshaped and remolded in the literature of women writers across the Caribbean region.

NOVELS BY WOMEN: A NEW CARIBBEAN ESTHETIC

The patriarchal mentality that dominates postcolonial Caribbean societies is twofold: a combination of structures brought across the Atlantic by slaves from Africa and systems introduced by their Europeans masters. These structures and systems inevitably bleed into every Caribbean institution, despite the overarching matrifocal structure of the region's societies. I submit that the complexity of this seemingly indomitable cultural framework acts as a catalyst for women writers to rise to the challenge of creating literature in which the centrality of decolonization becomes a mainstay in the Caribbean novel, particularly on perceptions of female characterization. As the Caribbean short story concentrated on deconstructing Eurocentric ideologies with orality as its central influence, postindependence women writers used the bildungsroman (novels of development) to guide their preoccupation with identity and migration. Their efforts resulted in classic Caribbean novels with strong female presence in the literary tradition of the region: Merle Hodges's *Crick Crack Monkey* (1970), Zee Edgell's *Beka Lamb* (1982), Michelle Cliff's *Abeng* (1984) and *No Telephone to Heaven* (1987), and Jamaica Kincaid's *Annie John* (1985) and *Lucy* (1990). Decolonization is placed in dialog with the complexities of being female in a postcolonial environment.

In *Crick Crack Monkey*, Tee leaves her rural home to live in the city with her aunt. The traditional African-derived values and culture from the village clash with the city's modern Eurocentric norms to reveal the unsettling psychological cost of surviving in a postcolonial Caribbean setting as a young female. In turn, teenaged protagonists Beka and Clare wrestle with complex social and racial stratification in multiethnic environments in their respective novels *Beka Lamb* and *Abeng*. Clare's journey continues as an adult in *No Telephone to Heaven*, as she combats the hybrid nature of identity within her country and herself. In *Annie John*, a teenaged Annie tries to compartmentalize conflicting emotions concerning familial love for her mother and her island-home contrasted with the need for freedom and independence. This theme continues in *Lucy*, as an adult Lucy strains against the same concerns with a backdrop of the metropole. In each bildungsroman, the writers acknowledge the African past of characters and communities, highlighting the Caribbean's inevitable link with African culture. I focus on three writers in this section: Michelle Cliff and Jamaica Kincaid, for their depiction of the unwavering female spirit in the face of institutionalized patriarchy, and the complexities of a Caribbean identity; and Nalo Hopkinson, for her Afrofuturistic glimpse into the future.

Michelle Cliff's *No Telephone to Heaven*

The structure of Cliff's *No Telephone to Heaven* appears random at first glance. The title "No Telephone to Heaven" insinuates that there is no easy access to unanswered questions. An enigmatic fusion of stories and characters counteracts the physical demarcation of titled chapters. The narrative constantly crisscrosses between time and space, dream and reality, and myth and history. The result is a fragmented pattern mirroring the protagonist's confusion as she tries to find her "self." The simultaneous switching between the present and the past, and different settings captures the illusion of time and space. For example, the second chapter, named after the book "No Telephone to Heaven," captures the wavering plot as it meanders from a party in real time to past memories. The setting oscillates between a noisy pool party to a quiet home. The constant movement of the plot is disorienting, and it is easy for the reader to empathize with Clare Savage's own baffled reactions to her identity dilemma.

Symbolism plays a major role in the continuous movement between the present and the past. It highlights the theme of dreams and reality. Clare Savage anticipates finding herself when she leaves Jamaica. Michelle Cliff uses the poem "Aurora Leigh"[25] to frame Clare's expectations,

> The child turned round,
> And looked up piteous in the mother's face
> "Oh, mother!" then, with desperate glance to heaven,

"God, free me from my mother," she shrieked out,
"These mothers are too dreadful."

The mother figure is plural and multifaceted. It applies to Clare's biological parent, the Jamaican society, and the "mother" country of England. As Clare tries to find herself, she realizes that race relations in the metropole are no different from the Caribbean. The same racism that plagues Jamaica exists in England, albeit in different forms. Just as "Aurora Leigh" appeals to God for freedom from "dreadful" mothers, Clare aches to understand herself without the cruelty and neglect sown into the collective fabric of her identity because of past colonial relations.

Cliff is specific in her praise of the female spirit in two short chapters called "Magnanimous Warrior" and "De Watchman." These chapters are odes to the strength of the female ancestors and a call to arms of her descendants.

Magnanimous Warrior! She in whom the sprits come quick and hard. Hunting mother. She who forages. Who knows the ground. . . . Warrior who places the blood-cloth on the back of the whipped slave. She who turns her attention to the evil doer. . . . We have forgotten her. Now that we need her more than ever. The nurses ignore her. The doctors make a game of her. The priest tries to take her soul. Can you remember how to love her? (163–64)

Cliff maps the journey of the ancestors, from African hunting grounds to Spanish Town, Jamaica. She uses a poetic register to paint a picture of a female warrior who can be any, and every woman. A "magnanimous" spirit is generous and forgiving; this big-hearted warrior refers to Clare, her mother, her grandmother, her country, or that of her ancestors. Cliff challenges her reader to forgive and move forward. The mythical magnanimous warrior aligns with historically accurate mothers such as Maroon queen "Nanny"[26] and a group of elderly women who died in the May 1980 "Eventide fire."[27]

Cliff uses the different layers of motherhood to highlight the difficulty of finding a distinct identity as a Caribbean woman. Clare searches for a specific mold in which to fit, but the Caribbean woman is a product of her multifaceted past. Belinda Edmondson (1993) views Clare as a symbol. She asserts that Clare is not a character in the traditional sense but more of an archetype—a representation of the collective West Indian "Other" who is in search of an identity and is constantly searching for a place to fit in. Clare travels the globe, but never finds contentment in who she is. Edmondson stresses that instead of descending to madness in a foreign land, Clare returns to Jamaica. Having come full circle, she finds the ultimate act of self-sacrifice by dying with fellow rebels during a guerilla attack. In Jamaica, she is no longer split as to who she is. She accepts her identity and dies proudly with other revolutionaries.

According to Davies and Fido (1990), Clare's death is her final attempt to wrest control over her identity (7). Antonia MacDonald-Smythe (1994) describes *No Telephone to Heaven* as an autobiography which allows Cliff a way to rewrite herself into a narrative of West Indian history. Her protagonist's determination to belong exposes how the quest for identity can collide with political reality and result in psychological fragmentation or death. Even so, Clare's trauma is useful in identifying migration as an inevitable part of the Caribbean woman's construct. It also highlights how Caribbean women draw on their cultural roots to find answers, no matter where they are in the diaspora. Furthermore, Claire's constant pursuit of wholeness is an extension of her need for connection, symbolic of the efforts of women writers endeavoring to forge links across regional and international borders through universal experiences, mutual understanding, and shared purpose.

Jamaica Kincaid's *Lucy*

The literature of the region was shaped by migration ranging from the forced passage of enslaved Africans across the Atlantic Ocean, to the voyage of indentured servants from China and India, and the exodus of eager migrants in search of a better life in Europe and North America. Stewart Browne (1999) sees migration as arguably the most defining experience of Caribbean being: its diaspora stretches across every continent, though more concentrated in America, Britain, and Canada. The region has earned its reputation as a center of modern migration. Hence, it is not surprising that the concept of migration is a major focal point for Caribbean women writers, most of whom reside in the diaspora.

Jamaica Kincaid, in an interview with Belinda Luscombe, identifies hatred as a form of love. Her outlook embodies the enigmatic dualism that characterizes her protagonists. Literary critics often categorize Kincaid's novels as autobiographical, but she admits that she finds the label annoying. In a *Huffington Post* interview with Joseph Erbentrant (2014), Kincaid insists that her work is a reflection on her life, rather than a carbon copy. Her novel *Lucy* tells of a Caribbean girl who sheds her sheltered postcolonial upbringing in Antigua for a job as an *au pair* in New York City. Paradoxically, she admires her new home, even as she is revolted by it. The novel's exploration of power relations presents an interesting discourse on colonial and postcolonial binaries.

Kincaid's work revolves around her relationship with her mother, her island-home and the metropole. In *Lucy*, the protagonist looks forward to embracing a new life in the United States. She is caught off guard by nostalgia (for her home and mother) as she wrestles with pride and loathing, an emotional conflict illustrative of the relationship between former colonies and the empire. Lucy dislikes her mother's influence, stating, "I had come to feel that my mother's love for me was designed solely to make me into an echo of her . . . and I felt that I would rather be dead than become just an echo of someone" (36). Lucy's desire for autonomy takes precedence over any emotional bond with her mother while she is in Antigua, yet once she is in New York, she yearns for her mother's companionship. This is emblematic of the way former colonies view the empire. There is a sense of pride in their independence, but there is also a lingering dependency, difficult to ignore with the Queen as Head-of-State, a position that outranks elected members of parliament in the commonwealth.

Lucy views her boss Mariah as a substitute motherly figure, but the emotional complexities that plague her relationship with her mother in the Caribbean surface in America. She admits that "the times that I loved Mariah it was because she reminded me of my mother and the times that I did not love Mariah it was because she reminded me of my mother" (58). She complains that "Mariah wanted all of us, the children and me, to see things the way she did" (36). Lucy realizes that Mariah mirrors her mother. This realization leads to an epiphany: emotional turmoil is not a tangible possession to be discarded on impulse. The psychological health of the female migrant is steeped in colonialist and patriarchal ideology. She is not familiar with the upkeep of her mental or emotional health because it was never a priority of former colonial masters. Female characters with mental problems in colonial and postcolonial texts either die or are locked safely away from society, facilitating the silencing of the female voice. Lucy's attitude may be seen as Kincaid's rejection of the female in a state of psychic collapse. She is a frustrated, lonely, and homesick character, but she refuses to submit to the trope of the "mad" woman. Kincaid offers an alternative course to deal with psychological healing that circumvents the recurring victim mentality found in earlier works of Caribbean women writers. Lucy shows that it is okay to be unsure, doubtful, and anxious; the problem lies in ignoring the emotions instead of addressing them. Her mother's assurance that she would "always be her mother" (128) makes it clear that even though Lucy physically removed herself from Antigua, her mother will always be a part of her. Her emotional conflicts are part of her identity and she must confront them in order to move forward. Lucy's attitude toward her mother, and Mariah, is a manifestation of her resistance to being controlled. It is also an indication of the relationship between former colonies and the new empire that mimics the "mother-country." The effects of United States were visible in the Caribbean long before the peak of the independence period in the 1960s.[28] The country's rise to prominence appealed to migrants, who saw it as the land of dreams. Women migrated to find opportunities to support their families. However, just like Mariah reminds Lucy of her mother, so too does the United States resemble England in the treatment of Caribbean immigrants.

The educational syllabus in the Caribbean is based on a European model, hence unfamiliar imagery dominated literature classes. As American content was added to the curriculum, Robert Frost[29] replaced William Blake,[30] but students were just as confused by "woods and frozen lake"[31] as they were by "Chimney-sweepers cry."[32] The age of television or the internet was not yet prevalent in the region, so there was little help with virtual imagery, except for photographs and drawings in some textbooks. Lucy's reaction to the daffodils illustrates some complications associated with a colonial-based education.

Mariah said, "These are daffodils. . . . I'm hoping you'll find them lovely."

How could I explain to her the feelings I had about daffodils—that it wasn't exactly daffodils, but that they would do as well as anything else? Where do I start? Over here or over there? I said, "Mariah, do you realize that at ten years of age I had to learn by heart a long poem about some flowers I would not see in real life?" (29–30)

Mariah is excited to share her love of daffodils with Lucy, but she does not understand why Lucy associates them with "sorrow and bitterness" (30). In fact, Lucy is confused by her own reaction: though she is repulsed, she says that she is "glad to have at last seen what a wretched daffodil looked like" (30). Lucy received a predominantly colonial education: William Blake's "I Wandered Lonely as a Cloud" is one of the staple poems on the literature syllabus. Lucy's hostility is therefore in reaction to the Eurocentric educational hegemony in the region. Lucy is not a fan of colonial binaries (Dianne Simmons 1994), thus her rejection of the daffodils preempts her refusal to be defined, thereby taking control of her own narrative. Her refusal to be coerced into postcolonial binaries is illustrated in her philosophical musings on a letter from her mother warning her of the perils of the big city. She compares these warnings with real hazards from Antigua, and wonders, "Why should my life be reduced to these two possibilities?" (21). Kincaid dismantles hegemonic power through her interrogation of binaries, organically creating new conversations for future writers. Moira Ferguson (1994) lauds Kincaid's explicitly counterhegemonic stance: through Lucy, she grounds whatever she sees in alternative visions, and refuses enclosures built by others while choosing her own margins. For Ferguson, Lucy represents the region at a transcendent level of decolonization. The treatment of colonial binaries in *Lucy* reflects a desire for fluidity. According to Justin Edwards (2007), Kincaid is projecting the idea that "one must find self-empowerment through the rejection of ancestry and antecedents while simultaneously recognizing that a complete rejection of the past can never be achieved" (14). Kincaid's work is a reminder to the reader of the complexities of Caribbean women: their love of family and home, their refusal to be policed, their determination to forge their own path—all culminating in the coming of age of the regional literary tradition. In essence, she introduces the possibility of being unapologetic in the face of resistance. Her attitude adds fuel to the symbolic forge where the links of patriarchal resistance and shared experiences have already been reshaped to fit an evolving society where women are calling patriarchy to task.

Nalo Hopkinson's *Midnight Robber*

Healing is the process of getting well again after an injury, and the Caribbean has been on the path to restorative health since its long bout with slavery. Traditional healers are an integral part of the Caribbean community: like the African griot, they come in many forms and serve various roles. They are educators, psychologists, and the keepers of spirituality and customs. Caribbean women writers shoulder the responsibility of healers in their narratives. Their search for a remedy to counteract the region's Eurocentric and patriarchal wounds has taken them across time to the past and present, but their quest—aided by the promise of fresh remedies from *Afrocentricity* and *Afrofuturism*—is also taking them into the new territory of the future. Molefi Kete Asante (2003) describes Afrocentricity as "a mode of thought and action in which the centrality of African interests, values and perspectives predominate" (2). He is concerned with positioning Africans within their own stories, claiming that they too often remain objects without agency. Moreover, he argues for an alternative perspective, which will place African people in the center of any analysis of African phenomena through their positioning within subject and place. In this way, Afrocentricity becomes a "transforming agent" which will invoke a new reality and introduce a new vision of Africa's role in the future (3). Kodwo Eshun (2014) builds on Asante's theory with the idea that countermemories aimed at the management and delivery of reliable futures are needed to contest existing colonial archives: these countermemories are dominated by arts, science, and technology. Nalo Hopkinson's (2000) use of the oral tradition to fuse Caribbean folklore with African myths in a futuristic setting not only places her protagonist in the center of her story but also shifts the narrative of the Caribbean experience to a reimagined space where there is a direct link to ancestral African influences.

In *Midnight Robber*, Hopkinson uses speculative fiction as an alternative form of analyzing the Caribbean experience. Freda Paltiel (1981) posits that this genre is a form of writing that develops scenarios for the future (13), a strategy that Eichler and Scott (1981) describe as "a way of breaking the time and space barrier" (v). The most significant feature in Hopkinson's alternative domain is orality, and with it, Asante's notion of Afrocentricity and Wiredu's vision of conceptual decolonization both flicker to life. In the novel, *Toussaint* and *New Half-Way Tree* are the names of Caribbean-colonized planets. Hopkinson establishes Caribbean and African history, myth, and folklore as integral parts of these terraformed worlds through her naming process. Each character, place, or thing has a name that connects it to either Africa or the Caribbean: Toussaint L'Ouverture (1748–1803) was a former slave who led his country in the Haitian Revolution, which ultimately resulted in Haiti's independence on 1804, and New Half-Way Tree is a small community in Kingston, Jamaica. Nanny and Eshu (Nanny was a Maroon Queen from Jamaica; Eshu is a trickster God/Orisha of the Yoruba people of Nigeria, West Africa) are part of Toussaint's powerful nanotech network[33] described by Hopkinson in the following manner: "[Everything] on Toussaint . . . had been seeded with nanomites. . . . one enormous data-gathering system that exchanged information constantly through the Grande Nanotech Sentient Interface: Granny Nansi's Web. They kept [the planets] protected, guided and guarded its people" (10). *Maka* (named after an ethnic group living in the forested areas of Eastern Cameroon) is one of Nanny's original programmers, while *Eleggua* (a manifestations of Eshu) is her original programming language. Hopkinson's use of historical, mythical, and folkloric legends as inspiration for the naming process results in an effective synthesis of Caribbean and African dynamics.

Hopkinson uses her protagonist, Tan-Tan to direct the reader's gaze toward a future multicultural, technologically advanced Caribbean community fully incorporated with its African and other ancestral heritage. Tan-Tan's father forces her to leave their idyllic life of comfort on Toussaint for one of abuse, hardship, and uncertainty on New Half-Way Tree. There, Tan-Tan encounters creatures she had only heard about in folklore: *douens, mako jumbie*, and *rolling calves*.[34] Her attitude sets her apart from other characters as she befriends mythical creatures and humans alike. Even so, her affability does not shield her from the incestuous abuse of her father, which, paradoxically, catapults her eventual evolution into her favorite carnival character and alter ego—*The Midnight Robber*—a popular traditional carnival character with an outlandishly wide brim hat, mask, skulls, gloves, a long cape, and weapon (knife, sword, or gun). Even before she migrates against her will to New Half-Way Tree, Tan-Tan is educated about socially constructed gender inequality and patriarchy from Eshu's data on the past: "Time was, is only men used to play the Robber King masque. . . . Earth was like that for a long time. Men could only do some things, and women could only do others" (28–29). Tan-Tan's reaction to this information implies that this philosophy is no longer a reality on Toussaint—"Why? What a stupid thing!" (29). The idea of such discrimination seems ridiculous to her, especially since her favorite carnival character is the Robber Queen. Unfortunately, Tan-Tan experiences the dark reality that Eshu related to her, the fantastical and the real, on New Half-Way Tree. She becomes Hopkinson's most powerful device in invoking a new Caribbean reality through speculative fiction.

In Hopkinson's futuristic Afro-Caribbean world of Toussaint and New Half-Way Tree, storytelling connects myths, memory, and history. Hopkinson weaves traditional signifiers, used to mark the beginning and end of an oral account in both the framing narrative and embedded tales of *Midnight Robber*y. Tan-Tan's story, as related by Eshu, begins "crick-crack, this is she story" (3), and ends, "Call that George, the story done. Jack Mandura, me nah choose none!" (329). These signifiers showcase the performance aspect of the oral tradition while drawing attention to the evolving process of transcribing orality to text. Many folklores are now being morphed into the written language of narration, converting hundreds of years of orality into text. Caribbean women writers are at the forefront of this movement, connecting the region's concerns, hopes, and dreams with its ancestral homeland and diaspora through their dynamic storytelling.

The performance quality of the oral tradition highlights the repetition and rhyming features of calypso, an enhanced form of protest and satirical songs on the plantation. In contemporary Caribbean society, it retains its original function of humorous social and political commentary. In *Midnight Robber*, when a scandal breaks out with Tan-Tan's family at the center, the calypsonian's commentary entertains and informs the public; "This woman greedy for so, you see? / One lover ain't enough for she! / She little bit, and she tallawah, oui!" (38). In her childish innocence, Tan-Tan doesn't understand the implications of the words, but she enjoys the tune, like most of Cockpit County.

Hopkinson creates a Pan-Caribbean atmosphere by fusing separate elements of festivals from various islands. She mentions *Jankanoo season* (18), *Parang* (19), *Jour Ouvert* (34), *Mummers* (night speech) (22), and *jab-jab devils* (314). All these events are celebrated in different countries across the region and the diaspora: from the Bahamas, Grenada, St. Vincent, and Trinidad to America. On Toussaint, carnival is more than a festival, it is a unifying agent for different races and ethnicities: "Finally, it was Jonkanoo Season. . . . Time to remember the way their forefathers had toiled and sweated together: Taino Carib and Arawak; African, Asian, Indian; even the Euro, ... All the blood flowing in one river, making a new home on a new planet" (18).

A major feature of Caribbean traditional festivals is the Masquerade. The custom started when African slaves began to mimic the mask balls of

European colonizers, but added their own traditions: reveling, drumming, stick fighting, stilt dancing, and speechifying. Spectators line the streets to observe the dancing and performance of *masqueraders* (individuals disguised in costumes and masks). This is referred to as *Playing Mas*. Masquerade is a unifying agent, but it is also an agent of justice. The Midnight Robber is an articulate and charismatic masquerade character. It brags about its ancestry and supernatural abilities while using a whistle to command the attention of its audience. Masqueraders in the Midnight Robber costume call themselves Robber King or Queen. After suffering many years of abuse at the hands of her father, Tan-Tan transforms into her favorite carnival character. Her final traumatic encounter with him pushes her over the edge. She spends months in exile trying to heal physically, mentally, and emotionally from the assault, before she finally uses the medium of carnival to expose her father's crimes from behind the mask of the Robber Queen:

> People, oonuh must understand. The Robber Queen father was a slick, sick man. The first time she did making baby for he, she was fourteen. . . . He rape she, beat she, nearly kill she. Lying under he pounding body she see the knife. And for she life she grab it and perform an execution. She kill she daddy dead. The guilt come down pon she head, The Robber Queen get born that day, out of excruciation. (324–25)

Tan-Tan's embodiment of the Robber Queen, and the retelling of her story, despite her trauma, is emblematic of women writers using literature as their agent to share their personal narratives, as well as the chronicles of a collective Caribbean memory. Telling their stories is a form of taking control of their own subjectivity. They are boldly positioning themselves as subjects with agency, and though they are not Africans, their claim to Afrocentricity lies in their connection to the African diaspora. Tan-Tan creates a chant mapping that connection, while emphasizing women's power and strength: "Nt woman; I name Tan-tan, a 'T' and a 'AN'; I is the AN-aconda, Taino redeemer; the AN-nie Christmas, Keel beat steamer; the As-AN-tewa; Ashanti warrior queen; the N-AN-ny, Maroon Granny; meaning Nana, mother, care-taker to a nation" (320). She embraces all of her ancestry, past and present, an ode to Derek Walcott's (1995) treatise in "The Muse of History," where he urges writers to embrace all of their heritage. Walcott views the Caribbean as an inheritance, and gift from ancestors (black and white) who have lost both Africa and Europe. Tan-Tan claims the region as a gift for both men and women, and in so doing, she dismantles notions of the inferior woman imbued in patriarchal ideology. In effect, she offers the final link of equality to the chain created by the four main Caribbean women writers in this discussion. The collected efforts of these writers result in improvements in the literary world of writing and critique; texts are interrogated with renewed partiality, more female experiences are collectively shared, resistance is probed instead of blindly criticized and ideas of revisions are closely examined. Improvements are also evident in the society as literature lay out a model for unity among women in the face of patriarchy. Women at home and those in the diaspora are aware of the advantages of tackling issues as a community, rather than isolated groups.

CONCLUSION: REDEFINING THE GAZE

Literary fiction influences the way we see the world, and conversely how the world views us. It is central to the way we tell stories about ourselves. It is important that every group be given the opportunity to tell their own stories, in their own way, and Caribbean short stories and novels are windows into its society. Caribbean women writers have proven that networking within the scope of literature has the power to alter present-day perceptions and inform new futures. They use orality as a major connective medium to create a new legitimacy: one which perpetuates a tradition of deconstruction in confronting various forms of inequality and injustice. Women writers have not only made the Caribbean woman's perspective valid but also ensured that it is an authentic addition to the collective regional depository.

Caribbean women writers are part of the transforming face of the region's cultural, economic, and political landscape. These writers not only establish a community of women whose collective efforts are changing gender politics and identity in the region but also command the gaze of global literary critics, slowly redefining the concept of Caribbean literature. According to Massiah (1990), as elsewhere in the world, women in the Caribbean have a pivotal role to play in the holistic development of their society. Senior, Cliff, Kincaid, and Hopkinson preserve the varied experiences of the Caribbean woman in their literature. Each writer disseminates knowledge of the region's heritage through their affiliation with numerous educational institutions worldwide. Sentiments, such as the need for a global understanding that change cannot be effectively implemented without women's political participation (Meghan Markle, Duchess of Sussex[35] 2015), are not new to Caribbean literary criticism. Evelyn O'Callaghan (1990) warns that we cannot ignore issues highlighted by women writers. She envisages the female self as a metaphor for society, with the society prone to all manifestation of illness subjected on the female person. With this premise in mind, inequality, in any form, is like a mutating viral infection that must be treated before inflicting damage on society.

Caribbean women writers encapsulate the past, present, and future in their work. They apply different techniques to arouse, rally, and then amplify the collective voices of Caribbean women, before validating orality through the transcription of the spoken word. They locate their individual voices and those of their voiceless sisters in the battle for social and political sovereignty. Our present-day reality reflects this phenomenon; literature heralds the appointment and election of women to leadership positions in government and churches across the globe. In recent years, eleven female heads of government served in the Caribbean. The work of women writers is now fundamental pillars of the Caribbean literary canon. They are integral to the preservation of links that connect the region to its African heritage. The maintenance of these links is even more vital, because they connect the Caribbean women writers to similar communities across the globe.

NOTES

1. Mary Prince was born into slavery in Bermuda in 1788. She is credited as the first black woman in England to publish an autobiography, or present an antislavery petition to Parliament. Her narrative was crucial to the antislavery movement in their fight for the abolition of slavery. Little is known about Mary Prince after 1833.

2. Mary Jane Seacole was born in Jamaica in 1805 to a Jamaican mother and Scottish father. She was christened Mary Jane Grant. She used her skill as a nurse to care for British soldiers during the Crimean War (1853–1856). Her work is largely overshadowed by that of English nurse, Florence Nightingale, who also cared for soldiers during the Crimean War. Seacole died in 1881 in London, England.

3. The French and Spanish share the island of Hispaniola, with the French nation of Haiti in the West, and the Spanish territory of the Dominican Republic in the East. The French and Dutch also share a northern leeward island. The Northern French side is called St. Martin, and the Southern Dutch side is St. Maarten.

4. Up until her death in 2016, Michelle Cliff had also been very involved in the women's literary circuit.

5. The name "Windrush" was taken from the *SS Empire Windrush*, a ship which carried almost 500 West Indians to England in 1948.

6. Una Marson (1905–1965) was a Jamaican feminist and writer. She was hailed as the Anglophone Caribbean's first major poet and a social activist. The BBC hired Marson during World War II. She became the first black woman to be hired by the broadcasting giant. She was also secretary to the legendary Haile Selassie (Ethiopia's last emperor).

7. Jean Rhys gives the power of personality, thought, and speech to Bronte's mad attic woman in *Wide Sargasso Sea*, a prequel to Charlotte Bronte's *Jane Eyre*. Antoinette Mason unsuccessfully attempts to navigate two incompatible worlds. She loses her sense of self and sanity when she is removed from the world she knows.

8. Paule Marshall's "Selina" struggles to overcome the conflicts that come with migration to the metropole, in *Brown Girl, Brownstones*.

9. In April 1988, Jamaica Kincaid, Paule Marshall, Michelle Cliff, Lorna Goodison, Olive Senior, and a host of other women writers, critics, and social commentators attended the first major conference on women writers of the English-speaking Caribbean. It was coordinated by Professor Selwyn Cudjoe who later curated an anthology of essays from the conference called *Caribbean Women Writers: Essays from the First International Conference*, which was published in 1990.

10. The first Anglophone Caribbean country to gain independence was Jamaica in 1962. The other ex-colonies became independent over a twenty-one-year period that ended in 1983 with St. Kitts' independence.

11. The Commonwealth Short Story Prize is an annual award for the best piece of unpublished short fiction in Commonwealth countries (the Commonwealth comprises fifty-three member states from across the globe, most of which are former British colonies).

12. Sharon Millar won The Commonwealth Short Story Prize in 2013 with her story "The Whale House."

13. Ingrid Persaud won The Commonwealth Short Story Prize in 2017 with her story "The Sweet Sop."

14. The Bocas Literary Festival is Trinidad and Tobago's premier annual literary festival. The festival's website describes itself as "a lively celebration of books, writers, writing, and ideas, with a Caribbean focus and international scope."

15. The OCM Bocas Prize for Caribbean Literature—a major award for literary books by Caribbean writers sponsored by One Caribbean Media. It is the only prize in the region open to works of different literary genres by writers of Caribbean birth or citizenship.

16. The CODE Burt Award for Caribbean Young Adult Literature—an annual award given to up to three English-language literary works for young adults (aged twelve through eighteen) written by Caribbean authors. The Award aims to provide engaging and culturally relevant books for young people across the Caribbean.

17. The JAAWP—an annual award, which allows an emerging Caribbean writer living and working in the Anglophone Caribbean to devote time to advancing or finishing a literary work, with support from an established writer as mentor.

18. The Frank Collymore Literary Endowment Award is part of The Frank Collymore Literary Endowment, established in 1988 to support and develop the literary arts in Barbados. The award, which began in 1999, is the leading literary award in Barbados. Women have won the top prize eleven times in its twenty-one-year history.

19. A griot is a West African historian, responsible for maintaining a tradition of oral history for his or her community/ethnic group that can be traced back several generations. The griot takes on several roles: storyteller, praise singer, poet, dancer, musician, or announcer. He or she also takes part in ceremonies such as weddings and funerals.

20. Louise Bennett-Coverley (1919–2006) affectionately called "Miss Lou" was a Jamaican poet, folklorist, and activist.

21. See Kwasi Wiredu's views on how orality may be used to decolonize in "An Oral Philosophy of Personhood: Comments on Philosophy and Orality." *Research in African Literatures* 40.1 (2009): 8–18.

22. Beccka is the protagonist in "Do Angels Wear Brassieres?" from Olive Seniors anthology *Summer Lightning and Other Stories*.

23. See "Mothertongue Voices in the Writing of Olive Senior and Lorna Goodison." *Motherlands: Black Women's Writing from Africa, the Caribbean and South Asia.* Ed. Susheila Nasta. New Jersey: Rutgers UP, 1992. 238–53. Pp. 245. Nasta quotes from interview with Anna Rutherford, "Olive Senior." *Kunapipi* 8.2 (1986): 11–20; 16–7.

24. See The Duino Elegies by Bohemian-Austrian poet Rainer Maria Rilke (1875–1926). The Duineser Elegien are a collection of ten intensely religious, mystical poems that weigh beauty and existential suffering.

25. "Aurora Leigh" is an epic poem by Elizabeth Browning, written in 1856. The poem's self-educated heroine is confident and successful.

26. Nanny is an eighteenth-century Ashanti slave transported to Jamaica. She escaped slavery and became the queen/leader of the Maroons, a group of runaway slaves who resided in the Blue Mountains of Jamaica.

27. The Eventide Home housed over 200 elderly women. On the morning of May 20, 1980, 153 occupants of Eventide perished in a fire of unknown origin.

28. The United States cemented their presence in the Caribbean with the 1904 Panama Canal project, their 1917 purchase of the U.S. Virgin Islands from the Danish, the establishment of an air force base in Trinidad during World War II, and their 1965 invasion of the Dominican Republic.

29. Robert Frost was an American poet (1874–1963). His poetry was celebrated for his depictions of rural life in America, particularly his hometown of Boston.

30. William Blake was an English poet (1757–1827), whose skills as a painter and engraver is showcased in one of his most famous work—*Songs of Innocence and Experience.*

31. See the poem "Stopping by Woods on a Snowy Evening," by Robert Frost.

32. See the poem "London" by William Blake.

33. Nanotechnology involves science on a subatomic level. For example, nanoparticles may make drug deliveries to specific cells to allow for direct treatment of diseases such as cancer.

34. The "Moko" is a West African Orisha (God) of Retribution, while "Jumbie" is a ghost/spirit. The Moko–Jumbie has legs up to 15 feet high. They stand at crossroads and block travelers at late night. Rolling Calves are enormous animal-like (bull, cat, dog, pig, goat, horse) creatures with blazing red eyes bodies wrapped in heavy chains.

35. HRH Duchess Megan Markle is vice-president for The Queen's Commonwealth Trust. Her role includes supporting young people, especially women and girls, throughout the Commonwealth.

REFERENCES

"Women Writers of the Caribbean." 2019. *Encyclopedia of African-American Culture and History*, July 10, 2019. https://www.encyclopedia.com/history/encyclopedias-almanacs-transcripts-and-maps/women-writers-caribbean.

Asante, Molefi Kete. 2003. *Afrocentricity: The Theory of Social Change*. Chicago: African American Images.

Benitez-Rojo, Antonio. 1996. "Introduction." In *The Repeating Island: The Caribbean and the Post-modern Perspective*. Trans. James E Maraniss. 2nd ed. Durham: Duke University Press.

Booker, Keith M. 1996. *A Practical Introduction to Literary Theory and Criticism*. New York: Longman.

Boyce-Davies, Carole. 1999. "Beyond Unicentricity: Transcultural Black Presences." *Research in African Literatures* 30(2): 96–109.

Brathwaite, Edward Kamau. 1984. *History of the Voice: The Development of Nation Language in Anglophone Caribbean Poetry*. London: New Beacon.

Brathwaite, Edward Kamau. 1995. "Nation Language." In *The Post-Colonial Studies Reader*, edited by Bill Ashcroft, Gareth Griffiths, and Helen Tiffin, 309–13. London: Routledge.

Brown, Stewart. 1999. "Introduction." In *The Oxford Book of Caribbean Short Stories*, edited by Stewart Brown and John Wickham, xiii–xxxiii. New York: Oxford University Press.

Cliff, Michelle. 1984. *Abeng*. Michigan: Penguin.

Cliff, Michelle. 1987. *No Telephone to Heaven*. New York: Plume.

Cooper, Carolyn. 1993. *Noises in the Blood: Orality, Gender and the "Vulgar" Body of Jamaican Popular Culture*. London: MacMillan.

Davies, Carole Boyce, and Elaine Savory Fido, editors. 1990. *Out of Kumbla: Caribbean Women and Literature*. New York: Africa World Press.

Donnell, Alison, and Sarah Lawson Welsh. 1996. "General Introduction." In *The Routledge Reader in Caribbean Literature*, edited by Alison Donnell and Sarah Lawson Welsh, 1–26. London: Routledge.

Edgell, Zee. 1982. *Beka Lamb*. Oxford. Heinemann.

Edmondson, Belinda. 1993. "Race, Privilege, and the Politics of (Re) Writing History: An Analysis of the Novels of Michelle Cliff." *Callaloo* 16(1): 180–91.

Edwards, Justin T. 1981. *Understanding Jamaica Kincaid*. Columbia: University of South Carolina Press.

Eichler, Margrit, and Hilda Scott. 1981. "Women in Futures Research." *Women's Studies International Quarterly* 4(1): v.

Erbentraut, Joseph. 2014. "12 Reasons Why Writer Jamaica Kincaid Is a Total Badass." *HuffPost*, October 24, 2014. https://www.huffpost.com/entry/jamaica-k incaid-interview-writing-badass_n_6036764.

Eshun, Kodwo. 2003. "Further Considerations on Afrofuturism." *The New Centennial Review* 3(2): 287–302.

Ferguson, Moira. 1994. *Jamaica Kincaid: Where the Land Meets the Body*. Virginia: University Press of Virginia.

Gallagher, Mary. 2002. Introduction. In *Soundings in French Caribbean Writing Since 1950: The Shock of Space and Time*, 1–13. Oxford: Oxford University.

Glissant, Edouard. 1992. "A Caribbean Future: Toward Caribbeanness." In *Caribbean Discourse: Selected Essays*, 170–94. Trans. J Michael Dash. Charlottesville: University Press of Virginia.

Griffiths, Gareth. 1992. "Culture and Identity: Politics and Writing in Some Recent Post-Colonial Texts." In *From Commonwealth to Post-colonial: Critical Essays*, edited by Anna Rutherford, 436–43. Sydney: Dangaroo.

Hodge, Merle. 1993. *Crick Crack Monkey*. Oxford: Heinemann.

Hopkinson, Nalo. 2000. *Midnight Robber.* New York: Grand Central Publishing.

Imbo, Samuel Oliroch. 2002. *Oral Philosophy: Okot P'Bitek's Legacy for African Philosophy*. Lanham: Rowman and Littlefield Publishers.

Juneja, Renu. 1996. *Caribbean Transactions: The Making of West Indian Culture in Literature*. London: Macmillan.

Kincaid, Jamaica. 1990. *Lucy*. New York: Farrar Straus Giroux.

Kincaid, Jamaica. 1995. *Annie John*. New York: Farrar Straus Giroux.

Kincaid, Jamaica. 2013. "10 Questions for Jamaica Kincaid." *YouTube Video, 6:00*, January 28, 2013. https://www.youtube.com/watch?v=YdHPZMfSOx8.

Levine, Robert S. 2017. "The Slave Narrative and the Revolutionary Tradition of African American Autobiography." In *Race, Transnationalism, and Nineteenth-Century American Literary Studies*, 63–81. Cambridge: Cambridge University Press.

Macdonald-Smythe, Antonia. 1994. "Autobiography and Reconstruction of Homeland: The Writing of Michelle Cliff and Jamaica Kincaid." *Caribbean Studies* 27(3/4): 422–26.

Markle, Meghan. 2015. "Meghan Markle UN Women." *YouTube Video, 9:40*, March 13, 2015. https://www.youtube.com/watch?v=Zkb-zg4JCLk.

Massiah, Joycelin. 1986. "Women in Caribbean Project." *Social and Economic Studies* 35(2): 1–29.

Massiah, Joycelin. 1990. *Economic Change, Structural Adjustment and Women in the Caribbean: Revised Version of Paper Prepared for Commonwealth Caribbean Regional Meeting on Structural Adjustment, Economic Change and Women.* Cave Hill: UWI Press.

Miller, Errol. 1988. "The Rise of Matriarchy in the Caribbean." *Caribbean Quarterly: A Journal of Caribbean Culture* 34(3/4): 1–21.

Mohammed, Patricia. 2012. "A Blueprint for Gender in Creole Trinidad." In *Humor in the Caribbean Literary Canon*. New York: Palgrave-MacMillan.

Morris, Mervyn. 1993. "Is English We Speaking." In *West Indian Literature*: *A Lecture by Mervyn Morris Delivered 21 October 1992,* 15. London: The British Library.

Nasta, Susheila. 1992. "Introduction." In *Motherlands: Black Women's Writing From Africa, the Caribbean and South Asia*, edited by Susheila Nasta, xiii–xxx. New Jersey: Rutgers University Press.

Nelson, Maldonado-Torres. 2007. "On the Coloniality of Being: Contributions to the Development of a Concept." *Cultural Studies* 21(2): 240–70.

O'Callaghan, Evelyn. 1990. "Interior Schisms Dramatized: The Treatment of the "Mad" Woman in the Work of Some Female Caribbean Novelists." In *Out of Kumbla: Caribbean Women and Literature*, edited by Carole Boyce Davies and Elaine Savory Fido, 89–109. New York: Africa World Press.

Ogundele, Wole. 2002. "Devices of Evasion: The Mythic Versus the Historical Imagination in the Postcolonial African Novel." *Research in African Literatures* 33(3): 125–39.

Paltiel, Freda L. 1981. "Shaping Futures for Women." *Women's Studies International Quarterly* 4(1): 13–25.

Pollard, Velma. 1988. "An Introduction to the Poetry and Fiction of Olive Senior." *Callaloo* 36: 540–45.

Senior, Olive. 1986. *Summer Lightning and Other Stories.* New York: Longman.

Simmons, Dianne. 1994. *Jamaica Kincaid.* New York: Twayne.

Talib, Ismail S. 2002. *The Language of Postcolonial Literatures: An Introduction.* London: Routledge.

Thorpe, Marjorie. 1998. "Myth and the Caribbean Woman Writer." In *The Caribbean Woman, the Writer and Caribbean Society*, edited by Helen Payne-Timothy, 34–40. Los Angeles: Regents of University of California.

Tiffin, Helen. 1992. "Transformative Imageries." In *From Commonwealth to Post-Colonial: Critical Essays*, 428–35. Sydney: Dangaroo.

Vazquez, Sam. 2012. *Humor in the Caribbean Literary Canon.* New York: Palgrave-MacMillan.

Wa 'Thiong'o, Ngũgĩ. 2008. "The Language of African Literature." In *African Literature: An Anthology of Criticism and Theory*, edited by Tejumola Olaniyan and Ato Quayson, 285–306. Oxford: Blackwell Publishing.

Walcott, Derek. 1995. "The Muse of History." In *The Post-Colonial Studies Reader*, edited by Bill Ashcroft, Gareth Griffiths, and Helen Tiffin, 370–74. London: Routledge.

Wiredu, Kwasi. 2009. "An Oral Philosophy of Personhood: Comments on Philosophy and Orality." *Research in African Literatures* 40(1): 8–18.

Chapter 6

Networks of Collective Memory

Women's Narratives of Injustice in Northern Kenya

Irene Awino

INTRODUCTION

The Kenyan Truth Commission was set up following a wave of unrest in 2007–2008 to investigate historical injustices and human rights violations. The Commission established that Northern Kenya had been the epicenter of gross violations of human rights and noted the Wagalla Massacre of February 1984 that occurred in Wajir County as a tragic story of how the government tortured and killed its own citizens. The Wagalla Massacre has generated much attention but it has been largely treated as a one-time event, erasing complex and gendered experiences of the Wajir community that prevailed before, during, and after the conflict. This chapter attempts to go beyond the dominant, androcentric, and superficial narratives of the massacre to deconstruct the role of patriarchal power in laying fertile ground for the Wagalla atrocities. This analysis explores how, by adding their voices to a space long manipulated by a patriarchal-capitalist-imperialist establishment, the women of Wajir engaged in a unique, critical moment of truth-telling, disrupting hegemonic interpretations of the Wagalla Massacre as a singular event. Accordingly, this chapter problematizes the commonly held assumption of women's victimization amid shared oppression that erases the nuances of collective, networked struggle for gender justice. In my study, the truth-seeking process allowed the women of Wajir to connect the individual and the collective through narratives of injustice that represent their Wagalla experiences beyond the massacre to unveil a historical, multilayered system of oppression.

A narrative analysis of women's testimonies about Wagalla highlights their reconstruction of patriarchal power in Wajir. During this process, as women demanded their rights, their personal stories informed, and were informed by the network of strength and solidarity they found themselves in. In this case, they drew on their individual experiences to identify shared oppressive state structures and called for interventions to question the status quo and initiate change. Their testimonies produced discursive strategies of mobilization, exhortation, and solidarity for agency, while disrupting the androcentric notion of the Wagalla Massacre as an attack on male Degodia clan members.

THE WAGALLA MASSACRE

On February 10, 1984, a security operation conducted in Wajir District, North Eastern Kenya resulted in the mass torture and killings of civilians at the local Wagalla Airstrip, hence the popular reference to the Wagalla Massacre. The scale of atrocities at Wagalla was unprecedented even for a region that had previously undergone violence (Anderson 2014). The Truth, Justice and Reconciliation Commission (TJRC), which was mandated to investigate Kenya's history of injustices after violent conflict that followed the 2007 election, noted that "the Wagalla Massacre is by far the most spoken about massacre in Kenya" (TJRC Vol IIA 2013, 221) and has been identified by the United Nations as the worst massacre in Kenya's history (Slye 2018). To this end, the TJRC spent more time investigating this massacre than any other injustice during its tenure between 2009 and 2013 (Lynch 2018; Slye 2018). While the TJRC concluded that numerous atrocities committed by state security agents in Wagalla qualified as crimes against humanity, no one has ever been held accountable for this and other massacres to this date.

The TJRC (or the Commission) defines a massacre as "the deliberate killing of several members of a particular targeted group on a single occasion" (TJRC Vol IIA 2013, 152). By this definition, the Commission limits the suffering to a single event and one group. In the case of Wagalla, this simple definition raises at least two concerns: Firstly, the Wagalla attacks cannot be removed from the history of marginalization of the people of Northern Kenya. Secondly, dominant references to the Wagalla atrocities often highlight the suffering of the male Degodia clan members, leaving out the experiences of many women who were also tortured, maimed, killed, and also bore the brunt of state repression.

In Kenya, human rights violations, including the economic marginalization of Northern Kenya, are well documented by human rights organizations like the Kenya National Human Rights Commission, and in media reports (Anderson 2014). However, there are hardly any discussions of gender relations before, during, and after conflict within the context of transitional justice. Articulating these conflicts simply through the rhetoric of equality and rights reinforces patriarchal power which has stood in the way of justice by suppressing the visibility of women as agents of change (Lambourne and Carreon 2016; Meintjes et al. 2001). Truth commissions, which are often off-shoots of patriarchal arrangements, have struggled to integrate transformative gender-responsive actions in their work. Despite acknowledgment of gender inequality and gender inclusive policies to "bring women in," the tokenistic treatment of women and their experiences has undermined their involvement and participation in conflict and peace-building (Moser and Clark 2001).

The drafters of the Truth, Justice and Reconciliation (TJR) Act, which established the Kenyan TJRC, acknowledged gendered implications of Kenya's history of injustices, where public discourse had been dominated by men, and women's voices were silenced (TJRC Vol IIC 2013, 10). The Commission therefore "provided safe and accessible forums for women to share their experiences" and hired female statement-takers in each community for women "who felt more comfortable sharing their stories with other women" (TJRC Vol IIC 2013, iv). The Commission then held special women's hearings at each of the locations where public hearings were held and recorded 16,377 statements from women. This represented 38 percent of the total statements received. Over 1,000 women attended the women's hearings across the country, with an average of sixty women in each hearing. A total of 161 women testified during the public hearings (TJRC Vol IIC 2013, 10). The TJRC's Final Report has a chapter dedicated to gender and "highlights the different ways that women experienced historical injustices and gross violation of human rights" (TJRC Vol IIC 2013, iv).

This study explores how the women of Wajir engaged in the truth-seeking process, going beyond predominant scholarly focus on sexual injustices. I argue that common debates on bodily harm are borne out of normative expectations during moments of transition rather than the desire to consider such experiences as a consequence of broader social, political, and economic conditions, prior to, during, and after conflict. Accordingly, this chapter confronts arguments in gender justice scholarship that Truth Commission testimonies risk reinforcing the retraumatization, restigmatization, and revictimization of women when they testify about their experiences.

CONTEXTUALIZING KENYA'S TJRC

The Kenyan TJRC was born out of the need to address the country's recurring history of injustices since independence. Scholars and activists alike believe these injustices contributed to the bitterness and animosity of the 2007–2008 postelection violence. The TJRC was established alongside other transitional justice mechanisms, which involves "a full range of processes and mechanisms associated with a society's attempt to come to terms with a legacy of large-scale past abuses, in order to ensure accountability, serve justice and achieve reconciliation" (UN 2010, 2). According to the International Center for Transitional Justice, the goal of transitional justice mechanisms (such as truth commissions and criminal trials) is to expose the truth about past atrocities, hold perpetrators accountable, provide reparations for victims, and fundamentally reform institutions that normalize atrocities.

Much has been said and written about the Kenyan TJRC. However, some salient factors surrounding the Commission's work stand out as factors that shaped its work. Firstly, right from the onset, the Commission faced credibility challenges over Chair Bethwel Kiplagat's alleged culpability in past wrongdoings (TJRC Vol 1 2013; Slye 2018; Lynch 2018). Incidentally, one of the major allegations against the chair was that he had been part of a government meeting in Wajir which led to the infamous Wagalla Massacre (TJRC Vol 1 2013; Lynch 2018; Slye 2018). At the time of the Wagalla hearings, the chairman had "stepped aside" and Tecla Namachanja was appointed acting chair of the Commission. Secondly, the Commission's work ran concurrently with the indictments of prominent Kenyans at the International Criminal Court. Some of the politicians involved in the ICC cases at The Hague were also mentioned at the TJRC hearings and investigations. This led to a highly politicized transitional justice process that prioritized elite political rhetoric at the expense of intersecting forms of violence that had plagued the country since independence. The ICC cases and other constitutional reforms agenda also undermined the visibility of the TJRC in the mainstream media (Lynch 2018).

The TJRC operated under a cloud of a *familiar performance* as just another commission in the fight against impunity (Lynch 2018). For many years before the Truth Commission was established, Kenyans had been subjected to various commissions of inquiry into economic crimes, assassinations, disasters, ethnic violence, electoral violence, among others. These commissions have been riddled with controversies, scandals influenced by elite political actors' competing interests (Africog Report 2007). The fact that no one has ever been held accountable for these crimes fueled the perception that the Truth Commission "represented repetition, continuity and impunity rather than transition change and justice" (Lynch 2018, 105). Lynch further describes this scenario as a sense of *once-againness* that conjures up past inaction against impunity. With the politicization of the TJRC Report, the Kenyan government never made it publicly available. Professor Ronald Slye, who was one of the commissioners of the Kenyan TJRC, has posted the whole Report on his institution's website for public access, that is, the

Seattle University School of Law website under a Digital Commons repository platform.

In contrast, the South African TRC remains the most studied and spoken about of all truth commissions. But while the Kenyan TJRC was inspired by the South African truth-seeking experience, it had major differences with the TRC in terms of context, mandate, visibility, and structure. The Kenyan TJRC was for one, given a broader mandate and was established under different circumstances. Nonetheless, similarities can be found largely in the public hearings of survivors and perpetrators of apartheid atrocities (Slye 2018; Lynch 2018).

The work of the Commission was structured into four overlapping phases: statement-taking, research and investigations, hearings and report writing (TJRC Vol I 2013). The Commission also received memoranda from individuals, groups, associations, and communities. In total, the Kenyan TJRC hired 304 statement-takers and collected 40,000 statements, the largest in the history of truth commissions (TJRC Vol 1 2013). The Commission conducted three kinds of hearings: individual hearings, women's hearings, and thematic hearings. "These sessions provided victims the opportunity to narrate their stories and in the process restore their dignity and commence a healing process" (TJRC Vol 1 2013). Hearings were held in public or in camera. These hearings began in mid-April 2011 in Garissa, North Eastern Kenya and concluded at the beginning of April 2012 in Nairobi. Thematic hearings focused on specific violations, events, or groups of victims.

GENDER AND TRANSITIONAL (IN)JUSTICE

Gender-responsive postconflict reconstruction as well as providing justice and redress for conflict-related abuses of human rights is at the core of transitional justice (Warren and Alam 2017). However, gender inclusivity in truth commissions is futile if the political and socioeconomic ecosystem is not gender transformative in postconflict contexts (Lambourne and Carreon 2015; Gready and Robins 2014). Many truth commissions have included chapters on gender and human rights violation and scholars have termed these approaches to engendering truth-seeking as superficial processes that have failed many women (Nesiah 2006). This criticism stems from arguments that transitional justice mechanisms often fail to remove structural inequalities (such as gender inequalities) at the root of violence, dictatorship, and war (Gready and Robins 2014).

Also on the table are observations that truth commissions (e.g., in South Africa, Rwanda, and Kenya) have led the way in addressing the history of power imbalances and gender inequalities in postconflict societies. For while truth commissions have faced criticism in their work—and rightfully so—they have nevertheless helped highlight neglected abuses and gendered violations, and have recommended reparations (Nesiah 2006). The TJRC's gender-responsive peace-building and reform process (Warren et al. 2017) was a critical juncture in Kenya's history of commissions of inquiry into mega-corruption scandals, assassinations, massacres, economic crimes, and so on that had largely involved elite male actors.

There is no universal approach to transitional justice. Instead, it is a complex, fluid, "incomplete and messy" (Franke 2005) process because individuals and societies experience conflict differently. Due to prevailing social roles and norms before, during, and after the conflict, the implications of transitional justice processes are often gendered (Warren et al. 2017). As Moser et al. (2001) argue, critical understandings of armed conflict and political violence rest on a gendered framework that recognizes "that violence and conflict are both gendered activities . . . where male and female roles are ideologically ascribed, women and men as social actors each experience violence and conflict differently and have differential access to resources (including power and decision-making) during conflict" (30). Any Truth Commission operating outside this understanding will more than likely fail to consider and reckon with women's multifaceted experiences (Ephgrave 2015; Warren et al. 2017; Bell and O'Rourke 2007). Therefore, gender-sensitive approaches allow us to examine how gender hierarchies influence our worldview, and how to avoid further exacerbating inequalities in postconflict contexts (Ephgrave 2015).

Women's experiences of oppression—sometimes referred to as "indirect" victimization—are often overlooked (Turkington 2017). In recent years, though, truth commissions have accommodated the views of women as legitimate in retributive justice. The Kenyan TJRC's women's-only hearings provided one of the most detailed records of the views and experiences of women arising out of a truth-seeking process (Slye 2018). But the "addition of women" into this process as a category of victims is reductionist and defeatist because women are sometimes perpetrators of violence, activists for change, or bystanders in conflict (Ephgrave 2015; Ross 2003; Franke 2006; Moser and Clark 2001; Warren et al. 2017; Meintjes et al. 2001). This a priori treatment of women as "victims" (Ephgrave 2015) of bodily injury such as rape, incest, and other forms of sexual violence lends credence to resubjugation of women in such cases as vulnerable and lacking agency (Ephgrave 2015; Ross 2003) or "as internally displaced persons, heads of households, and refugees" (Bell and O'Rourke 2007). Similarly, Utas (2005) warns against linear and static interpretations of women as victims. Alternatively, they should be treated as "tactical agents engaged in the difficult task of social navigation" (426).

As truth commissions grapple with gender-responsive processes of truth-seeking, care should be taken to ensure gendered experiences in transitional justice are subjected to context-specific analyses and approaches (Nesiah et al. 2006). Reductionist strategies may do more harm than good as they roll back the gains made with regard to gender equity during the postconflict process (Warren et al. 2017) and obscure reconstruction of patriarchal power (Meintjes et al. 2001). The focus of transitional justice should therefore account for these gendered differences (Warren et al. 2017; Meintjes 2009), wider systems of power, and on how gender is socially constructed and not biological determinism (Ephgrave 2015).

Through testimonies as "victims," women run the risk of retraumatization and stigmatization (Ephgrave 2015; Lynch 2018). During testimonies before truth commissions, men have been known to talk about their own experiences of injustices or violations, while women's truth-telling involves stories and experiences of others (Coombes 2011; Ross 2003; Holliday-Karre 2008). In a study of women's testimonies before public hearings of the South African TRC's Human Rights Violations Committee, Ross (2003) argues that the TRC focused on bodily harm rather than the roots of apartheid. This dominant focus on bodily integrity "fixes experience in time, in an event, and draws attention away from ways of understanding of that experience as a process that endures across bodies and through time" (49). The treatment of women as a category of victims, she notes, generally essentializes suffering and gender, the effect of which is "to displace questions of resistance, class, race, age and cultural difference in the making of apartheid's subjects" (Ross 2003, 25). Also, Ephgrave's (2015) study of women's testimonies in South Africa and Rwanda unveils how the narratives of both postconflict Rwanda's *gacaca* courts and the South African TRC create a "singular woman victim" that omits the complexity of women's experiences in collective memory. What emerges from the official discourse of these two truth-seeking mechanisms, she adds, is a single-dimensional female victim subject. Similarly, Lynch (2018) closely followed the Kenyan Truth Commission's work and observed that even though the women's hearings were well intentioned, they too fell prey to a metanarrative of inaction, poor planning, lack of political will, and unmet expectations that surrounded the truth-seeking process.

This chapter hopes to extend these conversations on engendering transitional justice by arguing that even though women's narratives may subject them to direct or indirect resubjugation, studies that explore their willingness to testify, to be heard, and their expectations reveal their hunger for justice in the face of previous indifference and inaction. Their framing of human rights abuses through multiple perspectives can be disruptive of dominant historical narratives. Indeed, even Lynch (2018) observes that the women's hearings in Kenya evoked deconstruction of dominant truth-seeking narratives of violations against bodily integrity to include tales of "structural violence, inequalities, patriarchal cultures and everyday harassment" (196). The women's testimonies before truth commissions should therefore be welcomed and promoted in every truth-seeking process.

Counternarratives that emerge from the testimonies can destabilize narrow and superficial singular truths (Ephgrave 2015) and pave the way for gendered truth (Meintjes 2009). Truth commissions should leverage women's voices to gain gendered understandings of the roots of conflict. This approach through testimonies, I argue, can be a source of shared healing when a community attempts to memorialize past injustices in ways that capture conversations on gender justice before, during, and after conflict. More so, by accepting to testify, the women of Wajir confront an unjust past through the shared hope that their voices can counter male supremacist ideologies that place women first and foremost as victims. In the struggle for justice, women cross the "victim" boundaries to share strengths that identify structural forces working to undermine their resourcefulness as individuals and as a collective. hooks (1986) argues for a bonding of women not through shared oppression but through shedding of victimhood to acknowledge their agency to fight for justice.

NARRATIVE ANALYSIS OF WOMEN'S TESTIMONIES

The Kenyan Truth Commission adopted nonretributive truth-telling in its efforts to provide women a space to talk freely about their experiences (Slye 2018). In nonretributive truth-telling, those who testify are "not cross-examined in an adversarial process designed to establish the guilt of the accused (like in criminal trials), but rather they were present in their own rights, speaking about what had happened to them, in a supportive environment" (Allais 2011, 333). According to Slye (2018), personal or narrative truth is the most important during Truth Commission hearings. Though subjective in describing what happened, the narratives also include stories of individual experiences. In the context of truth commissions, narratives influence interpretations of the past as people place meanings on their experiences so that they can come to terms with them (Buckley-Zistel et al. 2014).

According to the TJRC, 161 women testified during the public hearings, significantly lower than men. However, over 1,000 women participated in the women's-only hearings. The latter hearings were also much less formal, including singing and dancing. The Commission observed the women's willingness to testify among fellow women as compared to speaking in public hearings. Their gratitude and relief for such spaces was captured in the proceedings. As one woman stated to the Commission:

> We are grateful that you have separated us from men because yesterday we
> listened to what the men were saying and we could not talk. This is because

you would say one thing and leave the rest as we were oppressed in very many things. We could be punished in many aspects. Thank you for the knowledge and wisdom you used to decide that women should be separated in order for them to say their own things.

By participating in the special hearings, the women's narratives create a sense of involvement in their narrated experiences for the audience (Foss 2018). This chapter examines the stories of women who testified before the Commission's special hearings in Wajir District. The transcripts of the testimonies were obtained from Seattle University School of Law Digital Commons where all documents pertaining to the Commission's work are archived and available online. I conducted a narrative analysis to interpret the stories as told within the context of transitional justice. The women's testimonies about the Wagalla Massacre are treated here as narratives that are unique in their structure, functions, and themes (Parcell and Baker 2018). I analyzed the transcripts with the following questions in mind: What do the women's narratives convey about their objectives in testifying about Wagalla? What narrative strategies did the women employ to testify about the Wagalla Massacre? What are the implications of the women's testimonies on dominant understandings of the Massacre?

After a "long preliminary soak" (Hall 1975) into the data—in this case, the TJRC transcripts—I conducted a three-step subdivision of content (see Hallihan and Riley 1987). The first category is procedural issues and opening statements from the commissioners in attendance; the second, comments to other participants that are not necessarily testimonies; and the third, considers storylines (narratives that tell the story of participants). This subdivision of data was necessary so that my ensuing analysis could capture the most relevant content from the transcripts and give more attention to the women's narratives. Following the subdivision process, I analyzed the data using a grounded coding process to identify objectives, strategic features, and implications of the narratives (Foss 2018). Through initial coding I segmented the captured data into in vivo codes. I finished with a focused axial coding where the in vivo codes unveiled salient themes from the narratives (Charmaz 2006). The following section presents a section of the findings.

OPENING STATEMENTS AND PROCEDURAL ISSUES

The TJRC designed the women's hearings as safe spaces so women could talk freely about violations specific to them. These hearings were framed as *"conversations with women"* and presided over by female commissioners and staff (TJRC Vol IIC 2013, 9–10). At the women's hearing in Wajir, TJRC staff and commissioners asked participants to express themselves freely, even in Somali language. The hearing session was presided over by two commissioners, one who acted as the chair following Bethwel Kiplagat's resignation. Also present were two interpreters and one member of staff who guided the session.

The procedures and the statements from the commissioners and staff provided a *structure* of the hearings. The opening statements from the commissioners and staff, though procedural, set the tone for the hearing session. The acting chair of the Commission, Tecla Namachanja expressed concern about the "violation the women underwent" during the massacre, thereby encouraging testimonies on violations of bodily integrity.

The initial statements also inquired into the experiences of single mothers and widows. The acting chair, Commissioner Namachanja, wanted to know "what are the problems that you have undergone as a widow or as a woman who is taking care of her children without a man?" The commissioners acknowledged the women's marginalization in education, cultural practices, health, and lack of infrastructural development that had hampered the Commission's truth-seeking operations in the region. However, they expressed optimism that the women's testimonies would not be in vain, that this was the beginning of a new conversation that would be carried through to future generations, and that such atrocities would not happen again. The acting chair also alluded to the catharsis of sharing experiences about the massacre, stating that "it is only through sharing that they will heal." The other commissioner, Shava, noted that it was time Kenyans knew what was going on in the region: "These are the issues we want the rest of Kenya to know about. What happens here in North Eastern Province is often hidden because of the difficulty of getting here. There is no communication, and people do not know what is happening here. Let us shout about it very loudly." The goal of the TJRC women's hearings was to encourage women's testimonies in the absence of men. According to the TJRC, this was informed by the experience of previous truth commissions and anecdotal evidence from a previous task force that women spoke "freely when fewer or no men were in attendance" (TJRC Vol IIC 2013, 10). The next session examines the women's narrative strategies both in their comments and testimonies.

COLLECTIVE DEMANDS FOR TRUTH AND JUSTICE

Narratives of Solidarity

The TJRC commissioners assured the women who testified of the legitimacy of their voices as they contribute to Kenya's stability. The women were also assured of justice, and in turn, expected it. Their testimonies therefore contain a collective demand for truth and justice with the knowledge and experience that this had not been delivered before. One woman whom I call Amburo[1] said, "We do not want to be lied to, we do not want the Commission to come here for nothing; we want the truth . . . I have written ten statements before but nobody did anything for me. This is the first time I have been told to talk openly about it." Another woman demanded that "justice be done" for "the generations who were born after me, including my age mates, and those who are older than me." The women also spoke against the injustice of official truth from the state. "You should not listen to what the Government is saying but you should listen to us since we do not have leaders to represent us in Nairobi," said Bishaaro.

In their testimonies, even though they distrusted the state to address their grievances, the women were grateful for the opportunity to be heard collectively as "women of Wajir." The hearings disrupted the culture of silence in the face of repression. As Bishaaro shared, "Thank you very much for giving us time as women, for addressing the state of women here. . . . This is a beginning because you let me talk. I have never talked about it but today, I did it because we are all women." The women used the testimonies to identify themselves as witnesses of state repression. And the Wagalla Massacre reminded them of such suffering. As Maua shared, "We are suffering, we are the witnesses and this is what is happening. There is no justice and the Government is just finishing us and as women, we do not know where we are heading to." Some of the women told the Commission they could not forget their experiences as they witnessed their community suffer under the very same government that was supposed to protect them. Some wanted to forget the atrocities because of past inaction and lack of accountability. These narratives of remembrance unveil an important identity of the women as witnesses of what happened in Wajir before and during Wagalla. They had witnessed a continuum of victimization, and survived to tell their story and those of others. This double identity as witness and survivor disrupts the hegemonic treatment of women as a special category of "victims."

Narratives of Exhortation and Restitution

Narratives of exhortation represent women's efforts to mobilize their voices to claim their rights. One speaker emphasized a need for collective empowerment and action toward reaching such rights:

> I urge women to stand up whenever there is a problem. Which justice can we get if we are not together? The Commission can only help us if we are also ready. Who are we waiting for to come and help us? Let us help ourselves and ask for our rights. . . . We have to be united, so that we can get our rights. The Government cannot give us our rights if we do not come out. We can stand in unity and all will come to an end. —Kesi.

Similarly, Penda encouraged women to insist on their rights. She shared: "Let us stand in unity. Let us be together as that is when our problems will come to an end . . . I am calling upon women as we have to come forward. The TJR Commission, is telling us that we have to be aware of our rights. We need to claim our rights, so that we can be given land and education." As evident from Kesi and Penda's testimonies, women used the strategy of exhortation as narrative device to not only encourage unity among themselves but to use such solidarity toward seeking restitutive justice. In this case they supported one another to collectively claim their rights to land and education. Both the latter rights have been beyond women's reach due to the region's marginalization, even before the Wagalla Massacre. The women's stories transcended space and time to reconstruct a version of events surrounding the Wagalla Massacre. Their stories brought to the fore how the political and cultural climate in the region constituted fertile ground for state repression and injustices. Such repression, as some women shared, was often based on ethnic association. The salient themes that emerge from these narratives are aligned with the context under which the Truth Commission was operating and the Commission's own acknowledgment of hegemonic domination at the intersection of a patriarchal gender system and economic inequality.

The Injustice of Tribal Othering: "We are the Degodias"

The women's narratives reconstructed their experiences as ethnic minorities. This included Wagalla attacks by Kenyan security forces as a consequence of frequent targeting of the Degodia clan in Wajir. The Wagalla Massacre was as a result of tribal othering of the community and its resources. The subsequent marginalization of the community and the lack of justice affected men and women in different ways. The women's testimonies revealed how the Degodia targeting had reproduced their subjugation. In addition to gender discrimination, women also endured ethnic marginalization.

Single parenthood, poverty, stigma, and rejection in the community and within government on both gender and ethnic grounds are especially evident in Jawaahir's testimony. She shared that "when we go to the hospital, we are asked where we are from . . . they then asked us from which clan we were and we told them that we are Degodias . . . we were told that they only wanted the Degodia tribe. . . . We saw the people who were shot after they said that they were Degodias." In addition to limited access to health services, women also experienced rejection when it came to employment and access to government services. As Calaso stated during her testimony, "I cannot get a job here because my tribe is different. . . . Even my children cannot get jobs because I am from a different tribe . . . I cannot even get family relief like my neighbour because those who give out the family relief money are not from my tribe." Sentiments such as these shared by Calaso, underscoring her sense of exclusion from broader economic activities, are also present elsewhere, especially where state-level participation is concerned. In other cases, women's testimonies described state repression, with some women asking about the brutality from the government that was supposed to protect its citizens, and impunity from such attacks. And the women often used metaphors to articulate such brutality. Bishaaro stated that "the Government that should protect us ate us like a hyena eats a goat. We are now in the stomach of the hyena." Along the same lines, Maua shared: "We were told that they were the police . . . we were crying and asking why the Government was killing us." By bringing these sentiments to the fore, women used their testimonies to actively alter the discourse surrounding their experiences during conflict. They are doing so by voicing their concerns around political exclusion and state repression.

Injustice of Patriarchal Entanglement: "My Children Do Not Have a Father"

The women's testimonies reified the imbalanced gender relations in Wajir before, during, and after the Wagalla Massacre. This prevailing gender system allowed for the essentialization of their gendered experiences as running concurrently with their fight for justice. By reconstructing the Wagalla narrative, the women reaffirmed the dilemma of fighting injustices while being entangled in a web of patriarchal power. Several women decried their helplessness without their men, or as breadwinners in the absence of husbands. Such testimonies are mostly likely in light of commissioners treating single motherhood as an area of interest. "They [police] took all the men . . . people have problems when there is no man," one women said. "We no longer have any resources, all our brothers and grandfathers are dead," expressed another speaker. "My children do not have a father and I am struggling to take care of their education as a single mother," Fawzia stated.

In some cases, the gendered injustice of patrilineality is evident in the economic and social marginalization of women who are expected to follow their husbands and identify with their husbands' families. This is the case in most Kenyan cultures.

> I was born in Isiolo but I am married in Wajir . . . My father was killed just a few kilometres from Garbatulla Town. All our resources got finished . . . I got married and came to Wajir in 1980 because my husband is from here . . . I am over 40 years and I cannot go back to my matrimonial home because I also have children. So, I am forced to stay with my children here at Wajir. —Calaso

As the testimonies of Calaso and other women point to injustices accompanying the Wagalla Massacre were merely single incidences in comparison to the more frequent and systemic injustices they have experienced. Such injustices were especially prominent as far as access to land and education is concerned. Such injustices include their sense of political exclusion from the state and its decision-making processes.

Narratives of Physical Injustices

The TJRC, like others before it, identified violations of bodily integrity as a major barrier to women's advancement in Kenya. The testimonies of the women of Wajir narrativized how their bodies became a site of repression during security operations in the region. Their targeting shaped broader debates about the Wagalla Massacre in which the Degodia men were tortured and killed while the women were victims of sexual violence. "The soldiers locked the doors of the houses and they took us as their wives," Fawzia testified. Their collective memories reaffirm their physical vulnerability but unveil narratives of torture and killings beyond the Wagalla Airstrip.

> They told us that they were now our men . . . they came and picked all the women though I cannot recall the number. No woman was spared; all the beautiful girls were each raped by ten or more men, others by three and others by seven. Some women ran away and some were killed in the incidents or at the wheels of the trucks. I had just come out of labour and others who were pregnant gave birth prematurely. I can remember that no woman or girl was spared. —Bishaaro

The women displayed their scars during their testimonies. Scars are mnemonic, a constant reminder of the massacre. Therefore, the weight of the massacre lives on in the women's scars:

> They cut my leg, burnt part of my house and asked me about Wagalla. The Kenyan soldiers cut off my leg, injured my sister and killed my mother. My sister and I were in hospital for five months and you can even see the leg that was cut. —Amburo

Hani, another participant, stated: "Five men caught me and threw me next to a big stone. As I was crying, another one came, tied my mouth and covered my face and I cannot see properly now. . . . Right now, I have many scars where I was beaten." Targeting the women's bodies was a double violation of their rights. Along with the violence, such targeting stripped the women of their dignity. Such traumas resulted in shame and self-stigmatization which were often exacerbated by the patriarchal system in their predominantly conservative community.

While the physical violence stripped the women their dignity, their testimonies reveal their awareness of structural violence and unequal treatment of the girl-child in the region and how it was a precursor to the Wagalla attacks:

The rights of many girls are being violated because of cattle herding. Women are not valued; men do not value education for girls, and so they are left to look after cattle. That is why men take advantage and violate the girls' rights . . . when a woman, or a girl has been raped, they do not go to report it immediately as they [must] continue taking care of animals. —Penda

The gender violence haunts the women as they pursue economic independence. The women testified about sexual harassment and demands for sexual favors before they could get jobs. This resulted in cases of HIV/AIDS as well as women being forced to parent their children alone, both of which were harshly judged in the community. "There are very many who are suffering from HIV/AIDS because they gave their bodies so that they could get jobs to take care of their fatherless children," Calaso testified.

Injustice against "Our Men"

Truth commissions treat women as a special category of victims, and also tend to essentialize them as caregivers. However, during the massacre, women took care of and provided for each other and the men too, nursing the injured and giving them food. "All we could do [for] the injured men was put some glucose on their tongues," Bishaaro asserted. "I went to carry my donkey, so that I could come to help the two people who were giving birth at the Griftu," said Hani. Several women testified about the torture and killing of their male relatives. "My three brothers died at the Wagalla Massacre . . . up to now, my brother's health has been bad. He cannot even sit properly," Hani narrated. Another participant explained, "The men were beaten up. They were bleeding everywhere and they were even vomiting. They were stepped on as they were sleeping on their stomachs and they were injured on their private parts."

IMPLICATIONS OF NARRATIVES ON EXPECTATIONS OF JUSTICE IN WAJIR

The TJRC touted the women's hearings as a "huge success" (TJRC Vol IIC 2013, 12), despite the Commission's challenges and the prevailing political climate. The women's testimonies presented before the Commission in Wajir convey salient narratives about their experiences before, during, and after the 1984 Wagalla Massacre. The women, having suffered through years of human rights violations, saw an opportunity to speak out during the truth-seeking period. For one, they demanded justice. They also sought solidarity in order to be heard and to achieve justice. And they testified to the various atrocities that they had been subjected to. Given that the TJRC had defined "massacre" as a single event, the Wajir women's narratives of the Wagalla Massacre disrupt this narrow definition. The women's testimonies reveal similarities with the experience of others in Northern Kenya who are frequently marginalized. This chapter echoes many scholars who assert that women's hearings resulting in retraumatization, stigmatization, and victimization are genuine. However, I additionally argue that the survivors of the massacre face an ongoing challenge. I also recognize the power of these women's testimonies as disrupting the typical essentialization to the "victim narrative" so often applied to women during truth commissions. Instead, the women in Wajir project an integrated identity as survivors and advocates for justice.

Even though the Truth Commission was another familiar performance (Lynch 2018) in Kenya's culture of inquiries, the women's testimonies raised the bar in mobilizing gendered truth. Women's narratives reveal how the Wagalla Massacre, which is often discussed in relation to the killing of male Degodia clan members, was a repudiation of women's rights. By denying the community its economic rights, the women were dependent on their men for livelihood, their status linked to their reproductive labor. However, killing the male "breadwinners" left the women subjected to economic hardships. Furthermore, the sexual violence women experienced led to self and community stigmatization and rejection from their men, who felt humiliated by their women's violation. The horrors of the Wagalla Massacre left scars and memories of suffering. The decision to speak up about the massacre unveiled the narrative truth about a structural, ideological, and physical massacre that had been prevailed long before the Wagalla Massacre. The Kenyan TJRC was far from perfect in its constitution, operations, and reporting and has been roundly criticized for its shortcomings. However, to its credit, the Commission instituted a number of support mechanisms for victims and other witnesses who testified before it. The Commission also hired counselors to offer psychosocial support before, during, and after the hearings to support the survivors as they shared their experiences as well as to help them move forward in their healing process (TJRC Vol I 2013, xiii).

CONCLUSION

Post-South African truth commissions have adopted public hearings as avenues for truth-telling. The Kenyan TJRC traversed the country collecting views from the public about historical injustices, promising justice and reparations. The work of the TJRC faced many challenges, which resulted in an uncertain climate. These issues could have caused many women to lose trust in the system. Others may have chosen not to get involved because previous commissions resulted in runaway impunity. Despite these setbacks, the advancement of women's rights and the timeliness of the Commission created an environment that was ripe to discuss the crisis from a gendered perspective (IPTI Report 2016; TJRC 2013). The Truth Commission echoed what Meintjes and others have asserted: that the inclusion of gender was a vital element in the administration of the Commission's proceedings. The women's-only hearings acknowledged the vital role of a gendered perspective when approaching the process of justice and reconciliation. This chapter has examined the narrative connections behind the testimonies of women from Wajir regarding the Wagalla Massacre. The Wajir hearings reveal a community that was ready to talk not only about atrocities in the region but also about how their bodies had been weaponized for the battle between state security agents and interclan rivalry in the region. The narratives reveal how the targeting of male Degodias profoundly hurt the women. More importantly, the women exerted their agency, flipping the script from victim to powerful agents of justice. They employed collective memories of solidarity and deployed their past experiences to demand justice in the present. The narratives reveal that the Wagalla Massacre in its popular discourse even within the Truth Commission mythologizes transitional justice as a panacea to unequal power relations. Framing female-only interactions as safe spaces is problematic (Lynch 2018) and publishing separate chapters for women's rights (Meinjtes 2009) is unhelpful if we are to understand the gendered truth of human rights violations. However, truth commissions still need to encourage women's voices and contextualize their reports within an understanding of how gender relations shape a society's willingness to come to terms with its past and to ensure that such atrocities do not recur.

Treating women as victims reifies patriarchal power structures. This study suggests focused analysis and attention regarding how truth commissions can further the interests of marginalized groups and help communities to heal. The women's testimonies could be analyzed through a wide range of angles, and this is only one of them. Therefore, this study is not conclusive enough to represent a complete analysis of the narratives. Future studies could explore other research questions that would contribute to the study of gender and transitional justice.

NOTE

1. In my analysis, I chose not to reveal the names of the twelve women who testified at the hearings even though the documents are in the public domain. I use randomly selected pseudonyms instead. Qualitative methods allow researchers to enter participants' worlds, and as such this move is meant to respect their dignity.

REFERENCES

"A Study of Commissions of Inquiries in Kenya." 2007. *African Center for Open Governance (Africog) Report*, 1–26. https://www.africog.org/reports/Commissi onsofinquirypaper.pdf

"Guidance Note of the Secretary-General: United Nations Approach to Transitional Justice." *United Nations*, March 2010. https://www.un.org/ruleoflaw/files/TJ_Gu idance_Note_March_2010FINAL.pdf

"Truth, Justice and Reconciliation Commission. Final Report." 2013. *Core TJRC Related Documents.* https://digitalcommons.law.seattleu.edu/tjrc-core/

"Truth, Justice and Reconciliation Commission. Public Hearing Transcripts." 2013. *Core TJRC Related Documents.* https://digitalcommons.law.seattleu.edu/tjrc-core/

"Women in Peace and Transition Processes. Kenya (2008–2013)." August 2016. https://www.inclusivepeace.org/sites/default/files/IPTI-Case-Study-Women-Ke nya-2008-2013.pdf

Allais, Lucy. 2011. "Restorative Justice, Retributive Justice, and the South African Truth and Reconciliation Commission." *Philosophy & Public Affairs* 39(4): 331–63.

Anderson, David M. 2014. "Remembering Wagalla: State Violence in Northern Kenya, 1962–1991." *Journal of Eastern African Studies* 8(4): 658–76.

Bell, Christine and Catherine O'Rourke. 2007. "Does Feminism Need a Theory of Transitional Justice? An Introductory Essay." *International Journal of Transitional Justice* 1(1): 23–44.

Buckley-Zistel, Susanne, Teresa Koloma Beck, Christian Braun, and Friederike Miet. 2014. "Narrative Truths: On the Construction of the Past in Truth Commissions." In *Transitional Justice Theories*, edited by Susanne Buckley-Zistel, 144–62. New York: Routledge.

Charmaz, Kathy. 2006. *Constructing Grounded Theory: A Practical Guide Through Qualitative Analysis.* London: SAGE.

Coombes, Annie E. 2011. "Witnessing History/Embodying Testimony: Gender and Memory in Post-apartheid South Africa." *Journal of the Royal Anthropological Institute* 17: S92–112.

Ephgrave, Nicole. 2015. "Women's Testimony and Collective Memory: Lessons from South Africa's TRC and Rwanda's Gacaca Courts." *European Journal of Women's Studies* 22(2): 177–90.

Foss, Sonja K. 2018. *Rhetorical Criticism: Exploration and Practice.* Fifth ed. Long Grove, IL: Waveland Press.

Franke, Katherine M. 2006. "Gendered Subjects of Transitional Justice." *Columbia Journal of Gender and Law* 15(3): 813–28.

Gready, Paul, and Simon Robins. 2014. "From Transitional to Transformative Justice: A New Agenda for Practice." *International Journal of Transitional Justice* 8(3): 339–61.

Hall, Stuart. 1975. "Introduction." In *Paper Voices: The Popular Press and Social Change 1935–1965*, edited by ACH Smith, E Immirizi, and T Blackwell. London, England: Chatto and Windus.

Holliday-Karre, Erin. 2008. "A Simulation of Truth: Reconciling Gender in the Media and the Truth and Reconciliation Commission in South Africa." *The Journal of the Midwest Modern Language Association* 41(1): 78–87.

Hollihan, Thomas A, and Patricia Riley. 1987. "The Rhetorical Power of a Compelling Story: A Critique of a "Toughlove" Parental Support Group." *Communication Quarterly* 35(1): 13–25.

hooks, bell. 1986. "Sisterhood: Political Solidarity Between Women." *Feminist Review* 23(1): 125–38.

Lambourne, Wendy, and Vivianna Rodriguez Carreon. 2016. "Engendering Transitional Justice: A Transformative Approach to Building Peace and Attaining Human Rights for Women." *Human Rights Review* 17(1): 71–93.

Lynch, Gabrielle. 2018. *Performances of Injustice: The Politics of Truth, Justice and Reconciliation in Kenya.* Cambridge, United Kingdom; New York, NY, USA: Cambridge University Press.

Meintjes, Sheila. 2009. "'Gendered Truth'? Legacies of the South African Truth and Reconciliation Commission." *African Journal on Conflict Resolution* 9(2): 101–12.

Meintjes, Sheila, Meredeth Turshen, and Anu Pillay. 2001. *The Aftermath: Women in Post-Conflict Transformation.* London: Zed Books.

Moser, Caroline ON, and Clark, Fiona C. 2001. *Victims, Perpetrators or Actors?: Gender, Armed Conflict and Political Violence.* London, New York: Zed Books.

Nesiah, Vasuki. 2006. *Truth Commissions and Gender: Principles, Policies, and Procedures.* New York: International Center for Transitional Justice.

Parcell, Sahlstein Erin, and Benjamin MA Baker. 2018. "Narrative Analysis." In *The SAGE Encyclopedia of Communication Research Methods*, edited by Mike Allen, 1069–72. Thousand Oaks: SAGE Publications. https://dx.doi.org/10.4135/9781483381411

Ross, Fiona C. 2003. *Bearing Witness: Women and the Truth and Reconciliation Commission in South Africa.* Anthropology, Culture, and Society. London: Pluto Press.

Slye, Ronald. 2018. *The Kenyan TJRC: An Outsider's View From the Inside.* Cambridge; New York, NY: Cambridge University Press.

Turkington, Rebecca. 2017. "Attacks on Tunisia's Transitional Justice Process Threaten Women's Advancement." *OpenDemocracy: Free Thinking for the World*, October 5, 2017. https://www.opendemocracy.net/en/north-africa-west-asia/attacks-on-tunisia-s-transitional-justice-process-threaten/

Utas, Mats. 2005. "West-African Warscapes: Victimcy, Girlfriending, Soldiering: Tactic Agency in a Young Woman's Social Navigation of the Liberian War Zone." *Anthropological Quarterly* 78(2): 403–30.

Vasuki Nesiah, Mark Massoud, Elizabeth Webber, Jennifer McHugh, and Bonita Meyersfield. 2006. "Truth Commissions and Gender: Principles, Policies, and Procedures." *International Center for Transitional Justice*, July 2006. https://ictj.org/sites/default/files/ICTJ-Global-Commissions-Gender-2006-English_0.pdf

Warren, Roslyn, Anna Applebaum, Briana Mawby, Holly Fuhrman, Rebecca Turkington, and Mayesha Alam. 2017. *Inclusive Justice: How Women Shape*

Transitional Justice in Tunisia and Colombia. Georgetown Institute for Women, Peace and Security, August 2017. https://giwps.georgetown.edu/wp-content/uploa ds/2017/08/Transitional-Justice.pdf

Warren, Roslyn, and Mayesha Alam. 2016. "Introduction." In *Women and Transitional Justice*, edited by Roslyn Warren and Mayesha Alam, 3–5. Georgetown Institute for Women, Peace and Security, July 2016. https://giwps.georgetown.edu/wp-con tent/uploads/2017/08/Occasional-Paper-Series-Volume-II-Women-and-Transition al-Justice-July-2016.pdf

Chapter 7

Revisiting Token Resistance and Its Effect on the Perpetuation of Rape Culture

Olushola Aromona

INTRODUCTION

Tweet 1a: "I said no, but he did not stop."
Tweet 1b: "True, she said no but she is a girl, her no means yes."
Tweet 2: "If I am in your bed and I said no, better believe that I mean yes."
Tweet 3: "I may say 'no, stop' during an intimate period. If
  you stop, that's the end of our relationship."[1]

These tweets were exchanges among some Nigerian Twitter users about an intimate picture of two heterosexual persons with a caption, "Stop, stop. In this kind of situation, stop = continue."[2] Those statements indicate problematic communication styles in sexual consent and intention that could pose dire consequences in the context of rape culture[3] and victim-blaming.[4] Related to problematic communication, token resistance is defined as "a woman's indicating that she did not want to have sex even though she had every intention to and was willing to engage in sexual intercourse" (Muehlenhard and Hollabaugh 1988, 872). Rooted in sexual and gender norms that place the burden of sexual propriety on the woman, token resistance is not synonymous with role-playing where an individual may flirtatiously perform a resistance to sexual advances as a part of the sexual interaction (Osman 2003). Rather, token resistance is a problematic [mis] communication style which engenders ambiguity in the understanding of consent which has implications in the domain of sexual assault. The performance of token resistance has been linked to a higher likelihood of sexual aggression in heterosexual relationships (Shafer et al. 2018). Although research indicates that there are cross-cultural differences in men and women's sexual attitudes and practices, including sexual communication, women are more likely than men to engage in token resistance (Beres 2010; Shafer et al. 2018; Sprecher et al. 1994). One of the reasons for this is due to the traditional script of women' propriety expected during sexual intimacy and may be attributed to the fear of being labeled promiscuous (Muehlenhard and Hollabaugh 1988). Sadly, discourses about the effects of these problematic norms and conventions are scant in the traditional media, due in part to the gatekeeping in traditional media ecosystem. However, the affordances of social media platforms provide the space for these problematic conventions and norms to be questioned. Research has begun to investigate the use of social media for online feminist activism (Keller, Mendes, and Ringrose 2018; Mendes 2015). From online and offline sexual harassment to sexism discourses, women are raising conversations to question problematic norms and expectations (Keller et al. 2018). For instance, in 2015, Nigerian women, using the hashtag, #BeingFemaleInNigeria, shared personal stories that are rooted in discriminatory cultural norms thereby exposing their daily experiences of sexism (Anyagwe 2015). Thus, women are using social media as tools to organize, to educate, and to redress conventions that are unjust; their use of social media to raise important questions also point to the importance of their organizing. For instance, by raising conversations on sexual harassment and scripts that govern sexual discourse, the continued problem of sexual violence becomes even more visible. Inspired by the ambiguity in the opening tweet exchange and its potential contribution to sexual violence, I suggest that revisiting sexual scripts research and refocusing attention to contexts and scripts governing sexual interactions, which are problematic, may help us better understand the effects of unclear sexual communication on consent and the prevalence of rape. I begin by reviewing the existing scholarship about token resistance and how the performance of token resistance contributes to ambiguous communication. Then, I report data from qualitative interviews with ten heterosexual Nigerian women on their perceptions and experiences with token resistance, finding that Nigerian women indulge in token resistance as a performance of the sexual scripts that expects women to be subservient in intimacy resulting in rape as a common implication of such performances. These findings also highlight that women use token resistance to communicate other concerns beyond sexual desire, reformulating social scripts as a means of reaching consensus with their partners regarding sexual intimacy and other relational matters. The performance of token resistance, I argue in this chapter and as evident in the tweets at the beginning of this chapter, is a problematic communicative script that can limit the understanding of consent and consequently, engender sexual violence.

REVISITING TOKEN RESISTANCE

Utilizing social media, the #MeToo movement has drawn global attention and exposed many stories of sexual harassment and assault (Depoint 2018). In turn, emerging scholarship on the movement has investigated the frames that were commonly used in these discourses as well as the effects of the #MeToo wave on sociopolitical landscapes around the world (Xiong, Cho, and Boatwright 2019). While these are important concerns to consider regarding the movement, some of the stories shared by survivors and those accused of sexual assault reflect an ambiguity in perception and understanding of consent. For instance, Cristiano Ronaldo, five times FIFA best player, was recently accused of rape by former model Kathryn Mayorga (Buschmann et al. 2018). A document released by Ronaldo's handlers reported Ronaldo allegedly acknowledging that "she said no, a couple of times" (Buschmann et al. 2018). However, could Ronaldo's response suggest that he may have assumed token resistance on Mayorga's part? Because of common social norms that dictate that women, in a performance of chastity, show some initial resistance to sexual advances that in fact they welcome, did Ronaldo in turn take on the traditional role of the man as the one to take initiative to "persuade" Mayorga to change her mind? This allegation is currently still under investigation, but the possible misinterpretation I highlight here strongly indicates the pertinence of revisiting this old phenomenon as it continues in our current realities. It is critical to understand the underlying factors leading to miscommunication and ambiguity about consent.

Despite decades-old conversations on sexuality, gender, and sexual violence, including rape, it is expedient to investigate some of the reasons why sexual harassment continues to be prevalent. An earlier study on sexual intentions and communications indicates that sexual interactions are largely shaped by sexual scripts which are guidelines for expectations and behaviors in a dating or intimate relationship (Metts and Spitzberg 1996). An understanding of the normalization of token resistance in heterosexual relationships is essential when creating sexual consent interventions and rape prevention plans. Since sexual scripts can be culture specific, a study with a non-Western sample can extend our understanding of these scripts. I use a qualitative approach to analyze in-depth interviews with heterosexual Nigerian women to evaluate the normalization of token resistance in sexual relationships. The study aims to articulate the implications of ambiguous communication on understanding sexual consent and the prevention of rape culture. In this study, I suggest that investigating the prevalence of token resistance and social scripts helps to understand the perpetuation of rape and other forms of sexual violence.

Sexual Script Theory and Token Resistance

Sexual scripts are the acceptable norms that guide sexual interactions which individuals, regardless of gender, embrace, internalize, and adhere to through socialization (Simon and Gagnon 1986). Essentially, sexual script theory is the idea that all social behavior, including sexual behavior, is learned through social interactions (Emmers-Sommer 2016; Wiederman 2015). Put another way, token resistance is a sexual behavior learned in social interactions (Muehlenhard and Hollabaugh 1988). The sexual script indicates the acceptable cultural behavior by both men and women in sexual discourse and relationships. A man learns to be aggressive, and forthcoming in communicating his desires, while the woman learns to be passive and ambiguous in her sexual communication (Mills and Granoff 1992; Shafer et al. 2018). These scripts pose dire consequences for individuals engaged in them, as well as those who do not engage in them.

Literature on sexual violence has suggested that sexual harassment, including rape, could be a result of miscommunication and ambiguous consent from both parties (Krahé, Scheinberger-Olwig, and Kolpin 2000; Osman 2003). In cases where the woman uses token resistance, men are likely to interpret the rejection as indicative of a desire that the man be persistent in his request for sexual intimacy. Earlier studies on the interactions of the traditional sexual script and attitudes toward sexual interactions indicate the existence of a belief that when a woman indicates a refusal to have sex, the man should take the initiative because the woman's refusal is only a token (Check and Malmuth 1983). Muehlenhard and Hollabaugh (1988) were among the first researchers to investigate and provide results that show the prevalence of token resistance. In a sample of 610 women, they found that 40 percent of the women have engaged in token resistance. Subsequent studies have found similar results and prevalence of the use of token resistance to sex by women (Beres 2010; Krahé, Scheinberger-Olwig, and Kolpin 2000). Other studies found that men "expect" that women would use token resistance and that a "woman must say 'no' an average of three times before they will start to believe that she actually means it" (Mills and Granoff 1992, 683; Rozee and Koss 2001).

A common theme in these studies is the idea that token resistance is based on the traditional sexual script that requires a woman to be chaste, receptive, and passive in terms of sexual interactions. Thus, token resistance can be viewed as a communication strategy that is based on the traditional sexual script that men are initiators of sexual advances while women are recipients of said advances (Krahé, Scheinberger-Olwig, and Kolpin 2000). This script is further enshrined in social norms which view women showing eagerness to have sex in a negative light. This tendency is even more pronounced in patriarchal societies where the woman is labeled promiscuous for wanting sex not only in casual relationships but also in a committed relationship. For example, women in most Nigerian societies are perceived as cheap and promiscuous for showing a willingness to have sex. Osman (2003) indicates that a woman is judged negatively and as nonconforming to the "traditional passive feminine role" (683) if she appears eager or takes initiative for a sexual interaction. In fact, for a woman to actively seek out sex is to be "almost desperate or dangerous" (Gavey 2013, 12). The implications of token resistance performance have been linked to sexual violence, including rape, as consent to sexual advances is difficult to determine due to the ambiguous communication that arises from the expectation that a woman is saying "no" when she means "yes" (Krahé, Scheinberger-Olwig, and Kolpin 2000; Shafer et al. 2018).

Token resistance is a [mis]communication tool rooted in traditional sexual scripts and linked to sexual violence. Thus, it is imperative to revisit this concept following recent developments regarding sexual harassment, especially the #MeToo movement. This chapter suggests that the old stereotype that women should engage in token resistance so as not to be perceived negatively could offer new perspectives on understanding recent sexual assault accusations. Based on existing research, I suggest that the normalization of token resistance is an essential factor in the ambiguity and misunderstanding of consent, and ultimately, in the perpetuation of rape culture. Currently, there is no consistently accepted definition of consent (Muehlenhard et al. 2016). Therefore, following the Twitter responses and quote from Ronaldo, I suggest that the concept of sexual consent is not fully understood by men or women. However, the concept of consent which assumes male privilege, placing the man as always initiator, and the woman having to respond, as such, needs to be reexamined. It is also, consequently, an important factor that should be articulated in understanding the prevalence of sexual violence, including rape. Unfortunately, sexual assault allegations have become predominant in many societies today. Thus, understanding how the normalization of token resistance plays a role in the perpetuation of sexual assault has practical implications. First, the normalization of token resistance might indicate a limited understanding of the concept of sexual consent (Ortiz 2019). Second, the normalization of token resistance may be an underlying factor in many assaults.

It is important to raise awareness about unhealthy social norms in order to address the negative effects from the root cause. Again, it is essential to note that this study does not view token resistance in terms of role-playing which is a flirtatious signal to indicate that sexual advances are welcome (Osman 2003). Moreover, this chapter does not suggest in any way that sexual violence could be reasoned away. Neither does this study unequivocally suggest that the prevalence of rape is due only to the practice of token resistance by either men or women. Rather, the current study aims to contribute to recent conversations about sexual assault by suggesting that academic discourse should revisit the old stereotype of token resistance in understanding why sexual violence continues to be prevalent in the twenty-first century.

With these caveats and clarifications in mind, this chapter is guided by the following questions: (a) what sexual scripts shape Nigerian women's sexual interactions, (b) to what extent do these women understand the concept of consent in a sexual relationship, (c) how do these Nigerian women view token resistance?

METHOD

For this study, I draw on findings from in-depth, unstructured interviews that were conducted with ten participants.[5] Participants were recruited on Twitter through a recruitment tweet seeking Nigerian women in heterosexual relationships who were willing to participate in a study about communication in sexual relationships using a snowball approach. Participants were required to give informed consent to use data from the interview in a study before the interview. Participants' ages ranged between twenty and forty years.

The interviews lasted between 50 and 70 minutes. The interview style was unstructured to allow participants to share their experiences in ways they were comfortable, to provide opportunity for new and in-depth insights, and to encourage rich responses that structured questions may not allow (Richards and Morse 2012). The interview questions were on a range of topics, including participants' understandings of sexual scripts, their relationship and sexual histories, their understanding of consent in a relationship, their uses of token resistance, and their perceptions of the tweets and responses shared at the beginning of this chapter. The interview data were transcribed and analyzed using thematic analysis (Braun and Clarke 2006) which focused on observed themes in the discussion and participants' understanding of the interview topics.

RESULTS/DISCUSSION

Emerging Themes from Nigerian Women

The analysis revealed that the women who participated in the study follow the sexual script that prescribes that women be passive "recipients" of their male partners' sexual advances. Participants revealed that expectations for token resistance performance are still prevalent; however, education, length of relationship, and personal preferences moderate how much performance there is in heterosexual relationships. Responses also indicated that there are subtle behaviors and nonverbal cues that accompany acceptance or refusal of intimacy that are different from token resistance performances.

Also, the women have unspoken knowledge about their willingness and their partners' willingness for sexual intimacy, and they could articulate their interpretation of willingness or unwillingness to be intimate. However, this does not translate into understanding consent. Participants suggest that engaging in sexual intimacy with their partners is not always reflective of their consent but rather, an indication of a "coerced" consent. That is, some of these women have sex with their partners because intimacy is expected in marriage and, as one participant noted, "A woman should not say no to her husband." Finally, participants' responses revealed how problematic token resistance is and its effect on rape and sexual violence, as well as on self-esteem. These findings suggest the need for education and sensitization aimed at highlighting the dangers of some of the scripts that govern social interactions, including sexual interactions.

Unspoken Knowledge and Relationship Type

When asked about their understanding of their partners' desires for intimacy, participants revealed that understanding when someone wants to be intimate is often easy. As one of the participants, Sade[6] (26), stated, "When your partner wants to have sex, you just know. There is something about the way they act and behave that you just know" (Sade, interview with author, December 12, 2018). When asked how they know, participants' responses suggest that the knowledge, although implicit, is sometimes couched in certain behaviors and in the context of the relationship. Thus, knowledge of the willingness to participate in sexual intimacy is also learned through nonverbal behaviors that may include helping with chores, closing the physical space or distance (e.g., a man moving close to the woman in the room), making eye contact, or playing with the partner's clothing. This knowledge is, however, dependent on the context of the relationship.

In a newly established relationship, the use of elaborate nonverbal cues is more prominent compared to an older relationship. As Asher (29) said, "Depending on the kind of relationship, it is easy to know when your partner's willing to engage in sexual intimacy" (Asher, interview with author, July 26, 2019). A committed relationship, more than a casual relationship, enables partners to be transparent and less ambiguous in communicating their willingness for intimacy. Sade, however, stated that certain behaviors also indicate this willingness to engage in intimacy. According to her, "Time when he gets pretty cozy to me and smile at everything I say; I can tell that he is willing to be intimate. Other times, we just say it, you know, like, hey, let's have sex" (Sade, interview with author, December 12, 2018). Also, the type of relationship is a huge determinant of how partners engage in communication. Another participant indicated that in a casual relationship, it may be less likely or socially applauded if partners, especially women, are verbal and able to freely communicate their willingness for intimacy.

Consent and Problematic Social and Sexual Scripts

When asked about giving consent for sexual intimacy, participants differed in their opinions about consent. Some participants revealed that it is important to have mutual understanding and need for sex before engaging in the act. This *mutual understanding* is a positive element in sexual interactions. When probed if this *mutual understanding* translates to consent, some of the participants indicated that it could be, depending on the relationship. For example, Bunmi (27) explains that in a marriage relationship, there is no use for consent, as sex is "a primary reason for getting married."[7] She asked, "Why should the couple require consent to sleep together after marriage?" (Bunmi, interview with author, July 26, 2019).[8] For other participants, consent is a prerequisite before sexual intimacy. For these women, regardless of the type of relationship, consent should be given before intimacy. When asked what consent looks like, these women said that consent could be verbal or nonverbal. Verbal could be the woman saying "yes, let's have sex," according to Rita (31), or it could be nonverbal by smiling and allowing the partner's advances without resistance.

When asked about the performance of token resistance, participants suggested that women often engage in token resistance because they do not want to be vilified. According to Nike (36), performance of token resistance, although prevalent among women, is even more rife in casual relationships. While interpreting and understanding token resistance is ambiguous, the context of the relationship, Asher (29) argued, is a determinant of the level of ambiguity as well as the need for token performance in the first place. Thus, token resistance performance in a committed relationship may indicate a cue for something else other than a script performance. For instance, Sade (26) sometimes says "no to my partner even though I intended to be intimate. However, my no is not always because I do not want to be vilified or labeled as promiscuous; most of the time, I say no when I remember my partner's wrongdoing and I want an apology" (Sade, interview with author, December 12, 2018). When asked if her partner understands that her no at such a time does not reflect token resistance, she responded that her partner always understood. She further stated that her partner's understanding at such a time is attributed to the length and context of their relationship as well as her own confidence in communicating or requesting and declining intimacy without ambiguous performances: "We have been together for a while and we know what we want and when we want it. Plus, I clearly ask when I want to, and I do not shy away from declining when I do not want to" (Sade, interview with author, December 12, 2018). This complicates the notion of intimacy as something that only the man initiates; consent as something that only the man in the relationship seeks and which the woman provides. Rather, this suggests a consensus between the partners that either partner can be the initiator of intimacy, seeker of consent, or giver of consent at different times.

Participants' responses further suggest that token resistance is unhealthy and poses severe problems, especially in understanding consent and avoiding sexual violence such as rape.

Miriam (age 23): I think token resistance is very unhealthy and nobody should be performing that in this age. Now that I think about it, I remember a case on Twitter where the girl visited the friend she met on Twitter and she said no to the guy's advances, then sex happened and she came back on Twitter to say she was raped and the guy's excuse that she said no but then he was certain that she did not mean the no. I think that token resistance does not make it evident or clear when someone is truly willing to go down with you. You know, that Twitter boy may just be thinking the girl was playing hard to get. It is very unhealthy. And it could also cause trouble too. Isn't that boy eventually arrested? (Miriam, interview with author, July 27, 2019)

Likewise, according to Lola (age 25):

So token resistance is like playing hard to get? It is sad that women still do that. Although I have also performed it, I think it is problematic and I think women should have sex whenever and however they want to without them thinking of being castigated or perform whatever we think govern individuals. (Lola, interview with author, December 12, 2018)

When asked if they had performed token resistance, the participants revealed that they had. Their responses, however, revealed that relationship context, education, and high self-esteem are moderating variables in the performance of token resistance.

Toju (age 30): Although I have played hard to get before when I cared about what people would say. I was also trying to be a prim and proper girl with my partner, I mean, no Nigerian lady wants to be seen or tagged as "loose." So, you pretend that you don't want to go down even though you really want to. If you ask me now, I don't do that thing again. If I like you, I ask you and if you say "no," then that's your loss, not mine. (Toju, interview with author, July 26, 2019)

When asked the reason for the change, Toju responded:

I think being educated and knowing my worth as a woman plus I place so much value on my time and emotions. I remember a time, during my undergraduate days, it must have been my first year, there was a guy I really liked, and he wanted to get down with me, but I was shy, and I thought if I let him so easily, he won't value me and would see me as a cheap girl. So, I said no, and I always said no every time he requests before I would let him. Now, I have evolved, read and educated myself on some of the cultural practices that are enshrined in our Nigerian culture which are deeply patriarchal. So, the change for me was under-standing that it is my body and I should call the shots. My self-esteem went through the roof and I don't really care if you like or label me after I decline your request. (Toju, interview with author, July 26, 2019)

And it is not just Toju who feels this way. Asher (age 29) states:

I think I stopped performing and playing hard to get after my engagement and wedding. Before my partner and I got engaged, I always engaged in token resis-tance but not because I do not want to be labeled as cheap but more because I wasn't sure if we were together for the long haul or not. But after we got engaged and now in my marriage, I don't perform anymore. I think being in a committed relationship versus a not committed one was what stopped me. (Asher, interview with author, July 26, 2019)

With further probes into how problematic token resistance is, participants' responses revealed that ambiguous communication could lead to sexual vio-lence and rape. Participants said that rural women or women with very low self-esteem may be more likely to perform token resistance, and the high rate of rape and other forms of abuse, sexual and domestic violence may be results of these sexual scripts. Although some Nigerian women in rural areas are often perceived to be more prone to engaging in token resistance compared to women in urban areas, perhaps due to the deeply enshrined and visible patri-archal tendencies, the findings from this study suggest that the performance of token resistance is not necessarily location dependent.

Unhealthy norms that characterize patriarchal societies may be more vis-ible in some societies and less so in others. For instance, sexism may be veiled in chivalry or in benevolence in cities but be more aggressively visible in villages. Slut-shaming[9] women for their choices and burdening them with the dangerous and oppressive double bind that is a result of the inability to communicate their needs and being vilified for the same needs transcends physical or geographical locations.

In what follows, I attempt to report on the internal and external factors that were at play as I interacted with the research process, particularly as I collected data. As Etherington (2004) noted, researchers do not operate in a vacuum, but rather on a multiple of levels that influence how they interact with the research process; it is therefore advised that researchers are aware of the personal as well as the epistemological levels from which they interact and respond to the research process (Dowling 2006).

Reflexivity

As I gathered data, I was constantly aware of the power dynamics in the mix. One, as the researcher, it was clear that I had some power in the choice of questions I asked, the questions I did not ask, and how much I was willing to probe my participant. Two, although I am a member of the ingroup as a Nigerian woman, I was not sure if my position as a researcher evoked negative feelings from my participants' points of view. Therefore, throughout the interview, I struggled with mixed feelings and concerns: What if my participant does not want to go on with the interview? What if the questions were too intimate, overwhelmingly cathartic, or evoked unpleasant memories? How do I help the participant if she needs help with some of the memories that the interview brings up? Because I was aware of these possibilities, I was careful to reassure and affirm a participant whenever she answered a sensitive question.

In retrospect, as a Nigerian, I found that my acculturation in the expectation of women's chastity before marriage was in constant friction with my desire to respect other people's choices as I interviewed my participants. When I asked if one of my participants, an unmarried young woman, had ever had sex when she did not feel like (more like, having sexual intimacy based on coercion and not on willful desire), I caught myself expecting my participant to say that she has never been in that situation, given that she has never been married.

The expectation that a young woman who had never previously been married is a script that feeds into the biased complexity that results in a double bind for women. For single women, sexual activity is associated with promiscuity. For single men, however, the script is different. This difference goes full circle back to the notion that men are hunters, predators, and inherently "wired" to hunt. If women are burdened with celibacy prior to marriage, one wonders where the hunting men are expected to get the game prior to marriage.

Finally, the sampling method does not present the researcher to participants who may be in different social classes. While Twitter is widely used
by Nigerians (Probyn 2016), recruiting participants solely from Twitter does
not provide the variety needed to fully understand a phenomenon that is
cultural. As participants' responses show, token resistance, while visible in
communications on Twitter and other social platforms, goes beyond social
media. Thus, snowballing on Twitter may only present researchers with
individuals who are educated, have internet access, and who may or may not
have performed token resistance. Likewise, snowballing could also present
researchers with participants who have always engaged in token resistance.
Although snowballing was chosen for this project because of the sensitivity
of the topic, it could be limiting in providing richer and varied insights into
the phenomenon.

CONCLUSION

This study investigated the performance and prevalence of token resistance
and how it engenders miscommunication and results in misunderstandings
of consent and perpetration of sexual violence. This study also extends the
scholarship on this phenomenon by examining the issue in a non-Western
context and provides an investigation into an age-long script to articulate the
prevalence of sexual violence. Findings support existing literature that token
resistance is a result of expected social scripts that places the burden to be
chaste on the woman; thus, women are socialized to say no to sexual advances
even though they intend to engage in sexual intimacy. This script puts the
woman in a double bind: on the one hand, they desire sexual intimacy, yet
social expectations demand that they feign chastity, and this expected performance amplifies ambiguous communication that is problematic for both the
woman and the man, putting them both at risk. On the one hand, the man is
unaware of and/or has difficulty ascertaining the true intentions of his partner,
and on the other, the woman is at risk of sexual violence as the man may take
her refusal as merely performance.

Token resistance performance leads to unclear communication, and consent or refusal therefore remain unclarified (Ortiz 2019). Because this script
is culturally enshrined, change will not happen overnight. However, engaging
in conversations such as those discussed in this chapter and evoked by this
research can be a major step toward educating individuals about the harm of
token resistance. One way to raise awareness about unhealthy gender norms
is to leverage the opportunities offered by social media platforms such as
Twitter. Social media platforms provide the space for "tough" conversations
about some of the problems of cultural scripts, especially in the African

context. In most Nigerian communities, women are expected to be seen and not heard, and this has contributed to the deeply enshrined gender biases and abuse. However, with platforms such as Twitter, women are using their voices and engaging in discourses that could birth change offline. Twitter conversations about the prevalence of sexual violence and the role of cultural scripts are essential for advocacy, education, and for creating a community of support.

NOTES

1. The Twitter thread with these tweets was suspended and the handles irretrievable.

2. The Twitter account that posted this picture had been suspended at the time of finishing this manuscript due to a violation of Twitter policies.

3. Rape culture refers to the entrenched attitudes and beliefs that normalize sexual coercion and violence such that rape and other forms of sexual violence are perceived as inevitable (Rozee and Koss 2001).

4. Victim-blaming is a feature of rape culture where women are blamed for the sexual violence that is perpetrated against them (Ray 2013).

5. Participants' identifiable information, including names, twitter handles, and specific locations, were withheld in line with IRB approval. Pseudonyms were used in place of participants' real names.

6. In place of participants' real names, pseudonyms were used. Participants' self-reported ages were used.

7. The notion that consent is not necessary in marriage relationship is traced to the biblical teaching of St Paul in 1 Corinthians 7: 3–5. This view, which was popular in "most countries of the world" in the past (Chika 2011, 41), is still held by some.

8. This notion that consent is not necessary in a marriage relationship is problematic as it could result into marital rape. Marital rape, also known as spousal rape, is a nonconsensual sexual intimacy in a marriage relationship where the perpetrator of the assault is the victim's partner (Chika 2011).

9. Slut-shaming "is the act of criticizing women or girls for their real or presumed sexuality or sexual activity, as well as for looking or behaving in ways that are believed to transgress sexual norms" (Karaian 2014, 296).

REFERENCES

Anyangwe, Eliza. 2015. "Everyday Sexism: What's It Really Like #BeingFemaleInNigeria?" *CNN.com*, July 1, 2015. https://www.cnn.com/2015/06/30/africa/being-female-in-nigeria/index.html

Beres, Melanie. 2010. "Sexual Miscommunication? Untangling Assumptions About Sexual Communication Between Casual Sex Partners." *Culture, Health & Sexuality* 12(1): 1–14.

Buschmann, Rafael, Andreas Meyhoff, Nicole Naber, Gerhard Pfeil, Antje Windmann, Christoph Winterbach, and Michael Wulzinger. 2018. "The Woman Who Accuses Ronaldo of Rape." *Spiegel Online*, October 16, 2018. https://www.spiegel.de/in ternational/cristiano-ronaldo-kathryn-mayorga-the-woman-who-accuses-ronaldo-o f-rape-a-1230634-2.html

Check, James, and Neil Malamuth. 1983. "Sex Role Stereotyping and Reactions to Depictions of Stranger Versus Acquaintance Rape." *Journal of Personality and Social Psychology* 45(2): 344.

Chika, Ifemeje Sylvia. 2011. "Legalization of Marital Rape in Nigeria: A Gross Violation of Women's Health and Reproductive Rights." *Journal of Social Welfare & Family Law* 33(1): 39–46.

DePoint, Lauren. 2018. "#MeToo: Personal Accounts of Sexual Violence on Facebook Analyzing Individual Stories to Reveal Themes About Gender, Power, and Intersectional Factors." Thesis. Rochester Institute of Technology. https://scholarworks.rit.edu/theses

Dowling, Maura. 2006. "Approaches to Reflexivity in Qualitative Research." *Nurse Researcher* 13(3): 7–21.

Emmers-Sommer, Tara. 2016. "Do Men and Women Differ in their Perceptions of Women's and Men's Saying 'No' When They Mean 'Yes' to Sex? An Examination Between and Within Gender." *Sexuality & Culture* 20(2): 373–385.

Etherington, Kim. 2004. "Research Methods: Reflexivities—Roots, Meanings, Dilemmas." *Counselling and Psychotherapy Research* 4(2): 46–47.

Gavey, Nicole. 2013. *Just Sex? The Cultural Scaffolding of Rape*. New York: Routledge.

Karaian, Lara. 2014. "Policing 'Sexting': Responsibilization, Respectability and Sexual Subjectivity in Child Protection/Crime Prevention Responses to Teenagers' Digital Sexual Expression." *Theoretical Criminology* 18(3): 282–299.

Keller, Jessalynn, Kaitlynn Mendes, and Jessica Ringrose. 2018. "Speaking 'Unspeakable Things': Documenting Digital Feminist Responses to Rape Culture." *Journal of Gender Studies* 27(1): 22–36.

Krahé, Barbara, Renate Scheinberger-Olwig, and Susanne Kolpin. 2000. "Ambiguous Communication of Sexual Intentions as a Risk Marker of Sexual Aggression." *Sex Roles* 42(5–6): 313–337.

Mendes, Kaitlynn. 2015. *Slutwalk: Feminism, Activism and Media*. Basingstoke, UK: Palgrave Macmillan.

Metts, Sandra, and Brian H Spitzberg. 1996. "Sexual Communication in Interpersonal Contexts: A Script-Based Approach." *Annals of the International Communication Association* 19(1): 49–92.

Mills, Crystal, and Barbara J Granoff. 1992. "Date and Acquaintance Rape Among a Sample of College Students." *Social Work* 37(6): 504–509.

Muehlenhard, Charlene, and Carie S Rodgers. 1998. "Token Resistance to Sex: New Perspectives on an Old Stereotype." *Psychology of Women Quarterly* 22(3): 443–463.

Muehlenhard, Charlene, and Lisa C Hollabaugh. 1998. "Do Women Sometimes Say No When They Mean Yes? The Prevalence and Correlates of Women's Token Resistance to Sex." *Journal of Personality and Social Psychology* 54(5): 872.

Muehlenhard, Charlene, Terry P Humphreys, Kristen N Jozkowski, and Zoë D Peterson. 2016. "The Complexities of Sexual Consent Among College Students: A Conceptual and Empirical Review." *Journal of Sex Research* 53(4–5): 457–487.

Ortiz, Rebecca. 2019. "Explicit, Voluntary, and Conscious: Assessment of the Importance of Adopting an Affirmative Consent Definition for Sexual Assault Prevention Programming on College Campuses." *Journal of Health Communication* 24(9): 728–735.

Osman, Suzanne L. 2003. "Predicting Men's Rape Perceptions Based on the Belief that 'No' Really Means 'Yes.'" *Journal of Applied Social Psychology* 33(4): 683–692.

Probyn, Justin. 2016. "How Africa Tweets." *How We Made It in Africa*, July 25, 2019. https://www.howwemadeitinafrica.com/study-sheds-light-africans-use-twitter/54249/

Ray, Jillian. 2013. "Rape and Rape Culture on College Campuses." *Sprinkle: An Undergraduate Journal of Feminist and Queer Studies* 5: 39.

Richards, Lyn, and Janice M Morse. 2012. *Read Me First for a User's Guide to Qualitative Methods*. Thousand Oaks: Sage Publications.

Rozee, Patricia, and Mary P Koss. 2001. "Rape: A Century of Resistance." *Psychology of Women Quarterly* 25(4): 295–311.

Shafer, Autumn, Rebecca R Ortiz, Bailey Thompson, and Jennifer Huemmer. 2018. "The Role of Hypermasculinity, Token Resistance, Rape Myth, and Assertive Sexual Consent Communication Among College Men." *Journal of Adolescent Health* 62(3): S44–S50.

Simon, William, and John H Gagnon. 1986. "Sexual Scripts: Permanence and Change." *Archives of Sexual Behavior* 15(2): 97–120.

Sprecher, Susan, Elaine Hatfield, Anthony Cortese, Elena Potapova, and Anna Levitskaya.1994. "Token Resistance to Sexual Intercourse and Consent to Unwanted Sexual Intercourse: College Students' Dating Experiences in Three Countries." *Journal of Sex Research* 31(2): 125–132.

Wiederman, Michael W. 2015. "Sexual Script Theory: Past, Present, and Future." In *Handbook of the Sociology of Sexualities*, edited by John DeLamater and Rebecca F Plante, 7–22. New York: Springer.

Xiong, Ying, Moonhee Cho, and Brandon Boatwright. 2019. "Hashtag Activism and Message Frames Among Social Movement Organizations: Semantic Network Analysis and Thematic Analysis of Twitter During the# MeToo Movement." *Public Relations Review* 45(1): 10–23.

Chapter 8

"The Revolution Is in the Everyday"

Women in the Namibian Liberation Movement

Mariah C. Stember

INTRODUCTION

In Namibia, as the apartheid regime gained control in the mid-twentieth century, increasingly implementing and enforcing their system of racial segregation, Namibian activists and revolutionaries became more and more restless. The antiapartheid movement in the country was growing and women were a vital (yet often overlooked) component of this struggle. Based on my analysis of primary sourced oral history interviews, I argue that not only did Namibian women make an indelible mark on Namibian independence, but their contributions were also significant in ways both extraordinary and quotidian. Further compounding their experiences was the "double jeopardy" they faced due to their identities as black women.

Women's roles during the struggle were possible due to the innovative, dynamic networks of support they forged and deployed. Women provided support and organized networks to further the liberation struggle in countless ways. This chapter discusses the ways in which women contributed to the prolonged battle to break free from apartheid rule. This chapter works in concert with other scholars (Akawa 2014; Nambadi 2016; Namhila 2009, 2013; Kudumo and Silvester 2016) to contribute to an alternative history, one which is inclusive of women's diverse roles in Namibia's liberation movement. Beginning with a theoretical framework, and then pivoting to discuss the combat as well as the "caring" roles played by women in the struggle, and the double jeopardy which compounded their experiences, I conclude with an analysis outlining the importance of these women's narratives.

THEORETICAL FRAMEWORK:
POWER OF THE QUOTIDIAN

Namibia was originally colonized by Germany in 1884. In 1915, toward the beginning of World War I, Germany lost control of Namibia to South Africa (Wallace and Kinahan 2011), and in 1921 the League of Nations (an international diplomatic group and precursor to the United Nations) formalized Namibia as a mandated territory of South Africa (History 2019; Wallace and Kinahan 2011). In 1966, the United Nations assumed responsibility of Namibia, but the South African government maintained de facto rule (Thornberry 2004; Wallace and Kinahan 2011). While previously South African occupation of Namibia had been contested, as of 1966 it was officially an illegal occupation. In protest, The Southwest African People's Organization (or SWAPO, Namibia's liberation movement and current governing political party) began waging war to gain Namibia's independence. The People's Liberation Army of Namibia (PLAN), was the military wing of SWAPO, leading the opposition movement. In 1990, Namibia won the struggle, overturning apartheid rule and gaining independence.

During the struggle, the everyday activities of Namibian women became revolutionary. A number of scholars have theorized the concept of the everyday in political movements (Borland and Sutton 2007; Sargisson 2010). Additionally, Tina Campt theorizes the quotidian as "not equivalent to passive everyday acts. . . . The quotidian must be understood as a practice rather than an action. *It is a practice honed by the dispossessed in the struggle to create possibility in the constraints of everyday life*" (Campt 2017, 4, italics added). Campt's framework encourages us to view Namibian women's quotidian actions as "engag(ing) instance(s) of rupture and refusal" (Campt 2017, 5). Namibian women embraced and led such ruptures. As one of the women I interviewed stated, "The injustice was just too much." Namibian women's refusal to accept a violent and racist reality as the norm culminated in everyday efforts becoming intentional practices of rupture that would assist in realizing the vision of a liberated Namibia. Without women's labor and contributions to the liberation movement, the struggle would not have succeeded.

Campt also urges us to embrace the power of the quotidian and to "look beyond what we see" at first glance (Campt 2017, 9). Further theorizing the quotidian, Campt cites George Perec (1974), who writes about what he calls the "infraordinary . . . (or) everyday practices we don't always notice and whose seeming insignificance requires excessive attention" (Perec 1997, 8). The idea of looking beyond what we see to notice the infraordinary can be applied to the women at the heart of this chapter. What may appear as an average woman may in fact be a liberation warrior transporting weapons in her headscarf and using such gendered performance to slip past a military checkpoint. Due to the extreme, violent circumstances of the struggle, the quotidian work of the domestic sphere became extraordinary. Using Campt and Perec's lens of the quotidian as a vehicle for inquiry, I examine the ways in which Namibian women carried their country forward in seemingly quiet, yet significant ways. Additionally, I assert that we must reexamine these seemingly ordinary acts in a new light. It is critical that we not overlook or minimize these quotidian contributions, but that they be recognized as the true heroics that they are.

While utilizing the ideas of quotidian and extraordinary as a lens to consider the Namibian context, I also consider how these categories became blurred. Maintaining a household and raising children is challenging under normal circumstances, but it becomes especially difficult during war. Over and over again, women artfully combined the quotidian and the extraordinary, blending the roles of mother and warrior. A key example of this is Namhila's (2013) oral history of Mukwahepo, an "ordinary woman" who blended the quotidian with the extraordinary. Mukwahepo trained as a soldier in the SWAPO's Kongwa military training camp while also caring for her own and many others' families and children (Namhila 2013, 1, 31–57). This meant that, in addition to her military service, Mukwahepo was a mother and thus subjected to the gendered roles accompanying motherhood and domestic life. Mukwahepo embraced the role of mother and care-giver during the struggle, by raising many children for comrades who had been sent into exile for education or military training (Namhila 2013, vii). In doing so, Mukwahepo did more than simply provide childcare. Her labor contributed to the struggle in the form of child-rearing, provided solidarity, continuity, and groundedness to the children she raised, and eased their parents' anxiety as they trained for battle. In turn, her labor fortified Namibian society. Her work, which would normally be done by the mothers or grandmothers of a Namibian community, became extraordinary in the context of the war.

Everyday forms of labor associated with women and their role in domestic spaces became exceptional when managed under the punishing circumstances of war. Navigating and embracing both the private and the public realm is a debate which has often appeared in feminist scholarship (Borchorst 2009; Wetterberg and Melby 2009). While in many places, the debate regarding if and when a woman's place is in the public or private sphere—or both, has been resolved, feminists of the past fought for a woman's right to work in and engage with the public sphere. The limitation of such an interpretation lies in the risk of diminishing the value and transformative potential of the domestic sphere. As Muwati and Gambahaya assert, "Even the often misinterpreted home as a private space, is in fact a strategic arena for the expression of women's agency" (2012, 11). Palmary (2005) has also asserted the importance of the family in matters of the state. In this spirit, we observe the ways in which during the War of Independence, Namibian women's every-day domestic routines were transformed into the realm of the extraordinary.

MORE THAN A ROLE: ORAL HISTORIES OF NAMIBIAN WOMAN IN THE STRUGGLE

Much more than simply being an accessory to the liberation struggle, Namibian women played a central and foundational role in gaining independence for their country. To learn more about this phenomenon, I conducted fieldwork research in Namibia during the U.S. academic year 2019–2020. I collected data via a series of semistructured oral history interviews with interviewees selected via "snowball sampling" (Hesse-Biber 2013, 316). I began with individuals I knew, and they in turn made recommendations regarding others knowledgeable on the topic. In this chapter, I draw from thirty oral history interviews. I conducted these interviews via Skype (from 2017 until the first half of 2019), and in person, during 2019–2020. My main focus is on the stories of women, but I also spoke with others who provided contextual information about the liberation movement and Namibian history in general.

For ease of organization, I will categorize women's contributions either as combat and military-related roles, or as those aligning more closely with "caring" roles. In doing so, Namibian women's contributions are certainly not exhaustively covered in these two groupings. My aim rather is to achieve greater recognition for the ways in which Namibian women made independence possible. Combat or military-related roles included military training, actual combat roles on the front lines of the struggle, military supervision, strategy, operations, intelligence and leadership, medical assistance on the battlefield and in refugee and military camps, and leading activism in-country in Namibia (vs. in exile). Caring roles encompass childcare for children of parents involved in the struggle, hiding and providing sustenance to pro-liberation fugitives, and organizing support such as food, material supplies, and emotional support for those detained as a result of their activism.

Military Combat

In terms of combat or military-related positions, women occupied many roles. They also deployed the perception of gender and societal gender norms in clever ways to further their cause. Women completed military training, and some joined the ranks of PLAN as combatants (Cleaver and Wallace 1990, 2). Women's direct contribution to the struggle took the form of combat, leadership, and intelligence, and also included contributions to services on the front, such as medical assistance.

As of 1974, the PLAN included women combatants in its ranks (Becker 2001, 228; Soiri 1996, 76). As Nambadi (2016) states, "The success of PLAN fighters . . . was mainly made possible by the determination and bravery of women" (98). One woman I interviewed, "Rinouua," commented that in PLAN, "The platoon leader (could) be a woman. So . . . a woman gives orders" ("Rinouua," interview with author, November 4, 2019). Rinouua also shared with me the sense of gender equality she felt during the struggle. Rather than woman or man, she said, "It was comrade—it wasn't like you are ladies or women . . . you are comrade. It was all comradeship" (Interview with author, November 4, 2019). "Sara" described how women took on combatant roles, "Those who went out let's say in Angola, Zambia, they were fighting, fighting, on the front fighting with the guns" (Interview with author, October 10, 2017). "Isabel" was a dynamic leader who managed a great number of responsibilities and made a significant contribution to the struggle. She shared with me the following:

> My role really was in leadership! I went into the strategic planning for the party, together . . . with (the) young men . . . we would plan and do strategies and carry them out. We would plan public rallies and so on. . . . My role really was to create information and raise awareness and make our people understand and work on the ground. So that was really my passion, to make sure that our people knew what they were fighting for and where we were going and our vision and so I spent most of my time mobilizing the community, informing them, and then protecting them, analyzing for them what is happening and how it is happening. ("Isabel," interview with author, October 19, 2017)

Isabel's testimony echoes what other scholars have written about Namibian women's contributions to the struggle. Cleaver and Wallace (1990) emphasize the broad range of women's roles during the struggle: "Women played a significant role in all aspects of SWAPO organization, including that of active combat. That women refused to be restricted to supportive functions, such as medics and couriers, but were fully trained and equipped as combatants, is clear evidence of a change in the perception of women's role within the movement" (Cleaver and Wallace, 6). Women also upheld their comrades by working as medical professionals, attending to wounded soldiers, and sometimes using their positions as nurses to good effect by stealing medicine and other materials for guerilla fighters (Akawa 2014, 43; Temu and Tembe 2014, 170). The *Hashim Mbita Project* documents many accounts of female combatants, such as Sara Kuugongelwa-Amadhila's active role on the military front as a PLAN combatant (Temu and Tembe 2014, 352). SWAPO selected many women for advanced military training (411). All of these roles were filled with great risk, and women participated "knowing very well that their loyalty to the liberation struggle could cost them their lives" (Namhila 2009, 47), because during this time, anyone believed to be assisting PLAN jeopardized their lives (Nambadi 2016, 95–96). Such risk and sacrifices were offset by women's commitment toward political change and freedom. As Isabel mentioned, doing this work was her passion, driven by a shared vision toward independence.

Frontline activism also came with risk; liberation fighters were jailed or under constant threat of imprisonment by the apartheid regime's South African Defense Force. "Celine" participated in an antiapartheid demonstration and was jailed:

> It was about 10 women and about 11 men or so. We went to picket . . . in front of the post office and we were jailed. . . . They took us in on . . . a Saturday morning. And we were released on the Monday because we had good lawyers . . . they said it was (*an*) illegal gathering. Even a weekend (*in jail*) is already bad enough! (Interview with author, December 9, 2019)

"Celine" also shared with me that she and others suffered from the emotional trauma of the constant fear "that you could be thrown into jail all the time." By underlining the many diverse forms of labor that were present, and acknowledging that they were all equally valuable, a more complete liberation struggle historiography is revealed.

"Caring" Roles

In addition to participating in the military, women also served in caring roles by providing protection, shelter, supplies, and emotional support. When the South African Defense Forces (SADF) unjustly arrested antiapartheid activists, women banded together and organized food packages, reading material, and visits for prisoners. Women provided support and organized networks to assist these people and show solidarity. As Isabel shared with me, "When strugglers were arrested . . . women would organize and provide hospital or prison visits. They would provide support and organize networks to assist these people and show solidarity" ("Isabel," interview with author, July 18, 2019). Other women harbored fugitives and provided food and shelter to combatants (Kudumo and Silvester 2016, 92–93; Namhila 2009, 59–89). "Sara" confirmed women's role in caring for combatants:

> The women played a major role in the liberation of Namibia in many . . . ways. Even ordinary village women, not only their sons, the freedom fighters, they hid them. They provided hiding places for them, for their guns, they gave them information. (Interview with author, October 10, 2017)

These unsung heroes provided countless hours of physical toil and emotional labor, and ultimately provided the unseen work that made Namibian liberation possible.

Other caring acts played out in the realms of medical care and general support for fellow comrades. During the struggle, nurses sometimes stole medicine for PLAN fighters so that combatants could obtain the necessary medical care (Nambadi 2016, 103). Others worked in domestic or care roles supporting the movement and tending to the children in the guerilla camps (Akawa 2014, 60–61). Sharing parenting roles took different forms depending on if the strugglers were in the rural or urban environments. "Celine" was an activist in Windhoek (Namibia's capital city) and described how parents there worked together: "When the fathers are in jail, then those of us who had (*driver's*) licenses could now help to pick up their kids and drop them at school, because as you know, there's no reliable public transport here" (Interview with author, December 9, 2019). Older comrades also mentored younger women activists: "As women, we also encouraged women to join the struggle. We were sort of like role models for the younger people" ("Celine," interview with author, December 9, 2019). In considering such caring roles, it is clear that the boundaries between the quotidian and the extraordinary cannot be sharply demarcated. Through these women we see a myriad of ways in which they employed a wide range of caring techniques and methods to support the liberation struggle.

The Deployment of Gender

In a fusion of the military realm and the world of "care" most often attributed to traditional feminine gender norms, activists and militants in many contexts "deploy gender" in creative ways to meet their objectives. The strategic deployment of gender is a strategy that has been well documented (Cock 1992; Cockburn 2001, 2007; de Volo 2018; Turshen 2016; Turshen and Twagiramariya 1998). Consider the case of Helena Ndapuka, a SWAPO activist who manipulated perceptions of gender to her advantage when she hid "a petrol bomb and matches in (her) handbag" (Temu and Tembe 2014, 425). Tactically, women may use pregnancy as a cover for smuggling weapons, or they may be more effective at planting bombs or landmines because they attract less attention than men. A Namibian scholar shared with me that during the struggle, women would wrap boxes of medicine on their back, easily slipping past SADF soldiers who assumed they were carrying their babies on their backs. Similarly, Cock (1992) found that in opposing apartheid, "Women were used a lot as decoys and couriers . . . they were used a lot to smuggle arms and explosives" (230). Women cleverly manipulated gendered stereotypes, using them to their advantage to assist with the storage and movement of weapons (Nghidinwa 2008, 44). One of the men I interviewed, "Alatinius," confirmed such occurrences:

> The South Africans, when they see women carrying the basket, they don't worry about that, thinking it is only men who can carry arms. But some of these women, they are carrying baskets on their head . . . taking food to SWAPO soldiers. Some would be carrying some supplies to help those people, so they can liberate the country. (Interview with author, November 6, 2017)

During the Namibian struggle, women "were the ones giving shelter, water, and information to our freedom fighters" (Temu and Tembe 2014, 377). Women cooked for PLAN fighters and "used to call the PLAN fighters their children" (Temu and Tembe 2014, 501). They embraced their maternal roles as part of their contribution to the antiapartheid struggle and engaged perceptions of gender in clever, unique ways to advance liberation. Women's deployment of gender is yet again another example of the ways in which we witness the quotidian surfacing in ways that, though they initially appear mundane, upon closer inspection reveal a deft combination of the extraordinary in the everyday—in this case via the vehicle of gender norms being put to good use to further the independence struggle.

THE DOUBLE JEOPARDY OF WOMEN AT WAR

Further compounding Namibian women's involvement in the liberation movement was the idea of "double jeopardy." This concept was coined by African American sociologist Deborah King to characterize the multiple, compounding effects of racism and sexism inflicted upon black women (King 1988). During the Namibian antiapartheid struggle, women combatants were doubly targeted: first, for the dehumanizing status assigned to them by the racist apartheid regime, and second, for their gendered identity as female soldiers. Many scholars have described sexual violence and the heightened stakes of double jeopardy that it created for Namibian women combatants during the struggle (Akawa 2014; Britton and Shook 2014; Turshen and Twagiramariya 1998).

The reality of double jeopardy was equally present in the oral history interviews that I have conducted. One woman confided in me that "It's always the question of, when women and men work together . . . traveling, and over weekends we have to camp out. . . . There (were) always some of the older men that took advantage of the younger women . . . we had to really fight hard against that and say, 'If you say that you are a freedom fighter, then you're not supposed to do these things'" ("Celine," interview with author, December

9, 2019). "Surihe" corroborated a climate of double jeopardy that was present during the struggle:

> You were seen maybe as a sex object. That the senior commanders would approach you and when you don't want or if you refuse to give them that sexual favor, then you will be punished directly or indirectly. You will not maybe have opportunities like another person who has given that favor—who would be sent maybe for additional scholarships. Or to be taken out of that camp where you are. The time I was still in the military training, soldiers would come to our parades.[1] And they will stand around there and they would call you and would want to propose (*proposition*) you. . . . I was called out in a parade, and warned, that I must listen to comrade. Because comrades want to talk to me, and I am refusing to talk to them. And I knew why they wanted to talk to me; that is why I didn't want to talk to them! And then that in itself became a crime. (Interview with author, November 1, 2019)

Surihe stated, "Even in the dungeons where some women gave birth to the guards' children—uh, I wouldn't call that consensual. It was a power play."[2] Surihe also spoke of her friend who "(went into) exile at a young age of 16 or 17 years of age . . . She was at the front (and) was abused by this senior commander. This is something that has stuck with her . . . she has that trauma in her, where she was abused by an elder man. That was way older than her— maybe 20 years difference. Just because he has the power!" Despite such threats, women formed invisible networks of support to protect each other. Akawa (2014) has written extensively about these networks, for example, in the ways in which older women comrades warned younger, newer recruits of the dangers of unwanted sexual advances (110). By forming such networks, women were able to take strides toward ensuring their own and others' safety. In studying Namibian history and women in the liberation struggle, it would be an incomplete account without considering women's increased risk due to the double jeopardy that they faced. In the context of war, double jeopardy compounded women's experiences, creating heightened levels of danger and oppression due to the women's intersectional identities as black individuals living under the racist and violent system of apartheid, and as women combatants at risk of sexual violence at the hands of their male comrades.

Given the heightened stress of double jeopardy outlined above, Namibian women were "everyday heroes" during the antiapartheid struggle. Women hid strugglers, provided them with food and supplies, and worked covertly within networks to organize protests and other antiapartheid actions. Consistently, women were much more than passive victims in need of protection; they were on the front lines of battle and key to the underground movement. They faced violence, uncertainty, and possible death throughout the war. Goldblatt and

Meintjes perfectly sum up this amalgamation when they write, "Even though the women's role in resistance often saw them defined within their maternal function, women used this definition as a means of lifting themselves out of the private realm and entering the public arena" (1998, 233). As I discuss, the public arena often meant combat and military roles. It is in documenting and appreciating all facets of contributions to the struggle, including women's "behind the scenes" as well as their frontline roles, that we can come to more fully understand and appreciate the entirety of the antiapartheid struggle history.

CONCLUSION

Namibian women propelled the liberation movement forward in ways both overtly heroic and in ways more subtle and understated. Employing the categories of quotidian and extraordinary, I have asserted the importance of Namibian women's contributions to the liberation struggle. Women were military combatants fulfilling many various positions and also contributed vital "caring" work such as childcare, nursing, and teaching. All of these contributions are equally important. In the realm of the extraordinary, women fought on the front lines of battle, trained other soldiers, and organized and deployed military strategies. Equally vital were the "caring roles" such as managing households, raising children, caring for cattle and other livestock, and generally keeping their families and communities together. Far from being done in isolation, women banded together and formed ingenious support networks to advance the liberation struggle, and to keep their families and communities intact in the meantime. Further complicating women's everyday achievements was the fact that their work was done in a state of continual uncertainty and danger. Women's contributions to PLAN, as well as their maintenance of domestic and community spheres during a time of great danger and uncertainty, is a key factor which made the Namibian liberation struggle successful.

Namibian women are the unsung heroes of the liberation struggle. We see in these women the transformative potential of the everyday. The examples discussed in this chapter work toward a more complete and nuanced understanding of southern African and antiapartheid historiography, while highlighting women's contributions therein. In this way, the strong, creative ways in which women activists propelled the antiapartheid movement forward will hopefully emerge more clearly from the annals of history.

Providing a more complete history of the antiapartheid struggle which documents and highlights the contributions of women is important for a number of reasons. First, these contributions provide compelling historical accounts that accentuate the central place of Namibian women in antiapartheid history. Second, the oral history stories of Namibian women during the struggle illustrate the ways in which the quotidian became extraordinary due to the context of war. They furthermore bring to light the intense challenge of their "double jeopardy." Third, these narratives also provide evidence of women blurring gender norms and creating enduring ruptures to gender norms in southern Africa.

Lastly, a more complete and nuanced account of Namibian women's contributions in ways both quotidian and extraordinary can motivate and inspire women today. Isabel underlined this when I spoke to her in a follow-up interview: "I have a deep belief that (*the situation in Namibia*) can be different. If things are good, they can be much, much better. And if they are not good, it can be changed . . . I am not really afraid . . . to take on challenges" ("Isabel," interview with author, January 6, 2020). We gain courage from learning about these pioneers' resilience and ability to transcend and transform a deeply oppressive and violent reality. These interventions offer evidence that Namibian women of the past have provided a roadmap for ways in which to exert their power and wisdom to craft the futures they envision. Furthermore, these narratives of resilience trouble problematic realities of high rates of GBV and femicide in Namibia and globally. As this edited volume speaks to, these accounts point to women's agency and ability to realize better lives for themselves, their families, and their communities. As Sara declared, during the struggle "you knew that you could die at any time, but you just accepted it and went about your life. We were committed to a cause much greater than ourselves." Sara and many others fought for, and achieved, a free Namibia. Meintjes et al. (2001) assert that "conflict opens up intended and unintended spaces for empowering women, affecting structural social transformations and producing new social, economic and political realities that redefine gender and caste hierarchies" (7). By offering ourselves as students to these leaders of the past, we can harness the possibilities outlined by these unsung heroes who have so often been omitted, but who rightfully deserve their places in the history books.

NOTES

1. In this context, "parade" refers to a morning gathering organized by SWAPO during the struggle in their military camps to set the agenda for the coming day.

2. While somewhat contested by various political leaders in Namibia, scholars have documented the abuse and torture of Namibians who were accused of being spies while in exile in military camps. For more information, refer to Groth (1995).

REFERENCES

Akawa, Martha. 2014. *The Gender Politics of the Namibian Liberation Struggle.* Basel: Basler Afrika Bibliographien.

"Alatinius" (pseudonym used). Interview by author. Digital recording. Lawrence, KS, USA (conducted via Skype with individual in Windhoek, Namibia), November 6, 2017.

Becker, Heike. 1995. *Namibian Women's Movement, 1980 to 1992: From Anti-Colonial Resistence to Reconstruction.* Oslo: IKO.

Becker, Heike. 2001. "'We Want Women to Be Given an Equal Chance': Post-Independence Rural Politics in Northern Namibia." In *The Aftermath: Women in Post-conflict Transformation*, edited by Sheila Meintjes, Anu Pillay, and Meredith Turshen. London and New York: Zed Books.

Borchorst, Anette. 2009. "Women-Friendly Policy Paradoxes? Childcare Policies and Gender Equality Visions in Scandinavia." In *Gender Equality and Welfare Politics in Scandinavia: The Limits of Political Ambition?*, edited by Kari Melby and Christina Carlsson Wetterberg, 27–43. Bristol: Policy Press.

Borland, Elizabeth, and Barbara Sutton. 2007. "Quotidian Disruption and Women's Activism in Times of Crisis: Argentina 2002–2003." *Gender & Society* 21(5): 700–722.

Britton, Hannah, and Lindsey Shook. 2014. ""I Need to Hurt You More": Namibia's Fight to End Gender-Based Violence." *Signs: Journal of Women in Culture and Society* 40(1): 153–175.

Campt, Tina. 2012. *Image Matters: Archive, Photography, and the African Diaspora in Europe.* Durham: Duke University Press.

"Celine" (pseudonym used). Interview by author. Digital recording. Windhoek, Namibia, December 9, 2019.

Cleaver, Tessa, and Marion Wallace. 1990. *Namibia: Women and War.* London: ZED.

Cock, Jacklyn. 1992. *Women and War in South Africa.* Bullock: Pilgrim Press.

Cockburn, Cynthia. 2001. "The Gendered Continuum of Violence and Conflict: An Operational Framework." In *Victims, Perpetrators or Actors? Gender, Armed Conflict and Political Violence*, edited by Caroline O.N. Moser and Fiona C. Clark. London: Zed Books.

Cockburn, Cynthia. 2007. *From Where We Stand: War, Women's Activism and Feminist Analysis.* London: Zed Books.

de Volo, Lorraine Bayard. 2018. *Women and the Cuban Insurrection: How Gender Shaped Castro's Victory.* Cambridge: Cambridge University Press.

Goldblatt, Beth, and Sheila Metinjes. 1998. "A Gender Perspective on Violence During the Struggle Against Apartheid." In *Violence in South Africa: A Variety of Perspectives*, edited by Elirea Bornman and Yvonne Muthien. Pretoria: HSRC Press.

Groth, Siegfried. 1995. *Namibia, The Wall of Silence: The Dark Days of the Liberation Struggle.* Wuppertal: Peter Hammer Verlag.

Hesse-Biber, Sharlene Nagy. 2013. *Feminist Research Practice: A Primer.* Newbury Park: Sage Publications.

History. n.d. "League of Nations (website)." Accessed September 10, 2019. https://www.history.com/topics/world-war-i/league-of-nations

"Isabel (interview 1)" (pseudonym used). Interview by author. Digital recording. Lawrence, KS, USA (conducted via Skype with individual in Windhoek, Namibia), October 19, 2017.

"Isabel (interview 2)" (pseudonym used). Interview by author. Digital recording. Chicago, IL, USA (conducted via Skype with individual in Windhoek, Namibia), July 18, 2019.

"Isabel (interview 3)" (pseudonym used). Interview by author. Digital recording. Windhoek, Namibia, January 16, 2020.

King, Deborah K. 1988. "Multiple Jeopardy, Multiple Consciousness: The Context of a Black Feminist Ideology." *Signs: Journal of Women in Culture and Society* 14(1): 42–72.

Kudumo, Marius, and Jeremy Silvester. 2016. *Resistance on the Banks of the Kavango River.* Windhoek: Museums Association of Namibia.

Meintjes, Sheila, Anu Pillay, and Meredith Turshen. 2001. *The Aftermath: Women in Post-Conflict Transformation.* London and New York: Zed Books.

Muwati, Itai, and Zifikile Gambahaya. 2012. "The Private/Public Space Dichotomy: An Africana Womanist Analysis of the Gendering of Space and Power." *Western Journal of Black Studies* 36(2): 100.

Nambadi, Aaron. 2016. "Resistance on the Banks of the Kavango River." In *Resistance on the Banks of the Kavango River*, edited by Marius Silvester and Jeremy Kudumo, 92–104. Windhoek: Museums Association of Namibia.

Namhila, Ellen Ndeshi. 2009. *Tears of Courage: Five Mothers, Five Stories, One Victory.* Archives of Anti-Colonial Resistance and the Liberation Struggle Project.

Namhila, Ellen Ndeshi. 2013. *Mukwahepo: Women Soldier Mother.* Windhoek: University of Namibia Press.

Nghidinwa, Maria Mboono. 2008. *Women Journalists in Namibia's Liberation Struggle, 1985–1990.* Basel: Basler Afrika Bibliographien.

Palmary, Ingrid. 2003. "Family Resistances: Women, War and the Family in the African Great Lakes." *Annual Review of Critical Psychology* 4: 54–65.

Perec, Georges. 1997. *Species of Spaces and Other Pieces.* London: Penguin.

"Riann" (pseudonym used). Interview by author. Digital recording. Windhoek, Namibia (conducted via Skype with individual in Cape Town, South Africa), November 22, 2019.

"Rinouua" (pseudonym used). Interview by author. Digital recording. Windhoek, Namibia, November 4, 2019.

"Sara" (pseudonym used). Interview by author. Digital recording. Lawrence, KS, USA (conducted via Skype with individual in Windhoek, Namibia), October 10, 2017.

Sargisson, Lucy. 2001. "Politicising the Quotidian." *Environmental Politics* 10(2): 68–89.

Silvester, Jeremy. 2015. *Re-viewing Resistance in Namibian History.* Windhoek: University of Namibia Press.

Soiri, Iina. 1996. *The Radical Motherhood: Namibian Women's Independence Struggle.* Vol. 99. Uppsala: Nordic Africa Institute.

"Surihe" (pseudonym used). Interview by author. Digital recording. Windhoek, Namibia, November 1, 2019.

Temu, Arnold, and Joel Tembe. 2014. *Southern African Liberation Struggles: Contemporaneous Documents 1960–1994.* Vol. 3. SADC Hashim Mbita Project. Dar es Salaam: Mkuki ya Nyota.

Thornberry, Cedric. 2004. *A Nation Is Born: The Inside Story of Namibia's Independence.* London: Gamsberg Macmillan Publishers.

Turshen, Meredeth. 2002. "Algerian Women in the Liberation Struggle and the Civil War: From Active Participants to Passive Victims?" *Social Research: An International Quarterly* 69(2): 889–911.

Turshen, Meredeth. 2016. *Gender and the Political Economy of Conflict in Africa: The Persistence of Violence.* Abingdon-on-Thames: Routledge.

Turshen, Meredeth, and Clotilde Twagiramariya. 1998. *What Women Do in Wartime: Gender and Conflict in Africa.* London: ZED.

Wallace, Marion, and John Kinahan. 2011. *A History of Namibia.* London: C. Hurst & Co.

Wetterberg, Christina Carlsson, and Kari Melby. 2009. "The Claim of Economic Citizenship: The Concept of Equality in a Historical Context." In *Gender Equality and Welfare Politics in Scandinavia: The Limits of Political Ambition?*, edited by Kari Melby and Christina Carlsson Wetterberg, 27–43. Bristol: Policy Press.

Chapter 9

Finding Home

Displaced African Women in Rural Southwest Kansas

Debra J. H. Bolton

INTRODUCTION

This chapter explores the African diaspora, specifically its women, in Southwest Kansas, United States. This region boasts a history of being *that* place where people come to find their riches, be it on the railroads, in irrigation water systems (Blanchard 1931), in livestock or crops, in meat processing (Stull 1990), in land development or in other industries (Sanderson 2014) that depend on human capital for operations. Garden City, a hub of Southwest Kansas city, is considered a "best place" by market researchers, possessing economic viability, boasting low unemployment, and living costs 18 percent lower than national average.[1] Demographers state (Sandoval et al. 2012) that these characteristics tend to be a natural pull factor for refugee and other migrants looking for a place to settle. After large-scale beef processing operations moved into Southwest Kansas in the early part of the 1980s (Stull 1990), the region became, and continues to be, a place where refugees from war-torn countries receive offers of sponsorships by churches, families, and social service entities. Not unlike other market citizenship[2] economies (Grace, Nawyn, and Okwako 2017), new arrivals to Southwest Kansas quickly accept employment opportunities in the meat processing industries.

In the 1980s, Southwest Kansas received refugees from Southeast Asia (Stull, Broadway, and Griffith 1995), and by the mid-1990s, African refugees began to arrive following conflicts in Somalia, Ethiopia, Uganda, and Kenya. Ongoing conflicts in the twenty-first century in Eritrea, the Democratic Republic of Congo, Sudan, Chad, and Burundi resulted in increased numbers of both individuals and families seeking refuge in Southwest Kansas, resembling trends in other Midwestern U.S. American states, including Michigan (Grace et al. 2017) and Minnesota (Heger Boyle and Ali 2010; Kebba 2003). In addition to populations from seven Asian countries and six Meso, Central, and South American countries (Bolton and Dick 2013), the African diaspora in Southwest Kansas adds to a region labeled as *Majority-Minority*,[3] meaning that ethnic minorities comprise the *majority* of the population. This rural region's population tends to reflect metropolitan areas, but since the nearest major city is 300 miles, Stull and Ng (2016) label it as *a micropolitan*.[4] While many metropolitan regions designate as *Majority-Minority* (Frey 2011) or nearing such a standing (Grace et al. 2017), few rural communities with *Majority-Minority* status emerge to compare with Southwest Kansas' demographics (Lichter 2012) as economic hope for small towns and the most important demographic change in the past twenty years. This chapter contributes to developing knowledge of the diaspora of African women settling in rural Midwestern United States (Grace et al. 2017). More specifically, exploring quantitative data and rich narratives collected between 2008 and 2017, this research sought to answer questions about the health, well-being, social networks, and community integration of African women living in Southwest Kansas.

Developing and maintaining social connections is integral to communities' social well-being. According to political scientist Robert Putnam (2000), people from differing backgrounds learn to trust one another and build social networks upon which they can call in times of need and return those favors, known as reciprocity (Elliot and Yusuf 2014), when needed. Putnam made the argument that people's limited ability to connect to others with differing levels of access to good and services can threaten livelihoods. Establishing and maintaining social connections, or *social capital*, on the other hand, can strengthen people's livelihoods and overall social well-being. I use a social capital framework to illustrate a sense of resilience among women of the African diaspora. Such resilience links to the advantages of bonding social capital, resulting from intragroup connections and the celebration of common identities, and bridging social capital, that emerges from social networking and connectivity between different groups of people. The establishment and strengthening of such networks tend to support individual feelings of safety, well-being, and even job acquisition (Coleman 1988, 1994). Social networks also increase people's collective access to vital human services (Glaeser 2001) and can facilitate better social and communal integration (Elliot and Yusuf 2014). The theoretical construct of social capital therefore speaks to increased emotional support, the benefits of social support systems, trust, and connections through individual and collective networks. As a theoretical framework, the concepts of social networking, and accompanying social capital, helped me to observe the women through objective lenses in my interactions, data gathering, and analyses over time.

About twenty-three years of interaction with and study of rural Southwest Kansas migrant communities allowed me the opportunity to become acquainted with women from the African diaspora. In this chapter, I draw specifically from these experiences (Bolton and Dick 2013, 2017; Bolton and Hernandez 2017). My first twelve years of working with the women took place in an adult education center, where the women came to learn English, socialize, and continue the educational process toward high school diplomas. My former students and recently arrived migrants continue to settle with their families. Families who came ten years ago make connections to recently arrived families as they all work to integrate with the dominant Anglo cultures and other ethnicities that represent the majority demographic of Southwest Kansas (Bolton and Dick 2013; Frey 2011). In the process of acculturation[5] these women describe their feelings of an unprecedented sense of safety and peace, though they remain traumatized by the long-term effects of war, human rights abuses, hunger, and poverty.

Narratives collected during these times together with supportive quantitative data allowed me to consider the women's experiences as migrants. What were the financial and emotional costs (Nikolova and Graham 2015)? Was it worth it? I had other questions around their "settling in." What are their roles in the acculturation of their families to rural life in Southwest Kansas? What are their individual methods of navigating social, political, health, educational, and employment systems (Zuccotti et al. 2017)? How do they address their social needs while working to earn livelihoods for their respective families? (Hendriks and Bartram 2019). By analyzing these narratives, I sought to capture the hopes and aspirations of women in the African diaspora in terms of finding ways out of poverty, addressing their fears, attending to traumas of the past and present—all while establishing social networks (Putnam 2000; Coleman 1994) and building their lives in communities quite different from their countries of origin. In their stories, I recognize a remarkable resilience in the face of devastating challenges. I echo Gersmehl's (2014) claim that such resilience marks migrant women's lives as they find sense of place in a new homeland.

HUMAN DISPLACEMENT AND EMIGRATION

To understand the reality of African emigration to rural areas in the U.S. American Midwest, we must acknowledge the conditions that brought us to this point. The combination of war and accompanying malfunctioning state structures force individuals and families to flee their home countries. This includes the conflict that won Eritrea its independence in 1991, together with violence in Ethiopia, Somalia, and Burundi in the 1990s. Also culpable is the mid-1990s fighting in Uganda and continued conflict in South Sudan and the Democratic Republic of Congo in the 1990s and 2000s. These conflicts extend into the present, contributing to the dismal conditions of *forced displacement* (Crisp 2010; McLoughlin 2015, 343; Misago and Landau 2005). In addition to violent conflict and war, people continue to be subjected to ineffective and/or nonfunctioning state structures. In *Survival Migration,* Alexander Betts (2013) offers a strong statement about such states and the breakdown of responsibility toward their citizens. Betts asserts, "Through malevolence, incompetence, or lack of capacity, many governments cease to ensure that their citizens have access to fundamental conditions for human dignity" (1). Betts adds that when people cannot access basic human rights and feel threatened in the process, they seek alternative solutions. As a result, people subjected to forced displacement tend to live with ongoing stressors such as fear, harm, poverty, and general vulnerability (Kaplan 2016). In these conditions, as Krause (2015) argues, women experience particularly high levels of trauma, including sexual and other forms of physical and emotional violence.

Facing few alternatives, displaced people often seek refuge in other countries, including the United States. They emigrate with hopes for an end to their struggles and the possibility of, eventually, improving their lives; the first sign of optimism comes from offers for political asylum. As Emma shared (Emma with Debra Bolton, Garden City, 2018) and emerging from other scholars (Monsour 2019), the emigrant finds that receiving asylum tends to be followed by the realization of leaving what is familiar to make a journey to an unknown land while contemplating other trials that may lie ahead.

African Emigration and Southwest Kansas

Kansas continues to offer resettlement to groups of Somali and other African immigrants to its rural Southwestern communities, because of the demand for unskilled labor within agricultural food production (Brown 2018).[6] Southwest Kansas counties receiving African migrants, include the counties of Ford, Finney, Seward, Gray, Kearny, and Grant. I focus only on Finney County (population 36,611) because it appears to be the most welcoming to immigrants. Many attributed such openness to the city's progressive government and its history of receiving Hispanic and German immigrants since the early 1920s (Blanchard 1931; Stull 1990; Broadway and Stull 2006). Newspapers, social media publications, and other news outlets continue to cover this region's unique approach to integrating refugees and other immigrants. Filmmakers Steve Lerner and Reuben Aronson's 2019 film *Strangers in Town* tells the story of newcomers and continues to be shown on university campuses, in civic settings, and at film festivals. The filmmakers worked hard to draw from a representative sample of the community's inhabitants, including a short clip with me, this chapter's author, speaking about the concepts of social integration. The film focuses on the long history of Garden City, specifically, and its welcoming spirit. This includes the community's coming together when a near tragedy hit the Somali community, an event discussed later in this chapter.

However, not all Southwest Kansas communities have the welcoming spirit like that of Garden City. For example, Ford County and its county seat, Dodge City, displayed examples of segregation by housing refugees and other immigrants in a part of the county set away from the city proper (Sandoval and Jennings 2012; Ott 2011). Ford County received attention on state and national news because it provided only one polling place for the entire community, of nearly 34,000, set outside the city for the 2018 city and state elections, according to a KWCH television news report on November 1, 2018. After the backlash, the city offered rides for voters via radio and television. Regardless of these challenges, people seeking political asylum still see opportunity in Southwest Kansas (Bolton and Dick 2013; Bolton and Hernandez 2017; Stull and Broadway 1995; Stull and Ng 2016) as it provides peace and safety, and job security.

Similar anti-immigrant sentiments also arose in 2017 when Garden City residents became concerned over the possible economic ramifications imposed by Trump administration on so-called sanctuary cities and states actively recruiting workers from so-called Third World Countries. In the *Garden City Telegram* of February 10, 2017, Finney County sheriff Kevin Bascue stated that while the Center for Immigration Studies has the county listed as a "sanctuary city," Immigration and Customs Enforcement (ICE) does not. The newspaper article noted that sanctuary cities have no precise definition, but some communities tend to adopt the designation to signify protection of undocumented immigrants.

While such challenges reflect whole communities, looking at what confronts the African women in the process of integration helps in understanding individual social, emotional, and financial costs and gains in emigrating from one place to another. Is it rational to ask migrants coming from war-torn countries and arriving with low skills and in extreme poverty to be self-sufficient in six months? (Nawyn 2010). Do we understand the creativity it takes to navigate and build networks that, ultimately, contribute to well-being? Collectively, building social networks, in terms of community involvement, contributes to skills development and expanding capacity for "increasing tolerance among people and supporting actions for strengthening autonomy" (McBride et al. 2006, 152). Because migrant women have double expectations of providing economically for their families (jobs), and raising children to be productive citizens (childcare), scholars argue that structural inequities are inherent in the system's requirements of being self-sufficient in six months. What does a migrant mother omit in her efforts to meet the requirements? She cannot forego employment to care for her family. She cannot care for her family efficiently when the only work available to her requires non-family-friendly work schedules. These challenges require resilience, which comes from persistence, which Hendriks and Bartram (2018) call one of the most important strategies of migrants to integrate into their host communities. As seen in the narratives, the joys of their new lives mixed with the effects of previously experienced trauma contribute to a complicated process of social integration for both "economic" (J. Thome, personal interview, 2017) and political refugees (Ndika 2013). Of key importance to the broader receiving community remains an understanding that acculturation does not happen overnight. Effective integration and acculturation stands as an interactive and continuous process (Lakey 2003, 105) that evolves in and through communication between the newcomer and their new sociocultural environments. Researchers agree that migrants in Southwest Kansas, work hard to integrate into communities quite unlike their own places of origin. Perhaps we may allow ourselves to learn from them about resilience in the face of challenges, if we simply listen to their stories.

STORYTELLERS AND RESEARCHERS

While Southwest Kansas remains a favorite site of exploration for scholars interested in, among others, social dynamics, immigration, and rural development, most conduct their studies in English (Easterling et al. 2007; Bolton and Hernandez 2017; Stull and Ng 2016). While a small percentage conduct studies in Spanish (Sanderson 2013; Lerner 2019; Bolton 2011; Bolton and Dick 2017), few consider the myriad of other languages spoken in the region. Equally important, scholars have yet to collect the stories of women from the African diaspora currently living in this region.

Collecting data in the respondents' native tongues proves to be powerful because it gives respondents an opportunity to tell personal stories in their own languages (Cenoz and Gorter 2019), especially when answering questions on delicate topics (Lee, Sulaiman-Hill, and Thompson 2014). Sociologist Matthew Sanderson (2014) speaks to the advantages of gathering data using respondents' first language. He asserts, "Language gives us the ability to 'see' (or not 'see') the world around us by placing socially-agreed upon words on things . . . (ideas, thoughts, material objects, etc.). Speaking with people in their native languages allows us to 'see' their world from their perspectives" (personal communication, March 2015). This emphasis on seeing the world through people's native languages, encouraged my approach to data collection.

A further impetus for gathering data in respondents' mother tongues came from a social capital study completed in 2007 by Easterling and their colleagues. Among four other communities across Kansas, the group focused their work on Garden City, Finney County. To participate, respondents had to speak English and possess a landline telephone, a method that favored the dominant culture, which is not the majority, and led to limited participation by immigrant groups (Bolton and Dick 2013). My research sought to include what the Easterling et al.'s (2007) study excluded—the voice of the *majority*, as opposed to the dominant culture's perceptions about the underrepresented[7] groups.

In addition, I chose to bring to light the lives and experiences of women living in these rural communities. While scholars have been interested in Southwest Kansas' immigration patterns and populations, ranging from an interest in immigration and education (Stull and Ng 2016) to the region's employment sector (Stull, Broadway, and Griffiths 1995), the realities of women, particularly those of the African diaspora, remain absent. As Tippens (2019) argues, migrant women use strategies of persistence, their resilience moves communities away from deficit-centered approaches and toward strengths-based programming and research. Mental health experts (Kawachi and Berkman 2001) posit that focusing on the women's assets rather than deficits appears to be a more sustainable strategy toward integration, community-building, and community well-being. When we consider the socioeconomic and socioemotional hardships the women and their families undergo, displaced from their homelands because of governmental conflict, it becomes an opportunity to invite women to tell stories about their taking chances to build new lives in the United States.

METHODS

The data I reflect upon in this chapter was part of a larger mixed-methods study conducted from 2010 to 2017.[8] My colleagues and I recognized a need among human services providers, educational entities, and city governments who wanted to deliver health, social, learning, and governing services to newcomers in the most efficient and effective way possible. Furthermore, charitable foundations wanted to understand human needs in order to grant their contributions in ways that would do the "most good." These needs pointed to localized research that expanded beyond English and/or Spanish-speaking respondents. With input from the region's human services, educational services, governing, and other professionals working with new populations, we designed a survey instrument in 2011 to study social connections. In 2017, we enhanced the 2011 survey to inquire about health, well-being, and safety. We collected 1,168 completed surveys (N=712 female, and N=456 male), of which 62 were completed in focused groups, and 417 completed online. Interestingly, African males responded at a higher rate (8.6 percent) than females (2.91 percent). For more information on data collection, please see this endnote.[9]

During this time, we collected field notes from face-to-face interaction and conversations, and interview data from semistructured interviews. In total, we interviewed 152 respondents of which thirty-eight were African women. For the purpose of this study, I draw mostly from the latter data set. I use pseudonyms for all the women quoted in this study. The respondents signed informed consents written in their native tongue.

For the purpose of this chapter, I disaggregated demographic data to focus on African-born women who emigrated to the United States in the past twenty-five years. Among those African women now residing in Southwest Kansas, 57 percent earn between $12,000 and $24,999 per year, which places them below the poverty line.[10] Most of the respondents read, write, and consider themselves fluent in English (46 percent) and speak an average of three other languages. Yet, most do not have a high school diploma (75 percent). Those who possess an education and speak English tend to navigate systems with greater ease. Of the thirty-eight African women interviewed, one possesses a professional degree and four have bachelor's degrees. We did note that the women coming with refugee status, as opposed to those who came as professionals, did report not having access to education in their own countries. In many cases, the latter group lived much of their adult lives in refugee camps. Nevertheless, those who come with refugee status possess a strong sense of survival and persistence, though they appear to have some cultural, social, and economic challenges (Bolton and Dick 2013; Zuccoti et al. 2015; Bolton and Hernandez 2017).

The regions' schools often reflect higher immigrant population percentages than the overall community since the schools represent a smaller sample size as compared to whole communities. In a general glimpse, the region's schools have student populations ranging from 70.12 to 80.08 percent of students of color with African students making up 1.48 to 1.75 percent of the entire student populations. The same communities show no more than 2.89 percent of African persons, but do not disaggregate for those born in Africa. Instead, this population falls into the same category as African American (Census 2018; Kansas State Board of Education 2019). Researchers and governments estimate the numbers of African diaspora families based on school populations, adult education sites, employer estimations, and through general contacts for this research. With these estimations, my research partner and I

(Bolton and Dick 2016) arrived at 1,200-plus families living in Southwest Kansas with approximately 500 in Finney County.[11]

AFRICAN WOMEN'S STORIES OF ACCULTURATION

The process of acculturation challenges many women from the African diaspora. This includes learning the laws, learning English, navigating school systems, and understanding social expectations of their new environments. Scholars write extensively on the connection between acculturation and psychological stress, with such stress especially prominent among women (Okigbo et al. 2009; Ellis et al. 2016). Rigorous social expectations of finding immediate employment, tending to the family's health, nutritional, educational, and social needs do create stress and appear to fall on the female as head of household, even when a husband or partner is present (Grace et al. 2017; Nawyn 2010; Gutierrez-Rodriguez 2010). Nnenna Ndika (2013) notes that the process of acculturation illustrates a combination of factors related to stressful life changes, which affect physical and mental health as well as general well-being. The women interviewed agreed on the importance of finding ways to destress, which includes gathering for coffee and conversations. One noted that moments of leisure may give the perception of wrongdoing. As Dora from Eritrea shared: "When we gather for coffee in the morning, it may be two or three hours long. The property owners suspect that we are 'up to something.' We grew accustomed to socializing around many cups of coffee for lack of other activities in refugee camps." Dora went on to say that fitting into this new land, learning the customs and traditions of the people, and understanding how their specific African cultures either blend or clash with the "mainstream" tended to be the challenge for many of her peers (Interview, August 2017). Dora's experience illustrates one of the processes of *acculturation* (Patil et al. 2009). She carried the stresses of acquiring a job, providing for her child and husband, who works at the same meat processing plant as Dora, preparing familiar foods, when she has access, and unfamiliar, when offered through an assistance program. As a researcher and later a friend, I found Dora's story to be the most compelling in terms of fight, flight, and resilience. She grew to trust me, and always referred to me as *mama*, a term of respect and endearment. I observed Dora as a strong and vibrant woman possessing leadership skills. The other women respected and honored her. Dora plays prominently in more of this story as the chapter continues to unfold.

The term *acculturation* relates to the changes that happen to groups when two different cultures meet (Phillimore 2011). The focus here relates to the changes women of the African diaspora make to adapt to their new communities. The women take on a big part of this process. Intertwined with their responsibilities of caring for family; navigating the health, social, and educational systems; and earning their livelihoods come other processes that can be challenging (Ndika 2013). The first of which includes finding adequate care for their children during work hours.

Child Care

Using a social capital to frame the networks of migrant women (Tippens 2019; Elliott and Yusuf 2014), an understanding of the creativity in meeting the needs of their families begins to unfold. Mothers working in shifts in the meat processing industry struggle to find adequate childcare. Kansas has no law requiring parents to put their children into licensed childcare facilities; however, certified childcare carries with it an assurance of care standards that may not be followed when having friends or relatives caring for children. Those safety measures may include cardiopulmonary resuscitation training, childcare food programs to assure proper nutrition, child proofing of the facility or home, and other safety measures regulated by Health and Human Services. When the mothers work in shifts, they must rely on friends and acquaintances in their social networks to care for their children since many of the shifts at the meat processing plant require overnight hours (from 2:00 p.m. to 1:00 a.m.) or early hours that require parents to be at work before the children wake up. "The hours at the plant are not 'family friendly,'" said Dora. She considers this one of her fights in meeting the needs of family while meeting the requirements of her refugee status.

Dora's daughter, Melody, came with her mother to Southwest Kansas. Melody speaks five languages (Tigrinya, Amharic, Arabic, Maltese, and English), all learned with each move the family made along the way from Eritrea to the United States. Melody's fluency in English led my own path-way into meeting and learning from her family. I met Melody one day at a local coffee shop. She was with a man, and she began to talk to my friend and me. After a while, I asked if the man was her father. "No. He's watching me while my parents are at work," she responded. By U.S. standards, that may be perceived as less-than-optimal childcare. Dora later told me that she hardly knew the man, but he was from her country. She had to rely on her connections and ties to fellow country-people as a strategy to survive while making a place for her and her family. Mothers also look for after-school and summer activities for socialization and cognitive stimulation for their children. "We need after school and summer programs for the children that teach educational crafts and other projects while the children are not in school." "We do not want them watching television or spending all their free time on their mobile devices," said one young mother. Nikolova and Graham (2015) agree with Bolton and Hernandez (2017) that the requirements of their shift work jobs' non-family-friendly hours, caring for the family, navigating the social systems, and experiencing the stress of acculturation, leave the women challenged with lack of sleep and other health-threatening conditions. But for many, their newly acquired benefits outweigh the cost of migration. As Dora noted: "While tending to all these duties to see to our lives in the U.S. can be stressful, they don't amount to the stress of living in poverty and war with no opportunities, which is why we had to flee our country."

In addition to childcare, mothers must also consider their children's education. Zuccotti et al. (2014) argue that migrant parents' ability to navigate educational systems and act as guides and tutors influences their children's social and economic futures. In order to assure their children's education, migrant mothers in Southwest Kansas learn quickly how and where to enroll their children in school. They learn the rules for school regarding age of entry, immunizations, and school readiness. The migrant mothers, in this study, rely on their networks for increased knowledge through information sharing (McBride et al. 2006) by asking acquaintances and their community leaders to look for places to learn English, often to find that classes are full at the community colleges, churches, community learning centers, and other entities offering this service. "I was astonished at the types of questions asked when we were enrolling our child into preschool, such as, 'Is education important to you?' We also had to learn about car seat laws," said Anna (Personal interview, October 26, 2018). Anna noted that through an acquaintance, she received a brand-new car seat from the Kansas Highway Patrol office, which proved to be important since Kansas has a car seat law for children weighing fewer than eighty pounds. Anna, a nurse, came from Ethiopia with her two children and husband, who is an agricultural climatologist. She added, "Even with educations, we had so much to learn about life in the U.S." Anna's story exemplifies at least two realities and accompanying strategies applied by the women with whom I spoke. Moving into a new community requires migrants to become familiar with rules and regulations pertaining to childcare. Such information is not always readily available, but rather is shared through acquaintances and their social networks. The women use their social networks to learn more about the laws and regulations of their new environments, driven by their commitment to stay on the right side of the law. And through such sharing they also gain access to additional knowledge, street smarts, so to speak, not necessary gained through formal education.

Official Processes

Other acculturating activities include obtaining the proper identification, processing their refugee status, and obtaining a work visa. Initially, most refugee and other migrants work with state-sponsored social services' refugee resettlement programs (Nawyn 2010; Zuccotti et al. 2015) in a case management model. In the case of Southwest Kansas, the women of this study received case management for six to nine months with minimal financial supports. In addition, they used settlement services of the International Rescue Committee before its closure in 2018, which was a great loss to the migrant community. Emma observed how these formal resettlement services provided fertile spaces for women to establish and develop social links and connections. Those networks provided information about resources such as food and clothing pantries at the local indigent clinic and homeless shelter. Information gathered at the morning coffee rituals proved to be advantageous for services from the pregnancy center. Social connections established at these more formal places not only emulated women's more informal social networking but also encouraged further social networking opportunities. For example, coffee gathering in the homes emerges as bonding practices where the women feel empowered to seek connections outside their immediate groups.

Access to Special Foods

The African women in this study capitalize on the advantages of having social contacts among members of their receiving communities concerning survival and integration strategies (Flores 2006) with hopes of it ultimately leading to greater socioeconomic outcomes. Dora noted (personal communication July 2018) that she began connecting with the local health coalition's neighborhood learning center. She connected with the teachers and other students to learn English, to learn about social expectations, and to get the latest news about her community. The African Store functioned as a place to buy their cultural foods, like their tomato base for making *sugo* or teff, a grain native to Ethiopia ground and used for baking *enjere*, their bread. The African Store also stocked clothing, various culturally related items, and some *Halal* foods, needed for religious dietary restrictions, which can be a great challenge to find. To demonstrate a creative way to use social networks and meet dietary requirements, the African community found a local sheep farmer and a local butcher who found a way to slaughter and process a lamb to meet Halal requirements, which greatly demonstrated intercultural collaboration. This process involved a white sheep farmer, a Mexican butcher, and a Muslim leader (Imam) on the phone with the butcher. The Imam walked the butcher through the appropriate prayers before and after slaughter, proper bleeding, and a prayer before processing, in accordance with religious law. These social interactions exemplify an increase in trust and reciprocity, which according to Putnam (2000) are direct outcomes of social networking and manifestations of social capital.

Transportation

Transportation proves to be another trial in the process of acculturation (Zuccotti 2014). Mothers and partners learn about modes of transportation and safe places to walk when needing goods, human services, and educational connections for their local networks (Dora and Tani 2018). Garden City possesses a, mostly, convenient "mini-bus" system, which stops at grocery stores, department stores, health care facilities, schools, and other human service entities. It costs one dollar each way, and some can acquire vouchers for reduced or free rides. The bus routes run only hourly. None of the bus routes goes to the beef processing plant, which is five miles from town and employs most of the women in this study. Some of the women I spoke with noted that the bus routes run from 7:00 a.m. to 6:00 p.m., but not on weekends. Others who want to learn to drive may avail themselves of a local Catholic sister who often teaches immigrant women to drive. This need to drive themselves echoes Elliot and Yusuf (2014) and often leads to a sense of independence and wellness. Again, the women set goals to work toward independence (Dora 2018), while challenges continue to present themselves; she notes that persistence wins the day.

Health and Wellness

As part of one of the fastest growing populations in the United States, new data continues to emerge on the general health of African women who find homes in this country (Carrol et al. 2006). Adjusting to the concept of consuming health care services stands as a great challenge, especially when matters of family, housing, employment, and the processes of integration take precedence. The stories of wellness differ depending on the status of the immigrant as refugee or professional. Women who came as refugees did not have access to medical care in the refugee camps, so trust of the health care system becomes an imperative, especially when a pregnancy occurs (Brown et al. 2010). That means use of the health care system could be a barrier to integration for some women. For the women who came to the United States as professionals, there tends to be a greater path to integration into community life, according to Emma, who came with a law degree from her country. "We learned the 'King's English' in our schools. In my case, I went to boarding school. Knowing the language brings about a set of different opportunities," she noted in contrast to her counterparts who came with refugee status. Emma worked in a visible job, and community leaders sought her advice on items of assisting others in the acculturation process. She offered her expertise to educators, community leaders, researchers, and others seeking information on best ways to understand the needs of refugees and other immigrants settling in this rural region (Emma, personal interview, August 12, 2018). She listed accessing the health care system and then learning to navigate its complexities.

Major challenges for the women and their families, who come with refugee status, continue to be accessing health care providers. Refugee status allows four to six months of supplemental income and state-sponsored health care cards. However, most health and dental providers within the rural communities do not accept state-sponsored insurance policies and payments. That means a trip to a metro area, which requires a three to six-hour, one-way, car trip—if one possesses a car—two days of lost wages, a possible hotel stay, and food costs. Some employer-provided insurances do not cover mental health services, which holds great importance for refugee families and individuals who have suffered trauma in their countries. The mothers or fathers must take time off and lost wages to arrange health care visits for themselves or their children.

While immediate medical care is a continuous concern, many refugee women often seek ways of staying healthy and accessing additional health care services. They wished for dentists who accepted new patients and accept both state-sponsored and other types of insurances. Shift work hours also do not fit with most dentists' office hours of 8:00 a.m. to 5:00 p.m. Some communities have medical facilities with a sliding scale that cater to resource-scarce populations; however, wait times take two to six months. Fortunate families have private physicians and dentists, but wait times, again, take three to six months. Often, the women with refugee status voice that they had not received dental services previously, so the costs appeared to be quite expensive. "It wasn't possible to have a dentist or a physician in our refugee camp. Some of us learn to live with our tooth problems," said Tani (personal interview, June 23, 2016). Another respondent reported that she continues to seek dental assistance. "I've been looking for dental help for a while. I live with a serious tooth problem and have lived these past 10-plus years with it, but dental care is way too expensive!" She added a wish for more dentists who would serve the poor.

Migrant women of Southwest Kansas also shared their frustrations with other types of wellness practices, including the lack of in-home care, nutrition advice, and exercise training. "I wish there was such a thing as physician assistants who could visit homes to check on the health of family members," said Grace in an interview (2018). Another mother noted that she worked at two jobs in order to provide health insurance for her children. In addition, Grace worried about her children's nutrition and health. She told us: "I would like to prepare healthier meals for the children since their food at school does not have vegetables and can have many starches." Grace's preference for food more familiar to her and her family is nothing out of the ordinary. In fact, this sentiment echoes scholars (Rondinelli et al. 2010) who speak to the importance of dietary efficacy for migrants in new lands. Abdi (Personal communication, May 2019), who is Muslim, added a challenge concerning her children in school: "They don't know what to eat in school since we have our food requirements."

Grace wished to have the ingredients to prepare her traditional foods, too. She made the connection between diet and recreation:

> I do not expect everything to be perfect for us. I want to tell you what I think. We are lucky to be here in Kansas. I was more active in my country. Not being as active outside of work has affected my health. We could use more recreational opportunities.

Other challenges migrant women voiced centered on effective time management, a new concept for some who came from refugee camps, and balanced demands of work and family. This often ends up negatively affecting their mental health (Mental Health Foundation 2016). For example, loneliness for newcomers tends to be another challenge for integration, which in turn correlates with short-term and long-term behavioral health issues (Kawachi and Berkman 2001). Some comments in a focus group (July 2017) underscored such loneliness: "I miss my parents and brother in Ethiopia, but I just want to be able to feel I belong to this community." Similarly, Abdi noted that some of the greatest challenges for refugee and other migrant women tended toward longing for familiar things. The isolation that comes with communication challenges and new cultural expectations, often, exacerbate these emotions. As Abdi shared:

> Africans tend to be shy, quiet people, so we stay together so that we're not scared. We will not complain when we feel afraid, or we do not get help. We do our best to make it on our own.

The process of moving away from loneliness requires a focus on learning new ways in a new place, a challenge not always easy to overcome. Yet, as women like Abdi (personal interview, May 5, 2019) confirm, these challenges are surmountable, especially through the support of their networks in community.

Community Well-Being

Whether women come as professionals or with refugee status, they strive to find their places in Southwest Kansas. The mostly friendly welcome from people in Southwest Kansas' rural communities gives them a sense of belonging, a critical ingredient in the process of adjusting to a new society

(Phillimore 2011). "For the first time in my life, I feel like I can make a home for me and my family. I don't own our apartment, but it feels more permanent than living in a refugee camp," said Dora. However, the sense of something more permanent does not dissolve feelings of loneliness. The women share a sense of grieving over a lost part of their lives, which threatens their well-being. Regardless, they move forward, exhibiting remarkable resilience. Scholars note (Sleijpen et al. 2017, 349) that mental health problems do not display a lack of resilience for refugee migrants. Often conditions like depression or loneliness prove to be reactions to great challenges. The gradual movement toward healthy adjustment demonstrates *resilience*. Some have a long process in learning about *American culture*, shared a focus group respondent. Yet, some community members seek ways of fast tracking this learning curve. For example, Grace, a Somali community leader, wondered if her community could collaborate more with local community members or leaders. She recognizes that isolation is a problem not only for individuals, but also for small groups. To address isolation for the woman of her group, who struggled to find ways to fill their time away from work, they gather to socialize. Grace shared the following:

> Often when we get together. The people in the apartment [complex] don't understand that we are passing the time. Sometimes, other people in the apartments may call police when my husband and his friends have coffee after work at 1:00 a.m. and visit until 3:00 a.m. They don't see the things people do when they're off work. (Personal interview, November 18, 2017)

She added that they must socialize a little differently because of work hours and carrying on a tradition of visiting for long hours over coffee. This tradition (Personal interviews, October 17, 2017) came from living in refugee camps when there was little else to do, a common narrative for the women interviewed.

Dora's story mirrors others in her community. "I came from Eritrea 10 years ago. I was in California and then in different parts of Kansas. I have been in Garden City for 5 years," said Dora. She added that as a group, African women work to make the best world for themselves and their families. As refugees, Dora noted that her community knew war, hunger, and overcrowded refugee camps. "So, it's nice to have an apartment and a place to call our own," added Dora (Personal interview, October 15, 2017). She hopes to return to California one day, but she knows that she will never return to Eritrea since her home place no longer exists, and she hopes to bring more of her family to the United States. As she shared: "We love the safety here. Melody likes the school and the people have been nice to us."

Tani said her family fled Eritrea because of conflict and war. "After we left Eritrea in 2011, we traveled to Sudan, then to Libya, then to Malta" (Tani, personal interview, July 21, 2018). She added that her family lived in refugee camps until they could come to the United States. First, they landed in Wichita, a city that felt too large for Tani and her family. Tani came as a single mother, having lost her husband in the war. She has a son, Gabe, and they both grew quite close to one of his teachers who was very helpful while they were in Wichita. When Tani realized that it was difficult to raise her son alone with non-family-friendly work hours, the teacher offered to be a temporary, legal guardian to Gabe. "There are about sixteen of us [African] families from different countries who moved to Garden City from Wichita at the same time," said Tani. "And we support one another for the most part" (personal interview, July 2018). Tani added that working in a meat processing plant was something she did not understand. "It's very hard reporting to start work at 2:00 p.m. and working until 1:00 a.m. It makes it very hard to find childcare for those hours," she said. I observe the women with whom I interacted came to the United States quite traumatized, emotionally and physically (Phillimore 2011). However, they demonstrated a strong desire to survive in their attempts to keep traditions alive, caring for their families, decorating their homes, and daring to dream of brighter days to come (personal group interviews, 2018).

Other mothers report general feelings of loss resulting from leaving behind that, which is familiar. Some identified the feelings as grief, which tends to go unaddressed. "I think there needs to be more support for families facing grief because of losing a homeland, losing loved ones, and learning to live new lives," Emma shared. She added, "It's especially hard for children to understand their own emotions around grief and loss." Emma noted that some women reported feeling better, when they helped others settle into their new communities. She mentioned that she and her friends help families find inexpensive items for their homes since many come with nothing more than the clothes they wear and a few personal items in a small bag. Once the women find jobs, they begin to navigate the child and health care systems, as mentioned previously (Emma, personal interview, August 12, 2018). This desire to help others proves valuable in building relationships among this diverse group of women from different cultures. Most important to note with the women are their social strategies, deliberate or not, that help with loneliness through dialog with other in their bonded groups, with acculturation through dialog with those in their linking networks (loose ties), and with economic prosperity through ties at work (Hero 2007; Putnam 2013). The supportive networks promote resilience through advancing well-being.

In addition, the African women's support for others extends beyond their immediate communities to include other diaspora communities, such as Asian groups. This includes people from Myanmar, who make up another significant refugee and immigrant group in the area. Dora noted that she feels less sad and has more energy when she helps people. She shared the following:

> I help my neighbor from Myanmar, because I noticed that she has struggles, which I have experienced. I try to direct her to things, like programs, that will help her to live a better life.

Dora also prefers the community programs and activities that help people feel healthier and connect them to others in similar circumstances. She said, "We would like to see those [programs] again. I met some new people there." The women interviewed echoed one another on the key survival strategies were interacting with one another on a daily basis, making connections to other people outside their groups to learn information critical for smoother integration, and helping one another toward living better lives. This resolve and resourcefulness demonstrated resilience. As Abdi noted: "We are working toward a goal, and it takes hard work and patience."

COMMUNITY ENGAGEMENT, SOCIAL NETWORKS, AND COMMUNAL SUPPORT

Part of my building trust and relationships with the women required me to play chauffeur on many occasions. One time, I took Dora to another apartment complex where Tani and another woman lived. A lively burst of Tigrinya ensued as they discussed Dora's gift of a rug along with some talk about a neighbor. Proudly, Tani showed me the balcony on her second-floor apartment where a rock dove was sitting on her nest of eggs. Tani noted her delight to be in the presence of this little mother working to hatch her eggs. "That is something I have never seen in my 34 years of life." That moment of beauty seemed to soften the blow of other challenges faced by Tani, in her process of integrating to her new environments.

Grace, a community leader from Somalia, shared that she looks for commonalities in the experiences of other women coming to the United States for similar reasons. She speaks of the African community as a whole, rather than specifying certain countries. She shared the following:

> We Africans have something in common. We came here to the U.S. to flee hardships caused by the dangers of governmental conflicts. There was no peace for our children, and we did not want to live in war. We had learned not to trust, which is not good for raising a family.

Trying to achieve a sense of normalcy after a life of conflict, fear, and danger appeared to be common denominators among the women. "It's like having lots of noise in your head," said Dora. She added that it takes a while to shut out the noise of the past and focus on learning a new way of life. She told me that she wants the best for her children who are here in the United States. Dora laments having to leave her older children in Africa, echoed by UNICEF (2016), noting a common reality of family members left behind during conflict and subsequent displacement. Dora and her husband continue to work through their networks in the process of getting their son and daughter to Southwest Kansas.

Tani and Dora share a close friendship. They frequently host the morning coffee for their friends and acquaintances from Africa. Often, they share stories about their homeland and of adjusting to new ways of living. During another morning coffee gathering, Tani reminded me of her story of not being able to support her son, now living with one of his teachers until Tani gets on her feet. The conversations seem to repeat as they work on their own social changes. For example, there continues to be the desire to learn more about the community, but they tell me that they find little time between work and caring for the family. "Sometimes it feels like all I do is go to work and go to the grocery store. I'm not sure I'm part of this community yet," said Dora. She added that she and her friends like to walk and go to the park and other places to allow children to play and to see friends. She knows of those who cannot leave home, because of fear or the lack of transportation. She worries about their loneliness and isolation and works to get them involved with others (Personal interview, 2018). Some reported that they continue to hold onto the fear that came from living in their country and spoke of needing more "road patrols" (from focus group, July 2017). All respondents appeared to agree that leaving their countries was a tough decision to make. "However, I know we're fortunate to be here, though it can be a great challenge every day," said Tani.

Navigating More Challenges

The task of navigating a new country, new people, and new policies and norms leads to many challenges. Hendriks and Bartram (2018), who look for ways to measure outcomes in refugee and other displaced communities, noted that there lacks little to no frameworks to understand or to examine all-encompassing outcomes for political migrants. Often, the ways immigrants and refugees engage with these challenges tend toward misperceptions by local community members, who may even accuse them of being disrespectful. Abdi, a female leader from the African community, shared a story of riding a bus from Minnesota to Southwest Kansas, in what she considered an early step toward her own life's lessons in a new place. As she shared:

> My experience on transportation in Africa was that the bus driver told us what to do. Here, in the U.S., I was supposed to know when to get off the bus. After I missed my destination stop, the bus driver was quite upset with me, and told me that I was being disrespectful.

She added that when there are no visibly printed rules, it can be confusing for newcomers. Amina, a community leader and close associate of Abdi, works with newcomers to get them situated with jobs, to complete forms and applications, and to write letters. The African community looks to Abdi and Amina for their support in teaching the way to *do the right things in this country* (Interview, May 2019). Amina gave the example of helping the people who have suffered with post-traumatic stress syndrome (PTSD).

"We have to talk about it to assure that sadness is natural emotion for anyone who has witnessed traumatic events like killing, starvation, abuses, and other horrors of war," said Amina. She noted that the effects of trauma on people often go undetected; thus, when trouble with the law arises, or if children have academic or social challenges in school, punishment can be harsh. "They [authorities] treat us like criminals rather than help us with the mental and emotional effects of the trauma that we've experienced!" added Amina.

One of the greatest roles the African women play in the community, alongside other leaders, includes educating one another about what to do and what not to do and other cultural expectations. Growing up in war gives people different ideas about cultural expectations. "We have to teach about the consequences for actions, especially where the law is concerned," said Emma. "If one of our men commits a crime, there is little consideration of past trauma that can lead to violence" (Emma, personal interview, July 29, 2018). Despite her desire for more compassion in policing policies, Emma added that she and her community do expect proper punishments for crimes.

A Great Threat

During the months preceding the 2016 U.S. Presidential Election, three white American men from Kansas plotted to plant and detonate bombs at an apartment complex housing more than one hundred Somali people and a Muslim Mosque. Because of Federal Bureau of Investigation (FBI) infiltration, police arrested and jailed the men. The trials in 2016 and 2017 eventually led to sentencing in the earlier part of 2019. At least ten media outlets scrambled to get the story once the arrests materialized. Most community members understood the gravity of the situation, had the men succeeded in detonating the massive car bombs. The destruction would have extended well beyond the apartment complex buildings to destroy a significant part of the city. During that time, I led a reporter of a major metropolitan newspaper to visit some of the Somali families. One of the leaders told the reporter, "In my country [Somalia], we would have been killed, but in the U.S., we are safe, and the law protected us." Amina added that war brings a lot of tension to the people. "There was a sense of relief when the sentencing of the three men was announced. They will have to serve time in prison for the injustice they planned on committing." Amina echoed the sentiments of the leader who talked about the safety of being here in the United States, which she considers a great joy for her people. Hendriks and Barkram (2019) measure the outcomes of migrant communities by asking them to evaluate their lives, post conflict and migration. In this case, Amina and her peers saw the threat to their community as similar to what happens in their countries of origin. "It did not happen, so we are happy," said Amina.

The Joys of Home

The African diaspora communities in Southwest Kansas note a development in joys of home and continue to forge strong bonds to support and uplift each other in their new environments. Within the communities, female and male leaders provide guidance on acculturation and integration. These local leaders work side by side with community members to ensure the smoothest transitions possible. Amina indicated that this sense of home became a welcome change from the insecurity of life in refugee camps, as refugee camps had no safety, and the people had no roots. Others in the community talk about the United States being their home now. They express happiness at living in peace and safety. Amina added, "Once the people realize that they have homes, they become greatly motivated to learn English, to learn the laws, and learn how to be good citizens" (Personal interview, May 15, 2019). She thinks the women are quite adaptable and have done well here in the United States. Amina demonstrates great pride in living in Southwest Kansas. "This is a great place. Nowhere else would we be accepted for who we are. Nowhere else would we have been protected from a threat. I am very proud to live here," said Amina. Others, like Dora, express managing to find joy amid the challenges. "I work to find purpose beyond my job and raising my family," said Dora. She hopes to stay for a long time.

Those who came earlier now consider themselves longtime residents who have chosen to stay and be active in the community. "We are fortunate to live here in Garden City because this is a very open-minded city that takes an interest in a variety of activities for our diverse populations. I love living here!" said Emma. Others noted the joys of stability, opportunities for their children to be educated, and for the ability to move about in the community without fear. "We are making friends with the local people who are not African, and we feel like this is a new home," said Amina. To be involved and give back to the community, Emma serves on her community's Cultural Relations Board. The board connects city government with the local community and works to prevent problems, and to address negative issues as they arise. She noted that a past project was to purchase suitable swimwear for Muslim women who use the city's large swimming pool. The project continues to be very popular for the women who take their children to the pool, and it demonstrates that the community welcomes its African immigrants.

CONCLUSION

I conclude with Dr. Nana Twum-Danso (2012), who reminds us that "When it comes to creating lasting change in the lives of African people, including those in the diaspora, [African women] must be at the center of any conversation around abilities of planning a family, raising children, becoming financially stable, and of 'insisting on personal rights.'" She adds that we may hear the voices of African women talking about what is best for her and her family. Twum-Danso et al. (2012) demand that the international community no longer view African women as helpless victims but rather as change agents working to improve their communities, locally and abroad. Migration researchers (Stanciu et al. 2018; Bailey 2012; Hofmann and Bukley 2013) further remind us of women's persistent place in global migration, and their contribution toward the feminization of migration. This chapter explored the African diaspora, specifically its women, in Southwest Kansas, United States. Despite the challenges of living in conflict zones and withstanding human rights abuses, poverty, and lack of opportunities to earn wages, the women of the African diaspora demonstrate remarkable resilience in their process of adapting to a new life in the United States. They do this through building social networks within the African and other refugee migrant communities to bridging across sectors effectively to meet their needs. Even with difficult work hours in beef processing plants, they continue to acculturate to their new social environments, regardless of how challenging this might be. Similar to what other researchers find (Stanciu et al. 2018; Bailey 2012; Hofmann and Bukley 2013), the women appear to develop networks of support by working with one another to find resources, exchange information, and to help each other in the journey of navigating social expectations and financial obligations.

In the process, newcomers contribute to their new communities through their rich cultural and ethnic heritage, adding to the overall fabric of rural life, as noted by Ramos (2016). The diversity of people currently living in

Southwest Kansas contributes to rich exchanges in cultural traditions around food, clothing, music, and celebrations. This chapter explored the processes in emigrating to the United States as a final stop. Although this course comes with the challenges of learning new laws, a new language, and new cultural norms (Elliott and Yusuf 2014), it also presents new opportunities for earning a living, and, perhaps, the joys of feeling safe and relatively peaceful.

As I built friendships and acquaintances with the African families, specifically the women, I recognized clear signs of trauma from their lives in the war-torn chaos of their homelands. In what social scholars (Stanciu et al. 2018; Bailey 2012; Hofmann and Bukley 2013) call "the feminization of migration," I noticed that the women play critical roles in the integration of their families into community. These mutual experiences, with commonalities that transcended their challenging home environments, resulted in their being bonded to one another, in networks, regardless of differences whether they came to the United States as refugees, who often had little to no opportunities to go to school, or as educated professionals. Faced with the challenges of being *displaced* from their origins and facing new challenges of adapting to new environments, the women expressed hopefulness for the futures of their families and themselves. They say they have much to learn, but I notice resilience (Bailey 2011; Ott 2011; Lakey 2003) and strength demonstrated by the women in Southwest Kansas' African diaspora.

In the meantime, more researchers may come to Southwest Kansas with a special focus on Finney and its surrounding counties. Most researchers tend to focus on the Latinx populations, but we begin to see interest directed toward African populations. Through my research, I hope to influence those researchers who tend toward rich ethnographic stories by becoming part of the community, as Stull, Broadway, Ng, Lerner and Aronson, and Sanderson had done with bilingual investigations, and as I have done with multilingual explorations. Multilingual data and stories appear to be the element missing in the research literature exploring human migrations to Southwest Kansas. I offer this chapter as a means to contribute to filling this gap.

NOTES

1. https://www.bestplaces.net/city/kansas/garden_city.

2. *Market Citizenship* The allocation of citizenship rights based on an individual's ability to possess economic power and participation in the labor market (Grace et al. 2017).

3. The terms *majority-minority* and *majority-minority* appear to be used interchangeably depending on author. The terms denote that an ethnic-minority group makes up the majority of a population.

4. A *micropolitan* relates to an urban area, but the population runs at least 10,000 people per square mile and fewer than 50,000 people per square mile. In the case of densely settled rural counties, such as Southwest Kansas (U.S. Census 2010), there tends to be no urban areas directly associated, or not fewer than 300 miles.

5. A process of becoming culturally fluent in a dominant culture different than your own family/community/country culture.

6. Though immigration greatly mitigated the rural population decline (Kulcsar 2019), communities see fewer people immigrating to the region because of political pressures, at the time of this writing.

7. See work by Easterling et al. (2007) on social capital research.

8. Kansas State University's Institutional Review Board deemed the research compliant for human subjects' safety.

9. The initial survey was in four languages, English, Spanish, Karen (a Burmese language), and Somali. We worked with bilingual community representatives to translate the survey from English to the corresponding languages and used back translation to English to assure that the integrity and original meaning of the questions remained intact (Perez 2009). We took steps to ensure our sample would be representative of five counties in Southwest Kansas with the largest populations of foreign-born people who had immigrated within the past twenty-five years to rural counties with predominantly white residents and settled in Finney, Ford, Seward, Kearny, and Grant counties. We distributed surveys in group settings and targeted gathering spots for newcomers, such as apartment complexes, ethnic stores and restaurants, religious spaces, adult education classes, refugee resettlement sites, and school enrollment sites.

10. Department of Health and Human Services: a family of three earning $21,330 annually, lives at 100 percent of poverty for 2019.

11. According to 2018 census estimates, the biggest population groups are as follows: White alone, 40.1 percent, Hispanic, 50.5 percent, Asia alone, 4.5 percent, Black or African American, 4.1 percent.10. Regularly scheduled hours based on the 24-hour clock.

REFERENCES

2019. "Kansas State Board of Education." https://www.ksde.org/Board.

Bailey, Olga Guedes. 2012. Migrant African women: tales of agency and belonging. *Ethnic and Racial Studies* 35(5): 850–867.

Betts, Alexander. 2013. *Survival Migration: Failed Governance and the Crisis of Displacement*. Ithaca: Cornell University Press.

Blanchard, Leola Howard. 1931. *Conquest of Southwest Kansas: A History and Thrilling Stories of Frontier Life in the State of Kansas*. Wichita: Wichita Eagle Press.

Bolton, Debra, and Shannon Dick. 2017. "Community Data Portal: A a follow-up study to determine changes over time in Finney and Kearny counties (quantitative) with qualitative data." https://wkssl.shinyapps.io/cap_v0_2/.

Bolton, Debra J. 2011. *Social Capital in Rural Southwest Kansas.* PhD diss., Ann Arbor, MI: ProQuest.

Bolton, Debra J, and Francisco M Hernandez. 2017. "Applying Global Perspectives on Fragility to Improve US Communities." *Advances in Anthropology* 7(1): 22–33.

Broadway, Michael J, and Donald D Stull. 2006. "Meat processing and Garden City, KS: Boom and Bust." *Journal of Rural Studies* 22(1): 55–66.

Brown, Corie. 2019. "Rural Kansas Is Dying. I Drove 1,800 Miles to Find Out Why." *The New Food Economy.* Newfoodeconomy.org.

Buckley-Zistel, Susanne, and Ulrike Krause. 2017. *Gender, Violence, Refugees.* New York: Berghahn Books.

Cenoz, Jasone, and Durk Gorter. 2019. "Multilingualism, Translanguaging, and Minority Languages in SLA." *The Modern Language Journal* 103: 130–135.

Coleman, JS. 1988. Social capital in the creation of human capital. *American Journal of Sociology* 94: S94–S120.

Coleman, JS. 1994. *Foundations of Social Theory.* Cambridge, MA: Belknap Press.

Crisp, Jeff. 2010. "Forced Displacement in Africa: Dimensions, Difficulties, and Policy Directions." *Refugee Survey Quarterly* 29(3): 1–27.

Darboe, Kebba. 2003. "New Immigrants in Minnesota: The Somali Immigration and Assimilation." *Journal of Developing Societies* 19(4): 458–72. doi: 10.1177/0169796X0301900402.

Easterling, Doug, Capri G Foy, Kate Fothergill, Lori Leonard, and David R Holtgrave. 2007. *Assessing Social Capital in Kansas: Findings from Quantitative and Qualitative Studies.* Topeka: Kansas Health Institute.

Elliott, S, and I Yusuf. 2014. "'Yes, We Can; But Together': Social Capital and Refugee Resettlement, Kotuitui." *New Zealand Journal of Social Sciences Online* 9(2): 101–110.

Ellis, B Heidi, Saida M Abdi, Vanja Lazarevic, Matthew T White, Alisa K Lincoln, Jessica E Stern, and John G Horgan. 2016. "Relation of Psychosocial Factors to Diverse Behaviors and Attitudes Among Somali Refugees." *American Journal of Orthopsychiatry* 86(4): 393.

Frey, WH. 2011. "Melting Pot Cities and Suburbs: Racial and Ethnic Change in Metro America in the 2000s." https://www.brookings.edu/wpcontent/uploads/2016/06/0504_census_ethnicity_frey.pdf.

Grace, BL, Nawyn, SJ, and Okwako, B. 2017. "The Right to Belong (If You Can Affort It): Market-Based Restrictions on Social Citizenship in Refugee Resettlement." *Journal of Refugee Studies* 31(1). doi: 10.1093/jrs/dew046. Oxford University Press.

Gutiérrez-Rodríguez, Encarnación. 2010. *Migration, Domestic Work and Affect: A Decolonial Approach on Value and the Feminization of Labor.* New York: Routledge. ProQuest Ebook Central. https://ebookcentral-proquest-com.er.lib.k-state.edu/lib/ksu/detail.action?docID=534221.

Heger Boyle, Elizabeth, and Ahmed Ali. 2010. "Culture, Structure, and the Refugee Experience in Somali Immigrant Family Transformation." *International Migration* 48(1): 47–79. doi: 10.1111/j.1468-2435.2009.00512.x.

Hendriks, Martijn, and David Bartram. 2019. "Bringing Happiness Into the Study of Migration and Its Consequences: What, Why, and How?" *Journal of Immigrant & Refugee Studies* 17(3): 279–298.

Hero, R. 2007. *Racial Diversity and Social Capital: Equality and Community in America.* New York: Cambridge University Press.

Kaplan, Seth. 2016. "Countering Centrifugal Forces in Fragile States." *The Washington Quarterly* 39(1): 69–82.

Kawachi, Ichiro, and Lisa F Berkman. 2001. "Social Ties and Mental Health." *Journal of Urban Health* 78(3): 458–467.

Krause, Ulrike. 2015. "A Continuum of Violence? Linking Sexual and Gender-Based Violence During Conflict, Flight, and Encampment." *Refugee Survey Quarterly* 34(4): 1–19.

Lakey, Paul N. 2003. "Acculturation: A Review of the Literature." *Intercultural Communication Studies* 12(2): 103–118.

Lee, Susan K, Cheryl R Sulaiman-Hill, and Sandra C Thompson. 2014. "Overcoming Language Barriers in Community-Based Research with Refugee and Migrant Populations: Options for Using Bilingual Workers." *BMC International Health and Human Rights* 14(1): 11.

Lerner, Stephen, and Ruben Aronson. 2019. *Strangers in Town.* Film. Directed by Lerner and Aronson. NGO Films/DeRussey Films. Lawrence, KS, Brooklyn, NY.

Lichter, DT. 2012. Immigration and the New Racial Diversity in Rural America. *Rural Sociology* 77: 3–35. doi: 10.1111/j.1549-0831.2012.00070.x.

Mansour, Rasha S. 2019. "Displacement, Identity, and Belonging: Iraqi Communities in Amman." *Journal of Immigrant & Refugee Studies* 17(4): 425–440.

Mcloughlin, Claire. 2015. "When Does Service Delivery Improve the Legitimacy of a Fragile or Conflict-Affected State?" *Governance* 28(3): 341–356.

Mental Health Foundation. 2016. *Fundamental Facts About Mental Health 2016.* London: Mental Health Foundation.

Minton, Mark. 2017. "City and County Officials Buck 'Sanctuary City' Label." *The Garden City Telegram*, January 27, 2017. https://www.gctelegram.com/da966d2e-1849-54f9-9693-9716e60bf2ac.html.

Misago, Jean Pierre, and Loren Landau. 2005. "Responses to Displacement in Africa: The Irrelevance of Best Practice." *Conflict Trends* 2005(3): 4–8.

Nawyn, Stephanie J. 2010. "Institutional Structures of Opportunity in Refugee Resettlement: Gender, Race/ethnicity, and Refugee NGOs." *The Journal of Sociology & Social Welfare* 37(1): Article 9. https://scholarworks.wmich.edu/jssw/vol37/iss1/9.

Ndika, Nnenna. 2013. "Acculturation: A Pilot Study on Nigerians in America and Their Coping Strategies." *SAGE Open* 3(4). doi: 10.1177/2158244013515687.

Nikolova, M, and C Graham. 2015. "In Transit: The Well-Being of Migrants from Transition and Post-transition Countries." *Journal of Economic Behavior and Organization* 112: 164–186.

Okigbo, Charles, Jennifer Reierson, and Shelly Stowman. 2009. "Leveraging Acculturation Through Action Research: A Case Study of Refugee and Immigrant Women in the United States." *Action Research* 7(2): 127–142.

Ott, Eleanor. 2011. *Get Up and Go: Refugee Resettlement and Secondary Migration in the USA*. UNHCR, Policy Development and Evaluation Service.

Patil, Crystal L, Craig Hadley, and Perpetue Djona Nahayo. 2009. "Unpacking Dietary Acculturation Among New Americans: Results from Formative Research with African Refugees." *Journal of Immigrant and Minority Health* 11(5): 342–358.

Pérez, Efrén O. 2009. "Lost in Translation? Item Validity in Bilingual Political Surveys." *The Journal of Politics* 71(4): 1530–1548.

Phillimore, Jenny. 2011. "Refugees, Acculturation Strategies, Stress, and Integration." *Journal of Social Policy* 40(3): 575–593. Cambridge University Press. doi: 10.1017/S0047279410000929.

Putnam, RD. 2000. *Bowling Alone: The Collapse and Revival of American Community*. New York: Simon and Schuster.

Ramos, Athena K. 2016. "Welcoming Immigrants: An Opportunity to Strengthen Rural Communities." *Journal of Extension* 54(3): 3COM1.

Rondinelli, AJ, MD Morris, and TC Rodwell. 2011. "Under- and Over-Nutrition Among Refugees in San Diego County, California." *Journal of Immigrant Minority Health* 13: 161–168.

Sanderson, Matthew R. 2014. "Networks of Capital, Networks for Migration: Political–Economic Integration and the Changing Geography of Mexico–US Migration." *Global Networks* 14(1): 23–43.

Sandoval, Juan Simón Onésimo, and Joel Jennings. 2012. "Latino Civic Participation: Evaluating Indicators of Immigrant Engagement in a Midwestern City." *Latino Studies* 10(4): 523–545.

Sleijpen, M, T Mooren, RJ Kleber, and Hennie R Boeije. 2017. "Lives on Hold: A Qualitative Study of Young Refugees' Resilience Strategies." *Childhood* 24(3): 348–365.

Stanciu, RM. 2018. "Feminization of Migration." *Cogito* 10(1): 88–92. https://er.lib.k-state.edu/login?url=https://search-proquest-com.er.lib.k-state.edu/docview/2298706108?accountid=11789.

Stull, Donald D. 1990. "'I Come to the Garden': Changing Ethnic Relations in Garden City, Kansas." *Urban Anthropology and Studies of Cultural Systems and World Economic Development* 19(4): 303–320.

Stull, Donald D, and Jennifer Ng. 2016. "Majority Educators in a United States Minority/Immigrant Public School District: The Case of Garden City, Kansas." *Human Organization* 75(2): 181–191.

Stull, Donald D, Michael J Broadway, and David Craig Griffith. 1995. *Any Way You Cut It: Meat Processing and Small-Town America*. Lawrence, KS: University Press of Kansas.

Tippens, Julie A. 2019. "Urban Congolese Refugees' Social Capital and Community Resilience During a Period of Political Violence in Kenya: A Qualitative Study." *Journal of Immigrant & Refugee Studies* 18(1): 42–59.

Trouth, Erin, and CJ Buckley. 2013. "Global Changes and Gendered Responses: The Feminization of Migration from Georgia." *Center for Migration Studies of New York* 47(3): 508–538. doi: 10.1111/imre.12035 508 IMR.

Twum-Danso, NA, G Darmstadt, and W Prosser. 2012. "Raising the Voices of African Women." *Bill and Melinda Gates Foundation*. Blog. https://www.impatien toptimists.org/Posts/2012/08/Raising-the-Voices-of-African-Women.

U.S. Census Bureau. 2018. Edited by United States Census Bureau.

Zuccotti, CV. 2014. "Do Parents Matter? Revisiting Ethnic Penalties in Occupation among Second Generation Ethnic Minorities in England and Wales." *Sage Journals: Sociology*. doi: 10.1177/0038038514540373.

Zuccotti, CV, HB Ganzeboom, and A Guveli. 2017. "Has Migration Been Beneficial for Migrants and Their Children?" *International Migration Review* 51(1): 97–126.

Conclusion
Future Interventions, Persistent Networks

The power of resilience, reliance, and resistance is exemplified in African women's interventions and networking efforts. Alongside our fellow contributors we wanted to use this volume to showcase some of these interventions, and in the process document how women cultivate and operationalize the power of networks toward futures of equity and equality.

The volume's different chapters encapsulate stories of these kinds of networks and the women who either develop and maintain, or draw support from them. More often than not such support comes in light of socioeconomic complexities, political struggles, gender inequality, and accompanying forms of discrimination and violence. We also recognized women's interventions toward social change. In some cases, women use their informal and formal networks to stage these interventions. Examples of this include protest actions in South Africa against GBV and women's mobilizations around legal representation in Zanzibar. In other instances, women draw from their individual strengths to alter oppressive discourses around women, gender, and sexuality. This includes Caribbean women authors' active reshaping of the literary canon and women in Nigeria critically reflecting on male-dominated sexual scripts. While describing and celebrating women's initiatives toward improving their immediate social realities is of the utmost importance, we see such descriptions as only the first step toward better understanding women's support networks and interventions. We argue that women's networking initiatives and interventions signify deeper structures of oppression. What these structures are, and how women's interventions work toward dismantling them should remain central to our analysis of women's networks and initiatives.

Throughout the chapters, our contributors therefore recognized and analyzed different manifestations of women's power as they emerge in response to gender inequality. Women exhibit power not only when *confronted by* the everyday challenges associated with womanhood but also when they actively *confront* obstacles to gender equality. Through such acts of resilience, resistance, and activism, women are reshaping the status quo. It is through such acts, and by employing their agency, that women actively recognize and confront embedded social structures that obstruct gender equality. Yet, we also see power in the way women depend on each other. Such reliance or dependency on others, in no way, demonstrates that women are unable or hesitant to be autonomous. Instead, it signifies how women see strength in both connecting with others and in the eventual and various networks of support that emerge from such interactions. There is power in solidarity. And, in turn, such solidarity enables change. As Amina Mama (2018) reminds us, "Change has really been about working in groups and organizations and creating structures here and there. Why do we make organizations? We make them do more than what we ourselves can do as individuals. It is only a collective action that can make real change" (location 1453).

Solidarity among women does not always look the same, nor are women's networking initiatives and interventions toward change similar in their characteristics or motives. Instead, as the chapters in this volume illustrate, there is diversity in how, where, and when women initiate change. The first of such diversity lies in the geographic spaces where women's networks emerge. And here we recognize not only African women within the continent's nation-states but also those women who are in the diaspora. An additional layer of diversity resides in the social and cultural spaces from which women's networks emerge. This ranges from private and domestic spaces with their accompanying ascribed gender expectations to those spaces that are considered more public, such as political and legal spaces. Additionally, our contributors also reflect on networks and interventions that are virtual and therefore function within nontraditional communicative arenas. Such counterpublics, as described in Ndakalako-Bannikov's chapter, use these virtual spaces to both critique and move beyond the nonvirtual status quo.

Regardless of where, when, and how women's networks emerge, they are not necessarily time bound. On the contrary, as our chapters show, interventions geared toward social change are forward looking. By mere definition, change involves the future. This means that by developing and strengthening their networks of support and considering how they can intervene in current realities that are discriminatory and rife with gender biases, the women featured in this volume are considering futures where their interventions and networks are no longer necessary. In such futures, women are no longer subjected to, or live in fear of GBV; they have the same legal rights as men and are recognized as political actors in their own right.

With this conclusion, we therefore encourage continued discussions regarding women's networks. This means ongoing arguments for a focus on African women's networking interventions, a deeper analysis of existing data, and the collection of additional empirical data to broaden our current scope of inquiry. This also means considering the unique perspectives that interdisciplinary approaches afford us. All of this is an effort to underscore the value and contributions of women's networks as interventions, not only in response to their current realities but also toward imagined futures of gender equity and equality.

In summarizing the volume's main points, we therefore consider how individual chapters open up additional channels of inquiry regarding gender and feminism. A starting point for such future possibilities is the volume's first chapter. Here, Riley captures the power embedded in Senegalese women's associations, describing how these associations have become integral to Senegalese societies in the way they provide their members with both social and monetary support. Additionally, by featuring two important Senegalese women, Riley confirms that women's associations act as productive and nurturing spaces from which Senegalese women can launch careers in local and national politics. Thus, women's associations increasingly act as readily available recruitment grounds for political parties that may need to adhere to national gender quotas. While such recruitment does get women through the door, it is still unclear to what extent Senegalese society takes seriously the political value of women's associations. Women's associations therefore continue to function, more often than not, within the "hidden public" (Beck 2003). Yet, they still provide women opportunities to develop their own patronage networks of support that have been historically and primarily beneficial to men. Future questions therefore include concerns over the visibility of women politicians emerging from such associations. Why are political conversations not always considering and recognizing women's associations as valuable spaces of political engagement? What will it take for these associations and their actors to be "seen," heard, and to become visible publics, recognized for their invaluable role in Senegalese society at large?

At the same time, we also ask questions around the longevity, persistence, and popularity of Senegal's women's associations and how this has shaped the country's approach to social development. Women's associations do provide their members with nonmonetary support and conjure notions of solidarity among members. But their ongoing presence does open up questions about women's access to financial institutions as well as the sustainability of depending so heavily on an individual's access to state resources for financial support. Does this dependence mean a lack of alternative options such as access to financial markets for women? And if true, what is the future role of women's associations in the development of Senegalese society?

While the networks Riley analyzes are primarily bounded by the nation-state, the networks and interventions featured in chapter 2 are not confined to national networks. Here, Ott complements the volume by presenting the unique case of women's rights activism and Islamic legal reform in Zanzibar. The chapter considers how a broad coalition of Zanzibari women's rights activists are working to expand the Islamic legal authority that women are able to practice by advocating for women's rights to adjudicate Islamic legal cases as *kadhis* (Islamic judges). In addition, these women's legal networks have championed measures to realize the equal division of matrimonial property, and to require that all kadhis earn a degree in Islamic jurisprudence. To achieve these goals, activists rely on broad coalitions of activist networks from the NGO sector, build upon the Swahili philosophical concept of *umoja* (unity, solidarity, and relational personhood), and draw from alliances with Muslim women's rights activists in Singapore, Malaysia, and Indonesia.

Ott's chapter begins to outline a future in which young women Islamic scholars work to depatriarchalize the Islamic legal system in Zanzibar. It also considers how women use both national and international networks to learn from, as well as to support each other. Through such networking Zanzibari gender activists gain valuable insights on how best to approach legal reform while remaining sensitive to religious beliefs and traditions. At the same time this chapter also illustrates how women seeking broader societal change often face significant pushback. In the case of Zanzibari activists, public statements from public figures condemning gender activists' actions yet again confirm that change will take time and ongoing persistence from activists. Nevertheless, Ott's chapter allows for exciting follow-up inquiry that not only continues to trace the work of Zanzibari gender activists but also analyzes the challenges they face along the way. Such an analysis can be a powerful reference for activists in other regions regarding how to effectively engage long-standing patriarchal structures. The chapter also opens further opportunities to investigate the role of transnational networking. To what extent do such networks support women's initiatives toward gender equality? Additionally, what are the challenges that come with such international connections and alliances, especially as far as ethnic and local nuances are concerned?

While the women in Zanzibar draw from both local and international networks to develop futures of gender equality in the legal realm, the actions of women featured in chapter 3 are primarily concerned with the injustices of GBV. Here Cloete introduces not only the reality of women in South Africa amid alarming high rates of GBV but also illustrates how networking efforts toward addressing such violence take on different formats. With the popularity of ICTs, virtual spaces have become a central place for South African women to seek short-term solutions as well as long-term structural changes regarding violence against women. Short-term solutions include online groups such as the WhatsApp group, GIRLS(ICE), that can provide immediate support for women who might feel threatened or who are in danger. Other longer-term actions include the rise of #TheTotalShutDown, a women's social movement that is directing frustrations around GBV directly at the state and political actors.

Drawing from the chapter's examples of women's networks we can come to at least one conclusion: South African women are actively seeking solutions to GBV. Whether in invisible and closed, online groups, or in visible, public appearances, women are frustrated with the impact GBV has on their lives and their community members and are demanding state action. At the time of writing, the #TheTotalShutDown movement has sustained its actions, maintaining a strong social media presence while continuing to keep the government accountable for the promises it has made toward addressing violence against women. Yet, in September 2019, South Africa saw another series of women's marches and nationwide shutdowns following a series of murders, including the death of Cape Town student Uyinene Mrwetyana in August 2019. As he did in 2018, President Ramaphosa again showed his support, vowing to initiate measures to address the country's GBV crisis. Women's public mobilizations around GBV are surely grabbing the attention of the government. But how exactly will the government follow through? What next steps will gender activists take to ensure that violence against women is taken seriously by those wielding political power?

In 2018, #TheTotalShutDown manifested in marches in neighboring Namibia, Botswana, and Lesotho. In early 2020, #TheTotalShutDown also showed their support, albeit virtually, to the 2020 Women's March in Lusaka, Zambia. This brings to the fore transnational networking around GBV, reconfirming yet again that violence against women is not limited to ethnic, cultural, or national boundaries. On the contrary, at least as far as Southern Africa is concerned, it is a widely felt concern that affects all women. Similar to Ott's chapter, Cloete's chapter therefore sparks conversations around transnational networking. How does such networking work and moreover, what potential lies in such international networks to disassemble underlying structures of gender inequality and bring us closer to societies free of violence against women?

In chapter 4, Ndakalako-Bannikov considers how a fictional digital narrative published on Facebook intervenes in the dominant discourse surrounding young women (called "Kandeshis") in Namibia. The Facebook platform is more than merely a space where the anonymous author can make their work available to readers. Rather, through Facebook's commentary features, the narrative's Facebook page also functions as a "discursive space." It allows the author to facilitate discussion with the readers about the Kandeshis in the narrative, and by extension, in society. In making space for an alternative and nuanced perception of these women, *The Dream* makes gendered inequalities in Namibia visible and calls for redress in Namibian society. This chapter begs the question: How else do women and feminists in Namibia (and beyond) use narrative to create alternative discursive spaces and to redress inequalities? And what are the long-term effects of these attempts? It also creates openings for follow-up research that considers the longevity of public discourse around women, their roles in society, and also their public appearance. Ndakalako-Bannikov's broader project explores these questions from a literary perspective that considers the relationship between feminism, feminist activism, and literary form. However, the long-term impact of these attempts to create agency for women using literature has yet to be explored in scholarship on Namibian women.

Chapter 5 highlights the transformative relationship between women's fictional narratives and Caribbean social realities. Cockburn traces the interventions made by Caribbean women novelists in Caribbean literature over time. These interventions have allowed for more women to write and have legitimized women's fictions, perspectives, and gendered concerns both in the literary field and in wider society. This writing draws from women's knowledge of oral tradition passed down to girl-children and women from their African ancestors across generations, forging another connection to the African continent that continues in the present. This knowledge shapes women's literary works to address gender concerns in Caribbean societies, decolonizing both the society from Western-inflected patriarchal ideology and oppression, and the literary world from a pre-dominantly male and neocolonial perspective. This chapter is an example of Africa's transnational connections and how this connection has shaped the Caribbean literary discipline and Caribbean society. In the context of this volume, this chapter contributes to continued scholarship in African studies that works to further develop and strengthen the connection between Africa and its Caribbean diaspora.

Chapter 6 focuses on the Kenyan TJRC, and specifically the Wagalla Massacre. Via a gendered analysis of the proceedings of the TJRC, Awino outlines the ways in which women challenged dominant narratives and deconstructed patriarchal power structures which contributed to the Wagalla Massacre. In contrast to scholarship which argues that truth commissions tend to retraumatize survivors, Awino argues that the TJRC provided a forum for survivors of the Wagalla Massacre to demand their rights and to forge networks of strength and solidarity to do so. Indeed, women participating in the TJRC seized the moment and identified the massacre as a *marker* of ongoing patriarchy and oppression of women, rather than an isolated event. The chapter reveals nuances of the TJRC that expose the strength and collec-tive, networked struggle for gender justice. Essentially, women's willingness to testify, to hear and to be heard, and to demand justice demonstrates their hunger for justice and also their nimble, innovative methods of disrupting patriarchal historical narratives. It also sets an example for women in other parts of the world to harness the power of their words and their conviction for gender equity, using the formal apparatus of a truth commission to seek justice.

In chapter 7, Aromona presents qualitative research highlighting the ways in which Nigerian women's Twitter conversations leverage online communities to highlight problematic communication styles such as "token resistance" which commonly appear in sexual interactions. Token resistance is defined as "a woman's indicating that she did not want to have sex even though she had every intention to and was willing to engage in sexual intercourse" (Muehlenhard and Hollabaugh 1988, 872). In her case study, Aromona demonstrates how women online networks reshape the traditional norms that determine what constitutes acceptable sexual conduct and to push back against rape culture. The digital forums, a kind of online network, both bring awareness to, and challenge norms of consent and how communication patterns such as "token resistance" are being identified and refashioned due to the awareness and pressure created by such online digital activist forums. In sum, women leverage social media platforms such as Twitter to resist and adapt systems of gender oppression—in this case, rape culture. They also bring attention to the problematic nature of sexual scripts and how in the worst-case scenario, they can result in sexual violence. This is an illustrative example of women working together to change society by leveraging the power of online networks.

Chapter 8 takes a historical approach, delineating an example of women's networks in the southern African context in which women reshape systems of gender oppression. Namibian women seized the opportunities presented via the liberation struggle to step into roles traditionally deemed to be in the "masculine realm." In countless ways, as Stember describes, Namibian women were vital to the country's liberation, playing key roles in nearly all facets of the struggle. Despite this, they remain often overlooked and omitted from historical records. Further compounding their wartime experiences of violence was the "double jeopardy" of being a woman and a combatant of color. To address this, women forged networks of support to overcome these challenges during the conflict.

Acknowledging this more complete account of history fleshes out the historical records, brings light to both the quotidian and extraordinary contributions of Namibian women, and transforms the way we think of gender norms. This chapter invites further discussions regarding the afterlife of the colonial experience as it manifests as GBV toward women in contemporary Namibia. In turn, how do Namibian women who were involved in the struggle perceive this correlation between GBV during the liberation struggle and the ongoing and high rate of GBV in the country?

After considering national, international, as well as virtual and imagined women's networks, the volume's last chapter brings the reader home. And although the home described by the women in Bolton's chapter is not their original home within their native countries, it is the new homes they are crafting for themselves following the trauma and violence of war. Chapter 9 considers the experiences of African women refugees as they adapt to life in the American Midwest. Not unlike refugee women elsewhere, their experiences in their new location are "lived 'inside' and 'outside' a 'displaced space'" (Bailey 2012, 854). Establishing and maintaining connections with other women within the refugee community is therefore of the utmost importance to the women featured in Bolton's chapter. These networks not only provide women with the information they need to access medical and social services, to enroll their children in local schools, but also to bring them in contact with other women who are going through the same experiences as them. While their own internally established networks are of incredible value, the women in Bolton's chapter also want to connect with networks external to their immediate surroundings. They are interested in connecting with American women and developing diverse networks. It is through such multicultural networks that they feel they can contribute to the communities that have provided them with new homes and a second chance at life following the trauma of war and conflict. It is exactly in this cross-cultural networking where future inquiry lies. What factors are preventing such networks from developing? Additionally, what underlying misperceptions are preventing such networks from emerging?

The themes that have emerged in this volume are stimulating not only for underscoring African women's current interventions but also for how they open up further questions. For starters we are encouraged by African women's ever-increasing use of ICTs, social media, and virtual networks and how such technologies are becoming part of their mobilizations toward critiquing gender injustices. Furthermore, in their actions, women are challenging and changing the dominant, often simplistic and dismissive discourses that surround them regarding their realities. Equally engaging are themes about transnational and cross-cultural connectivity that take into account the implications of Africans' historical and present migrations into other parts of the world. This asks for future inquiry into how these connections translate into structural changes while also maintaining the integrity of local contexts.

Lastly, as we think about the directions that the chapters in this volume open up, we consider the longevity of other women's networks and interventions which have outlasted political and societal changes and become normalized by the societies they function in. In other words, what were once women's survival strategies and activism toward social change have in many cases become standard practice. Nowhere is such absorption and normalization more explicit than in the development industry, and the emphasis of both private (e.g., international nonprofit organizations and international development agencies) and public (state-level social development institutions) entities to incorporate women and their social networks into their social and community development plans. Development initiatives designed around women, for women, and managed by women, found themselves on the undisputed understanding that women are most affected by underdevelopment, poverty, and poor service delivery. Women should thus be central to discussions, planning, and eventual actions around poverty reduction and social equality. But while some interventions do put women first, in many cases, the real work toward addressing poverty-related issues falls yet again back on women, their interventions, and their networks. The work of community development becomes another responsibility of women who are already overburdened by, and subjected to gender inequality. Therefore, to what extent this absorption into the status quo takes place, and, even more importantly, how women can safeguard themselves against it are questions that should remain central to scholars' research agendas.

In this volume we featured women not only for their bravery and acts of solidarity but also for their innovative ways of questioning the status quo. As many of our contributors illustrate, the magnitude of such innovation is not as important as the connectedness and rallying around common grievance and challenges. As this project is launched into the world, we emphasize again why these interventions are happening in the first place. They happen because of the persistence of gender inequality, the dominance of male-centric traditions and customs, and the lackluster support of legislators and other decision makers as far as gender rights are concerned. Our work is far from over. We therefore join Chandra Mohanty and Linda Carty's (2018) call for a decolonial, anticapitalist, and antiracial resistance that draws its strength from solidarity. It is through the creation of alliances and solidarities across gender, race, class, sexual, and national divides that we can best obtain gender equality and justice.

REFERENCES

Beck, Linda J. 2003. "Democratization and the Hidden Public: The Impact of Patronage Networks on Senegalese Women." *Comparative Politics* 35(2): 147–169.

Mohanty, Chandra and Linda E. Carty. 2018. *Feminist Freedom Warriors*. Chicago: Haymarket Books. Kindle.

Mama, Amina. 2018. "Bridging Through Time." In *Feminist Freedom Warriors*, edited by Chandra T. Mohanty and Linda E. Carty Chicago: Haymarket Books. Kindle.

Index

A3J. *See* And Jappoo Jëf ci Jamm
Aboud, Asha, 50, 63
Abu-Lughold, Lila, 10
accountability, 79–80, 146, 153
acculturation, 195, 198, 201–10, 213.
  See also integration
activism, 2–3, 77, 105, 182, 222; action-
  oriented, 76; against gender-based
  violence, 77, 82; feminist, 2–4, 224,
  226; grassroots, 5–6; for liberation,
  184; online feminism, 73–75, 164;
  political, 73; postcolonial, 117; public,
  77; visible, 75; women's rights, 3,
  43–61. *See also* media
advocacy: groups, 26; for national
  and women's literature, 116; social
  movements, 72
African folklore, 12–13, 113. *See also*
  Caribbean
African literary tradition, 94. *See also*
  Caribbean, literature; online fictional
  diary
African Socialism, 49–50
Afrocentricity, 9, 13, 131–32, 134. *See
  also* Asante, Molefi Kete
Afrofuturism, 9, 13, 131; Afrofuturistic,
  126. *See also* Eshun, Kodwo
agency, 3–6, 91, 94

American Midwest, 15, 195, 228
And Japoo Jëf ci Jamm, 21, 30–32
apartheid, 147, 149; antiapartheid, 179,
  188
Arab Spring, 11
Asante, Molefi Kete, 131. *See also*
  Afrocentricity
Asia, southeast, 10
asylum, political, 7, 196, 197. *See also*
  refugee(s)

BeingFemaleInNigeria. *See* hashtag
  feminism
Benitez Rojo, Antonio, 115
Benno Bokk Yaakaar, 22, 28, 33, 35;
  Femmes de, 36
Biaye, Baba, 26
Botswana: TheTotalShutDown, 68, 225
Brathwaite, Kamau, 115, 119
Brown, Stewart, 115, 118, 128
Butler, Judith, 7, 109n17

Camberene, 22, 34–35
campaign, 21, 23–24, 27, 31–33, 37, 38
capital: political, 32; social, 5, 22, 32–
  33, 38, 194, 199, 202, 204
Caribbean, 12–13, 113; culture,
  124, 133; diaspora, 118, 128,

About the Contributors

Olushola Aromona

University of Kansas

Olushola Aromona is a PhD student in the School of Journalism and Mass Communication at the University of Kansas (KU). Her research interests include the interaction of gender in political communication, gender stereotypes in the media, and the use of social media for advocacy and social change.

Irene Awino

University of Oregon

Irene Awino is a PhD candidate in Journalism and Communication at the University of Oregon. She holds a Master of Arts in Communication Studies and a Bachelor of Arts in English and Sociology. Irene has several years of experience working with leading Kenyan dailies in editorial positions. Prior to joining the newsroom, Irene worked with various non-governmental organizations that champion human rights and gender empowerment. Irene specializes in critical journalism, global media and technology, gender and media studies, human rights and peace studies.

Debra J. H. Bolton

Kansas State University

Dr. Debra Bolton is director of intercultural learning and academic success and faculty member in the department of geography and geospatial sciences at Kansas State University. Bolton plays a key role in fostering cultural advocacy, civility and intercultural learning, education, and training development at the university. She targets curriculum changes to improve the university's efforts to recruit and retain students, faculty, and staff of historically excluded and underrepresented populations.

Bolton previously served as an extension specialist for K-State Research and Extension and adult educator, based in the Southwest Region, for nearly twenty-seven years. Her specialty continues to be engaging multilingual populations in localized research focused on education, health, well-being, integration, and social networks.

Bolton is a National Geographic Society Explorer with a focus on introducing geospatial analysis and geography to high school aged females of color, a grossly underrepresented population in the geosciences.

Elene Cloete

Outreach International, Kansas City, Missouri
Centre for Gender and Africa Studies, University of the Free State, South Africa

As Director of Research and Advocacy for Outreach International, a nonprofit in Kansas City, MO, Elene Cloete has extensive experience in developing and coordinating community development programs. Such work includes working in both rural and urban communities, coordinating outreach programs, and conducting research on Southern African social and political dynamics. She holds a PhD in Social Anthropology from the University of Kansas. Elene holds a research fellowship with the Centre for Gender and Africa Studies, University of the Free State, South Africa.

Lafleur Cockburn

University of the West Indies—Cave Hill Campus, Barbados
Lafleur Cockburn is a Literatures-in-English MPhil student at The University of the West Indies, Cave Hill Campus, in the Department of Language, Linguistics, and Literature. Her interest lies in exploring the Caribbean literary canon, focusing on excluded works. She uses postcolonial and Afrocentric theories to interrogate how Vincentian works compare to established canonical texts. She is also interested in the intersection of Caribbean and African writers in exploring common themes such as orality, gender, and landscape.

Martha Ndakalako-Bannikov

University of Oregon
Martha Ndakalako-Bannikov is a PhD candidate in Comparative Literature at the University of Oregon. Her research engages Namibian literary culture within the context of the African literary tradition, African studies, global anglophone, and new media. Focusing particularly on literary works by and about women, her research considers the politics of literary production that these literatures highlight, and draws from African and black feminisms and postcolonial theory to engage their transnational connections.

Jessica Ott
Michigan State University

Jessica Ott is a recent PhD graduate from Michigan State University in the Department of Anthropology. She was recently awarded a Fulbright-Hays DDRA for her research on women's rights activism in Zanzibar. Ott's scholarly work examines how feminist activists in Zanzibar invoke historical rights discourses and gendered ideas from the past about rights worthiness in their women's rights advocacy. Existing anthropological studies of women's rights have described contemporary feminist activism as guided primarily by "new" transnational women's rights ideas. Through ethnographic and archival research, Ott builds upon existing anthropological understandings of transnational women's rights by exploring how Zanzibari feminist activists additionally draw from Zanzibar's long and rich history of engagement with women's and human rights ideas in their contemporary political advocacy. Her research contributes to human rights policy debates and understanding of the implications of depending on historical rights arguments and constructions of innocent victimhood for women's rights in Zanzibar.

Emily Jenan Riley
El Colegio de Mexico

As assistant professor and researcher of African Studies at El Colegio de Mexico, Emily Riley focuses on African Studies, political and legal anthropology, as well as the anthropology of religion and gender, with a particular focus on Wolof language. As a Fulbright-Hays fellow, she conducted research in Senegal to investigate the concept of *teraanga*—the Wolof word which encapsulates the generous and civic-minded qualities of individuals— as practiced by women in politics, as pursuits of piety, and social obligations.

Mariah C. Stember
University of Kansas

Mariah C. Stember is a PhD candidate at the University of Kansas (KU) in the Department of Women, Gender and Sexuality Studies. She has master's degrees in both public policy and women's studies, as well as graduate certificates in African studies and international development management. Mariah studies women's roles during war and conflict in sub-Saharan Africa and how gender was strategically deployed as a tactic of war. During the 2019–2020 academic year, she was in Namibia with the support of a Fulbright fellowship, analyzing the oral history narratives of women who contributed to the antiapartheid movement.

Lightning Source UK Ltd.
Milton Keynes UK
UKHW010807101120
373105UK00001B/22